About Island Press

Since 1984, the nonprofit Island Press has been stimulating, shaping, and communicating the ideas that are essential for solving environmental problems worldwide. With more than 800 titles in print and some 40 new releases each year, we are the nation's leading publisher on environmental issues. We identify innovative thinkers and emerging trends in the environmental field. We work with world-renowned experts and authors to develop cross-disciplinary solutions to environmental challenges.

Island Press designs and implements coordinated book publication campaigns in order to communicate our critical messages in print, in person, and online using the latest technologies, programs, and the media. Our goal: to reach targeted audiences—scientists, policymakers, environmental advocates, the media, and concerned citizens—who can and will take action to protect the plants and animals that enrich our world, the ecosystems we need to survive, the water we drink, and the air we breathe.

Island Press gratefully acknowledges the support of its work by the Agua Fund, Inc., Annenberg Foundation, The Christensen Fund, The Nathan Cummings Foundation, The Geraldine R. Dodge Foundation, Doris Duke Charitable Foundation, The Educational Foundation of America, Betsy and Jesse Fink Foundation, The William and Flora Hewlett Foundation, The Kendeda Fund, The Andrew W. Mellon Foundation, The Curtis and Edith Munson Foundation, Oak Foundation, The Overbrook Foundation, the David and Lucile Packard Foundation, The Summit Fund of Washington, Trust for Architectural Easements, Wallace Global Fund, The Winslow Foundation, and other generous donors.

The opinions expressed in this book are those of the author(s) and do not necessarily reflect the views of our donors.

Megaregions

To Thomas Daniel Boston
My best friend, closest colleague, and husband
and
Mr. and Mrs. A. J. Ross, my parents

Megaregions

Planning for Global Competitiveness

Edited by Catherine L. Ross

ISLANDPRESS

WASHINGTON • COVELON • LONDON

Library of Congress Cataloging-in-Publication Data

   Megaregions : planning for global competitiveness / edited by
Catherine L. Ross.
     p.   cm.
   Includes bibliographical references and index.
   ISBN 978-1-59726-585-0 (cloth : alk. paper) — ISBN 978-1-59726-586-7
(pbk. : alk. paper)
   1. Regional planning. 2. City planning—Forecasting. 3. Planned
communities—Environmental aspects. 4. Sustainable development. 5.
Globalization—Economic aspects. I. Ross, Catherine Laverne, 1948–
   HT391.M397 2009
   307.1′2—dc22 2008051521

Printed on recycled, acid-free paper ✪

Manufactured in the United States of America
10 9 8 7 6 5 4 3 2 1

Contents

Part I. Spatial Planning and Defining the Megaregion

Figures

Tables

Foreword

It's a mantra of the age of globalization that where we live doesn't matter. The world is flat, says *New York Times* columnist Thomas Friedman. Thanks to advances in technology the global playing field has been leveled, the prizes are there for the taking, and all of us are players, no matter where on the surface of the earth we reside.

Such predictions about the declining role of place in a global world are nothing new. Experts have been making such predictions for quite a while. First, the railroad revolutionized trade and transport. Then, the telephone made everyone feel connected and closer. The automobile was invented, then the airplane, and then the World Wide Web, perhaps the quintessential product of a globalized world. All these technologies have carried the promise of a boundless world. They would free us from geography, allowing us to move out of crowded cities and into lives of our own bucolic choosing. Forget the past, when cities and civilizations were confined to fertile soil, natural ports, or raw materials. In today's high-tech world, we are free to live wherever we want. According to this increasingly popular view, place is irrelevant.

It's a compelling notion, but it's wrong. By almost any measure, the international economic landscape is not at all flat. Today's key economic factors—talent, innovation, and creativity—are not distributed evenly across the global economy. They concentrate in specific locations. Welcome to the age of the megaregion.

In 1957, economic geographer Jean Gottmann first used the term *megalopolis*, derived from the Greek words meaning "very large city," to describe a new kind of economic unit, made up of multiple metropolitan areas composed of central cities and their surrounding suburbs. Gottmann identified several megalopolitan areas: Bos-Wash, running from Boston through New York to Washington, D.C.; Chi-Pitts, from Chicago through Detroit and Cleveland and over to Pittsburgh; and the bustling Tokyo–Osaka region of Japan.

In 1993, Japanese management expert Kenichi Ohmae argued that the nation-state was no longer the central economic unit of the global economy but was being replaced by a new natural economic zone: the "region state." "What defines them is not the location of their political borders," Ohmae wrote, "but the fact that they are the right size and scale to be the true, natural business units in today's global economy. Theirs are the borders—and connections—that matter in a borderless world."

More recently, geographers, planners, economists, and other social scientists have updated Gottmann's and Ohmae's work with empirical data, charting the scope and extent of megaregions in the United States and elsewhere. In a 2005 study, Robert Lang and Dawn Dhavale of the Metropolitan Institute at Virginia Tech found that the ten megaregions that power the U.S. economy are home to nearly 200 million Americans, more than two thirds of the national population, and are growing at faster rates than the nation as a whole.

My own research with Tim Gulden of the University of Maryland used satellite images of the world to identify a new geographic measure of economic activity we call light-based regional product. We used those baseline data to identify the world's megaregions as contiguous lighted areas. Gulden likes to say a megaregion is somewhere you can walk all the way across, carrying nothing but some money, without ever getting thirsty or hungry.

Megaregions are the underlying driving forces of the world economy. According to our research, the world's forty largest megaregions account for about 18 percent of global population but produce two thirds of global economic output and more than eight in ten of the world's innovations. And just the top ten, which house less than 7 percent of the world's people, account for 43 percent of global economic activity and more than half of all innovations. The trend is most pronounced in the emerging economies, particularly the "BRIC" nations—Brazil, Russia, India, and China—where megaregions literally are the economy. Brazil's Rio–Paulo megaregion is home to 10 percent of the country's population but creates 40 percent of its output. China's megaregions account for more than two thirds of the country's total economic output.

This book is a welcome addition to this important, growing field of empirical research. Catherine L. Ross has done the field a major service by pulling together a wide range of scholars and a wide range of topics on the increasingly important economic, social, and spatial roles of megaregions. Chapters by leading scholars cover the definition of megaregions, domestic and global megaregions, their economic role and functions, density, transportation and mobility, finance, the environment and resource management, social equity and the challenge of distressed places, and importantly, institutional structure, design, and governance. Taken together, the collected research in this volume brings much-needed clarity to the age of the megaregion and adds greatly to our knowledge about the way these incredibly important economic, social, and cultural units are transforming the world in which we live. Read on. Learn. Enjoy.

Richard Florida
June 2008

Preface

All over the world, cities—and the people who govern cities, and the people who live in cities—face immense challenges. Cities in the developing world are growing so fast that millions of their residents lack access to basic infrastructure. Wealthier cities in the developed world are concerned about global economic competition, sprawl, maintenance of existing infrastructure, and a lack of public resources to care for the most vulnerable. Cities throughout the world must deal with the rising prices of natural resources, including food and oil, and the potentially catastrophic effects of climate change. These are clearly not the same challenges as those faced by cities 50 or even 30 years ago (with perhaps the exception of oil). Information technology, corporate investment, and our understanding of the current impact on the natural environment have all shifted, necessitating a new approach to planning, policy direction, and the operation of our cities, regions, and states.

The subject of this book, the megaregion, is one new approach. *Megaregion* is the name given to one or a grouping of several urban areas, linked by social, economic, demographic, environmental, and cultural ties, joining together to make infrastructure and planning decisions. Megaregions influence planning at a lower level than the federal government and would involve multiple cities and, often, multiple states. This would enable policymakers working together to address key questions about competing globally for talent and investment, avoiding and reducing environmental damage and irreparable climate change, and building a transportation network that strengthens our economic position without reducing our quality of life.

Planning in the context of the megaregion acknowledges some fundamental truths about modern cities:

- They are interconnected through information exchanges; through movements of capital and labor; through the use of new technologies as people send e-mail, call each other on mobile phones, or meet for videoconferences; and through shared natural resources.
- They are inseparable from the regions in which they grow and from which they draw people and products.
- They are economic agglomerations whose continued, sustainable, equitable growth will be necessary to achieve, or ensure, continued prosperity, both for those inside the city and for those connected to it.

The concept of the megaregion acknowledges that no city is an island—not economically, not environmentally, not demographically, not culturally, and certainly not politically. A thriving city both draws from and contributes to a thriving region.

This is a lesson I have spent the last 7 years learning, again and again, as mayor of Atlanta. Atlanta by itself has had to deal with a rapidly changing economy, formidable infrastructure challenges, and new demographic trends. But Atlanta can also be seen in the larger context of the Piedmont Atlantic Megaregion (PAM), one of ten megaregions in the United States that have been defined by researchers. PAM stretches from Charlotte, North Carolina to Birmingham, Alabama and includes all or part of six states. It includes major interstate highways, two of the busiest ports in the nation, a major air freight center, and one of the busiest airports in the world. Its cities have different economic strengths and weaknesses, and particular issues of water resources, traffic congestion, public infrastructure, and economic growth vary by city and state. But just as PAM can be strengthened by a more economically dynamic and healthier Atlanta, Atlanta can be strengthened by functioning within a better-coordinated, more dynamic, and more sustainable megaregion.

These particular issues are not unique to Atlanta or to PAM. As a member of the Advisory Board of the U.S. Conference of Mayors, I have had the opportunity to speak with dozens of my fellow mayors throughout the country. They too are concerned about making sure their cities grow sustainably and safely and remain attractive places to live and work. They also recognize that whether they are in California, in the Rust Belt, in the Bos-Wash Corridor (what geographer Jean Gottmann presciently called the megalopolis 50 years ago), or in PAM, they cannot solve all the problems by themselves. Although each megaregion has different cultural characteristics and particular economic advantages, the need to take a new, collaborative approach to policy issues transcends geographic and political boundaries.

What can thinking as a megaregion do for cities such as Atlanta and for regional groupings such as PAM? I would say that incorporating an awareness of the megaregion into our thinking and planning brings us closer to solutions for two major challenges that are intertwined. One of these challenges is to continue to foster economic growth so that all of the current and future citizens within PAM can continue to enjoy a high quality of life, with clean, healthy, affordable housing, constant access to clean water and healthy foods, and the ability to seize social and economic opportunities. The other is to grow in such a way that we do not exhaust increasingly scarce resources, including water, fossil fuels, biodiversity, and clean air. Tied up with this second challenge is the need to consume these resources in a way that does not encourage excessive global warming.

Thinking and acting on a megaregional scale will help us answer questions such as the following:

- How do we remain competitive globally?
- How do we avoid the potential environmental and climate damage that will harm our citizens and might erode our attractiveness to investing firms?
- How do we balance the needs of struggling people and struggling areas—urban, suburban, and rural—with investment in areas of more rapid development? How do we make sure, as we forge ahead, not to leave anyone behind?

I believe that organizing at the megaregional scale will help to encourage innovations and new ideas among planners and policymakers. In January 2006 I participated in a forum hosted by Georgia Tech's Center for Quality Growth and Regional Development, which attracted public officials, business executives, concerned citizens, and media from throughout our megaregion. We can already see the potential uses for the megaregional concept within PAM: for sharing best practices without worrying about political jurisdictions; for recognizing new challenges, such as rapid immigration or the aging of our populations, more quickly; for gathering information on traffic patterns so as to build more sustainable and more useful transport infrastructure; and for creating new cooperative ventures. Based on my experience, further development and refinement of the megaregion idea will benefit not only Atlanta, and not only PAM, but other cities and megaregions throughout the country.

Moreover, I expect that this book will make valuable contributions to improving our understanding of the full potential of megaregions as a platform to embrace as we confront the future development of American cities. Dr. Catherine L. Ross has assembled a group of dedicated and thoughtful scholars to discuss the topic of the megaregion from many different angles: environmental sustainability, urban design, economic development, transportation infrastructure, and social equity. This is one area in which the discussions in an academic context, grounded in theory, can have immediate and practical results for those shaping policy. To look more closely at the megaregion is to acknowledge that the destiny of any city henceforth will be linked to the destiny of its surrounding area, its surrounding infrastructure, and its fellow cities. The sooner we all recognize this and work with it in mind, the better off we—and our cities and regions—will be.

Shirley Franklin
Mayor of Atlanta
June 2008

Acknowledgments

There are numerous people to thank for their contribution to the development of this book. I will start at the beginning and thank my students, who serve as an inspiration and who began this journey with me almost four years ago. They served a critical role in shaping many of the ideas put forth in this volume. Of course, it is friends and colleagues, chief among them Robert Yaro of the Regional Plan Association, Eugenie Birch of the University of Pennsylvania, and Armando Carbonell of the Lincoln Institute of Land Policy, who continue to lead the charge, insisting that America must be better prepared for its changing role in the twenty-first century.

I am most grateful to the Ford Foundation for their generous support and to Carl Anthony for his encouragement and continuing support of the progressive ideas that undergird the very foundation of American society.

I have been fortunate to have enjoyed the wide support of an extensive network of people who have stayed the course and continue to be the force behind this effort. They include my colleagues and friends in the College of Architecture, the School of Environmental and Civil Engineering, and particularly the faculty and staff in the City and Regional Planning Program at the Georgia Institute of Technology. Their constructive criticisms and patience in the face of my often unbridled enthusiasm are greatly appreciated. Other individuals that figure prominently in supporting this work include Shirley Franklin, Barbara Faga, Adjo Amekudzi, Cheryl Contant, Karen Leone de Nie, Andreas Faludi, Susan

Fainstein, Jason Barringer, Harry West, the Rockefeller Foundation, Shani Ross Boston, and Linje Ross Boston.

Finally, the completion of this work is the result of the input and hard work of the staff of the Center for Quality Growth and Regional Development at the Georgia Institute of Technology. A special thank you to Jessica Doyle and Amy Danner, both of whom made substantial contributions to earlier versions and provided unlimited energy and support.

Introduction

Catherine L. Ross

The "regional cities" of tomorrow will be nearly continuous complexes of homes, business centers, factories, shops, and service places. Some will be strip or rim cities; some will be star-shaped; others will be "satellite towns" around the nucleus core. They will be saved from traffic self-suffocation by high-speed transportation—perhaps monorails that provide luxurious nonstop service between the inner centers of the supercities, as well as links between the super-metropolises themselves.   —*Chicago Tribune*, July 23, 1961

Megaregions are networks of metropolitan centers and their surrounding areas. They are spatially and functionally linked through environmental, economic, and infrastructure interactions. Today the spatial and functional dimensions of activities that are most vital to the quality of life—economic, environmental, physical, social—are not contained within traditional jurisdictional boundaries. Increasingly, the most appropriate unit of social organization and economic coordination is not the city, not even the metropolitan area; it is the city-region or the region-wide network of cities. Globalization is forcing us to recognize the growing interdependency of social and economic networks. By one estimate, there are now 300 city-regions with populations exceeding 1 million and at least twenty city-regions (Ross and Harbour 2006) with populations of 10 million or more. In 50 years, 400 million people will reside in the United States according to estimates by the U.S. Census Bureau (2000), and approximately 70 percent will reside in or close to the country's projected eight to ten megaregions (see Figures I.1 and I.2). This population growth will place even greater pressures on our economic and social systems as well as our natural and man-made infrastructures. Increased population and new spatial configurations will challenge our creativity in providing adequate opportunities for all Americans. Many projections show greater connectivity and interdependence occurring between economic sectors and regions in different areas of the United States. Although cities will remain the center of these regions, changes will take place as America grapples with issues of spatial planning and its increasing importance in a changing global environment. Infrastructure is taking on a different role that is increasingly complex and includes the provision of greater mobility in the new megaregions. These regions will continue to be centers of economic growth, and it is critically important that they be explicitly linked to existing and emerging markets nationally and globally.

Before now, increasing urbanization was most readily apparent internationally, but today it is also easily observed in the United States. By looking into the future, it is easy to see the nation's emerging megaregions. The multiple cities they will include will cross state boundaries. It is expected that these areas will continue to grow in population, adding potentially millions of new residents. The emergence of megaregions forces us to confront a number of critical questions. How will these regions function and remain competitive in the changing global marketplace? How will people and goods be transported efficiently in and outside of the megaregion? How can we ensure access to our ports, seaports, rail lines, airports, and other global gateways for our trading partners? How can we use the economic engines operating at the center of megaregions to energize and expand economically sustainable growth to areas that are performing poorly? How do we develop methods and tools that support the global planning needed for these areas? How do we retool our competitive advantage so that these regions will be served by twenty-first-century infrastructures and innovative governance structures? What will creative financing tools look like, and are they adequate to promote internal development and enhance our global connectivity? Finally, what type of economic restructuring is needed so that we might maintain and enhance our commitment to equity and a high quality of life? These are among the most daunting challenges. They grow out of an awareness that the world is changing and so must we. It is for this reason that this volume was conceived.

Responding to these challenges will entail planning across current political and jurisdictional boundaries in ways we have not yet considered in the United States (Scott 2001). Spatial planning, as conceived and practiced under European Spatial Development Planning, also represents an attempt to address "issues of

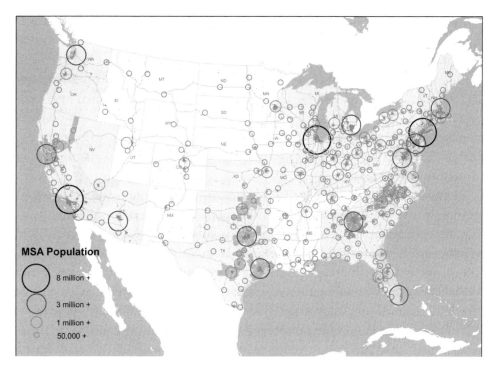

Figure I.1 U.S. Megaregions, 2000 Metropolitan Statistical Area, CQGRD.

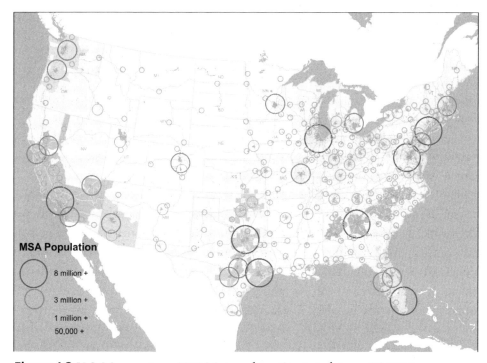

Figure I.2 U.S. Megaregions, 2050 Metropolitan Statistical Area, CQGRD.

global urban competition, environmental sustainability, social equity (spatial justice), and territorial identity" (Jensen and Richardson 2001). Recently, a great deal of attention has been focused on the emergence of the European Union and European spatial planning (Faludi and Waterhout 2002). Such planning has set the stage for a more competitive Europe. Given our projected population growth and the increasing global competitiveness we face, it is crucial for American planners, policymakers, developers, community leaders and residents to examine the history, feasibility, and usefulness of the megaregion and spatial planning in an American context.

Urban areas throughout the United States are facing increasing traffic congestion, worsening air pollution, and the challenge of providing and maintaining the infrastructure needed to move goods and people efficiently and effectively. The burning of fossil fuels and biomass has increased emissions that are changing the earth's temperature, the amount of precipitation, sea levels, and the incidence of extreme weather events. Land use changes affect climate change through urbanization, deforestation, and reforestation. These developments, in addition to reductions in land use cover and increasing exposure to solar radiation, establish climate change as one of the most pressing problems confronting our cities and regions. The continued reliance on diminishing fossil fuels makes the pursuit of alternative energy sources and regional responses to these challenges critically important. The implementation of climate change strategies and programs to minimize risks are more appropriately advanced under the framework of the megaregion.

The impact of changes in the financial markets of different countries on markets worldwide is easily observed in current times. Economic and financial downturns in one country influence market performance in other nations. This may lead to rapidly declining stock market values, mounting unemployment, bankruptcy and instability of financial institutions, and the unresponsiveness of the economy to numerous financial stimulus policies. In the midst of such economic chaos, we can learn many valuable lessons, one of the most important of which is that local jurisdictions cannot adequately respond to the challenges confronting them. In contrast, megaregions are best positioned to do so. History has shown that in times of worldwide declines in output and employment, the most effective prescription for stimulating the economy is New Deal–type fiscal stimulus policies. Policymakers may debate new stimulus policies that would be oriented toward expenditures on improvements such as highways, streets, bridges, and other infrastructure projects. These proposals typically encompass new government spending with a primary objective of jump-starting the economy while improving the nation's infrastructure, increasing its energy efficiency, and harnessing green technologies.

Megaregions, and not cities, are optimally positioned to respond to economic crises for a number of reasons. First, the economies of scale associated with large infrastructure projects usually dictate that such investments encompass regional or statewide jurisdictions rather than local jurisdictions. Second, economic crises severely strain government budgets and turn balanced budgets into large deficits. Tax revenues fall sharply as a result of declining retail sales and increasing social service payments, and state and local budgets are also severely strained. This means that cities can no longer act alone to meet the economic and social challenges they face. However, the megaregion may be a more effective alternative to marshal the necessary resources and implement the solutions necessary to meet these challenges.

Finally, megaregions are better positioned to absorb the shock waves accompanying economic downturns. Corporations shed thousands of workers, and many go bankrupt or close shop altogether. At the same time, consumers experience an unprecedented number of housing defaults. Although these kinds of economic shocks put extreme pressure on local jurisdictions, they are much more easily absorbed if all jurisdictions act in a regionally coordinated manner. Acting alone, cities will continue to experience immense economic distortions and unbalanced growth, but if they coordinate their actions through the megaregion, these major shocks will become minor market maladjustments.

Infrastructure throughout the nation is deteriorating, and the price tag for maintenance alone is expected to reach hundreds of billions of dollars over the next 15 to 20 years. This amount does not include what is needed for capacity enhancements. Sadly, the deteriorating infrastructure, escalating energy costs, increasing global competition, and increasing exhaustion of our natural resources and environment have driven us to consider alternative strategies to ensure our global competitiveness and quality of life. The megaregion must therefore become the footprint by which we ensure our global competitiveness and establish the domestic structures needed to respond to a changing environment.

This book is an edited volume containing contributions of a selected group of distinguished scholars and practitioners. Their contributions add to the growing theoretical development and understanding of the dynamics and underpinnings of megaregions. In this volume, these authors have addressed some of the most critical issues that will confront the growth and development of America during the next 50 years, critical among which is how we as a nation will position ourselves to confront increasing global competition. The authors not only address this issue but also examine particular ways in which megaregions may be useful in addressing equity and environmental sustainability. Therefore, the volume could not be timelier.

Today we confront the major issues facing cities and regions at a level dictated by jurisdictional propensity rather than functional efficiency. But the rising influence of the region and city-region and the challenges confronting American cities clearly signal that the megaregion is timely. More than ever it is the political, economic, and structural arrangement that is most capable of responding to the pressing problems we must confront.

The spatial dimensions that define the way we function have far surpassed the capabilities of traditional jurisdictional boundaries to provide optimal solutions. The new and dynamically growing patterns of urban space and functionality at the metropolitan and regional levels demand more creative forms of service delivery. For example, development patterns in one jurisdiction may lead to traffic congestion in others and often adversely affect the quality of life and health. These issues are interrelated; yet the decision and planning processes continue to take place discretely. Although the functional relationships already exist in space, their interactions have outstripped the outmoded political and planning structures we rely on to address them.

We do not mean to suggest that spatial mismatches between jurisdictions and functionality have been completely ignored. Over the last century, there have been many discussions of planning at the regional scale (see Wheeler 2002; Levine 2001). But in recent decades, regional planning and advocacy have focused more on economic growth nodes rather than the larger economic growth clusters that are represented by megaregions. We must develop a framework that provides an incentive and imperative to address spatial planning at the level of megaregions. Only then will we have the flexibility to address the myriad issues and opportunities that the current environment commands.

Megaregions will not replace the need for locally based planning, and it is not intended that they will usurp the sense of place and community also important to our cultural enrichment. Porter states, "While the relative emphasis is shifting, all levels remain important. . . . The task is to integrate the city-region with other economic units, and adopt a textured view of the sources of prosperity and economic policy that encompass multiple levels of geography" (Porter, 2001). The megaregion provides a rational framework within which we maintain both local identity and regional functionality.

Because spatial planning and megaregions are recent developments in the United States, I have sought to bring together academics and theoreticians who have the depth of understanding needed to elucidate the new regional dynamics. Each contributor was challenged to examine the emerging megaregions in the context of their disciplinary expertise. This volume therefore represents an opportunity to help define the theoretical, analytical, and operational underpinnings of an emerging paradigm that seeks to respond to an increasing population and rapidly changing spatial configuration in the United States. Contributors examine the spatial implications of local, regional, national, and global trends in the context of sustainability, economic competitiveness, and social equity. The volume outlines a new agenda and paradigm for American planning. This book is among the first of its kind to address the applicability of megaregions in the United States.

We believe you will agree that megaregions capture the economic, political, and spatial level of planning that should be conducted in order to respond to the challenges of agglomerations of economic activity and population. It also recognizes the new context in which large-scale regions exist and in which global economic and environmental developments are taking place. Megaregions provide the strategy that allows us to act globally while addressing local quality-of-life issues. They reflect traditional regional planning intellectual platforms and yet are responsive to the larger international context.

Global competitiveness and increased productivity will require more resources. They will mandate cooperation within and between regions and the subsequent identification of the strengths and characteristics of each. The specialization within regions offers the opportunity to reduce inefficient competition and focus on development strategies that take advantage of existing economies of scale and product differentiation. Cooperation on the construction of large-scale public works and on resource sharing and management are just some of the potential benefits associated with the megaregional approach.

The book is organized into three parts. Part I contains chapters that define spatial planning and megaregions and examines both the challenges and opportunities confronting the United States in the next half century. The authors extend their analyses to include past and present spatial planning efforts undertaken in Europe and Asia and resulting implications for the United States. Part II consists of chapters that examine changing household structures, environmental sustainability, economic growth, mobility, and social equity. This is done by examining the potential of the megaregion to respond to the changing environment, including an assessment of the mobility challenges of the Piedmont Atlantic Megaregion. Finally, in Part III the authors characterize the opportunities for megaregion planning in the context of global markets, growing global competition, and the potential to foster healthier, more competitive, and more resilient cities and regions.

The megaregion has been embraced by countries throughout the world and is emerging as a framework that holds great promise for the United States. As the importance of this topic grows we must develop the concepts, tools, and procedures that will allow efficient policy formulation by cities, towns, and regions.

Megaregions are an appropriate spatial and planning framework for the twenty-first century, and it is hoped that this volume will assist the reader in examining the applicability of this framework to the United States in greater detail.

References

Faludi, A., and B. Waterhout. 2002. *The Making of the European Spatial Development Perspective: No Masterplan*. Routledge, London.

Jensen, O. B., and T. Richardson. 2001. Nested visions: New rationalities of space in European spatial planning. *Regional Studies* 35(8):703–717.

Levine, J. N. 2001. The role of economic theory in regional advocacy. *Journal of Planning Literature* 16(2):183–201.

Porter, M. E. 2001. Regions and the new economics of competition. Pp. 139–157 in A. J. Scott, ed. *Global City-Regions: Trends, Theory, Policy*. Oxford University Press, Oxford.

Ross, C. L., and J. Harbour. 2006. Footprint for an international city: Transportation and redevelopment. *Georgia State University Law Review* 22(4).

Scott, A. J. 2001. *Global City-Regions: Trends, Theory, Policy*. Oxford University Press, Oxford.

U.S. Census Bureau. 2000. *Census of the Population and Housing*. Bureau of the Census, Washington D.C.

Wheeler, S. M. 2002. The new regionalism: Key characteristics of an emerging movement. *Journal of the American Planning Association* 68(3):267–278.

Part I

SPATIAL PLANNING AND DEFINING THE MEGAREGION

1

Scale Matters

Rethinking Planning Approaches across Jurisdictional and Sectoral Boundaries

Cheryl K. Contant and Karen Leone de Nie

American cities and metropolitan areas have reached an important crossroads in their growth and development. Will continued population growth and development be managed through local planning units based on current municipal and county boundaries? Or will cities, metropolitan areas, and states work cooperatively to address social, economic, and environmental challenges and opportunities? Can American prosperity be retained through competition between nearby metropolitan areas or suburban areas for growth opportunities? Or will cities, suburbs, and metropolitan areas work together to seek greater shared economic gains in total? Are there alternative geographic or functional scales that permit greater economic competitiveness, better opportunities to address social inequities, and enhanced protection of vital and limited natural resources?

All these questions occur in a context of unparalleled population growth and development in the United States. By the mid-twenty-first century, an additional 140 million people are expected to live in the United States, with much of that increase occurring in major urban areas (Carbonell et al. 2005). The U.S. Census Bureau (2004) projects a nearly 50 percent increase in population over current levels by 2050. Population and employment projections at the county level suggest that 70 percent of the population and economic growth will occur in extended networks of metropolitan regions linked together by transportation networks, environmental systems, economic activities, and culture. Along with this overall growth, the United States will witness significant demographic changes caused by aging of the population and increased racial and ethnic diversity (Regional Plan Association 2006).

Compounding this rapid growth are three sets of issues that are critical to our nation's future. First, globalization and its impact on American economic prosperity stand as key challenges for the twenty-first century. How will we adapt to a changing economic base in the United States? In what ways can we capture a niche in the global economy and do so without inefficient competition between regions within our own country?

Second, rising inequities between individuals and groups in the United States threaten the stability of our nation, question our commitment to all of our citizens, and challenge all of us to think creatively and purposively about distributive justice in our policies and plans. How can we address growing inequities between the haves and the have-nots within regions, within states, and within metropolitan areas? How can we plan for greater redistribution of economic resources among our citizens when we face structural features in our political economy that promote these inequities?

Third, the nation and the planet face new threats, including climate change and natural resource depletion. These threats all result, at least in part, from population growth and the actions of humans that capitalize on nature's abundance without taking into serious account the long-term negative consequences of resource extraction and use. Can we continue our economic prosperity in a manner that is less destructive to the planet and its resources? Is it feasible to create new human settlements that are prosperous, equitable, and more sustainable environmentally? All three of these issues call for more intentional planning at scales that rarely occur in U.S. planning practice and that may be better suited to address these critical questions.

The Need for New Planning Approaches

Population growth, an increasingly complex marketplace, social inequities, and the interrelationship of environmental, social, and economic systems are just a few of the challenges facing the United States in the twenty-first century. Many analysts have suggested that current planning efforts are not addressing these issues. This lack of success results in part from both the complex nature of the problems and the institutional structure of our current planning approaches.

Consider globalization, for example. Globalization no longer relies on proximity to raw materials, suppliers, and purchasers of manufactured goods. Instead, advanced communication technology, cheap oil (until recently) for moving goods, and knowledge-based and inexpensive labor allow workers, suppliers, and customers to be geographically dispersed. Salet et al. (2003) suggest that "regional economies have become more dependent on their position in global networks than on the traditional powers and investments of local industries and local entrepreneurs." This makes an area's competitiveness in a globalized economy reliant on its concentration of internationally linked and clustered knowledge resources and of inexpensive and rich labor pools, issues often not addressed through current local- or county-level planning.

As metropolitan areas expand and merge in economic activity and function, relationships between transportation systems, land consumption, housing availability and affordability, environmental quality, and natural resource availability become more complex. As a nation, we have more clearly recognized these relationships between human activities, social equity, and environmental degradation in the past decade. We understand that decisions to develop a parcel of land in one jurisdiction will probably have consequences for the mobility, wealth, environmental quality, and health of citizens both within that jurisdiction and in surrounding areas. Climate change researchers have even provided evidence that the type of development actions in a particular jurisdiction can have broader regional air quality and urban heat island effects (Stone 2008; Stone and Rodgers 2001). However, policy and planning solutions to these problems are often enacted independently by individual jurisdictions, with little cooperation and coordination across the borders.

Why have communities failed to plan for these problems that cross jurisdictional boundaries? First, the traditional U.S. scale of authority for regulating land use activities and impacts often rests at the local level, in municipalities or counties. Second, funding of local governments is linked to property values and the wealth of its citizens. Local governments therefore have an incentive to promote activities that increase property values and wealth even if they result in the export of pollution, congestion, and poverty to other nearby areas. When all local jurisdictions behave in this manner, the ability to think about interrelationships, social inequities, and clustering of economic resources becomes challenging, if not impossible.

This increased competition between nearby jurisdictions can result in regional inefficiencies. Levine (2001) suggests,

> Local decisions are often driven primarily by highly localized interests, which can result in minimal improvements in productivity and competitiveness at great cost: that is political autonomy creates a false sense of economic autonomy and produces decisions that are often zero-sum or even negative-sum for the region as a whole.

Without incentives to address broader spatial and functional implications of local decisions outside local political interests, there is little hope to expand overall economic activities and quality of life. In fact, Barnes and Ledebur (1998) found that interjurisdictional cooperation is rare and occurs in instances where significant economies of scale in service provision exist, significant spillover effects demand cooperative action, external threats force a collective response, or federal or state programs provide incentives for cooperative action.

Wheeler (2002) suggests that the current complexity of metropolitan areas in both physical form and social structure leads to jurisdictional fragmentation and piecemeal approaches to interrelated issues. He further suggests that this complexity would be best addressed through the integration of traditional disciplines of planning (economic development, housing, transportation, environmental protection) and the integration of various scales of planning (site, neighborhood, local, metropolitan, state, and national). This growing spatial mismatch between the existence of problems and the location for their potential solutions creates a demand for planning at scales larger than those of traditional planning approaches.

Given all the rationale for and theoretical benefits of planning at regional scales, why have new regional approaches been so slow to develop and slower to achieve success? Wheeler (2002) argues that fundamental political difficulties work against regional planning. Local and state governments are unwilling to relinquish power to a regional entity. Suburban voters are unable to see how their interests are tied to the well-being of the central city, and progressive voting blocs in central cities are reluctant to see their power base diluted by regional perspectives. In other words, the mismatch of local political power base and regional dilution of power further prevents the implementation of regional approaches to enhance economic competitiveness and address social inequities. Hershberg (2001) amplifies this point by stating that issues of race, class, and politics drive the existence of social inequities and environmental degradation. These same issues prevent the implementation of regional approaches to resolve these issues.

Megaregions and Megaregional Planning Approaches

Clearly, no one scale of planning can fully and effectively address the array of problems, opportunities, and challenges described here. Recently, numerous scholars and practitioners (Carbonell and Yaro 2005; Regional Plan Association 2006; Dewar and Epstein 2007) have suggested that planning at the scale of a megaregion may provide useful approaches to enhance future economic competitiveness, sustainability, and quality of life.

Megaregions are linked networks of metropolitan areas that serve as a functional unit for economic activity. Megaregions also consist of the areas that are tied to these economic engines by the natural environment (watersheds and drainage basins); flows of goods, services, and people; shared infrastructure, funding sources, and labor pools; and a social and cultural identity. The boundaries of megaregions are not fixed but are as dynamic as the functional relationships that create the megaregion.

America 2050 (Regional Plan Association 2006) defines a megaregion as a large, connected network of metropolitan areas that are joined together by environmental, cultural, infrastructural, and functional characteristics. Specifically, America 2050 states,

> The emerging megaregions of the United States are defined by layers of relationships that together define a common interest; this common interest, in turn forms the basis for policy decisions. The five major categories of relationships that define megaregions are: environmental systems and topography, infrastructure systems, economic linkages, settlement patterns and land use, and shared culture and history. (Regional Plan Association, 2006)

The definition of a megaregion comes on the heels of several alternative regional definitions. Perhaps the first to engage in this scale of analysis in the United States was Jean Gottmann (1964) in his book *Megalopolis*. His megalopolis combined counties in the metropolitan areas in the northeastern United States. Scott (2001) proposed the use of the term *city-regions*, consisting of spatially overlapping or convergent urban areas with a surrounding hinterland. Hall and Pain (2006) identified an emergent development pattern of clusters of towns and cities that are highly connected by information flows, which they defined as global mega-city regions.

Our definition of the construct *megaregion* builds on these earlier definitions by characterizing a connected set of activities with common resources, cultural identity, and economic opportunities. As such, a megaregion contains the economic, social, and population core of a region and delineates the natural, economic, and social connections between cities, metropolitan areas, and rural places. As a concept, it captures key features missing in earlier regional definitions. It explicitly recognizes the economic functionality of a region; the social and political character of the place and therefore the implicit inequities associated with race, class, and politics; and the environmental features that define the landscape and the impact of human activities on the region's future.

Can the megaregion be a useful construct for understanding and solving planning challenges in the twenty-first century? As a new concept in the regional planning field, megaregions hold great promise as a spatial unit for addressing problems, defining solutions, and implementing policies. However, the effectiveness of the megaregion construct has not been examined in any depth, except perhaps by its proponents in the America 2050 movement.

A New Call for Innovation in American Planning

The megaregion construct is not unlike the regionalism efforts of earlier decades. Recognizing the erratic success of past attempts at regionalism, it is reasonable to ask, "Why are we revisiting this subject?" We are revisiting it because our present context and projections for the future, some bleak, call for new ways to respond. The convergence of the aforementioned challenges facing the United States—population growth and demographic change, new construction, and expanding economic opportunity; a strained natural environment and limitations on natural resources; an evolving and more complex marketplace; and limited public resources and funding—necessitates the exploration of innovations in American planning.

References

Barnes, W. R., and L. C. Ledebur. 1998. *The New Regional Economies: The U.S. Common Market and the Global Economy*. Sage, Thousand Oaks, CA.

Carbonell, A., M. Pisano, R. Yaro, P. Hidiysan, and W. Fu. 2005. *Global Gateway Regions*. Regional Plan Association, New York. Retrieved June 2, 2008 from www.america2050.org/pdf/global gatewayregions.pdf.

Carbonell, A., and R. Yaro. 2005. American spatial development and the new megalopolis. *Land Lines* 17(2).

Dewar, M., and D. Epstein. 2007. Planning for "megaregions" in the United States. *Journal of Planning Literature* 22(2):108–124.

Gottmann, J. 1964. *Megalopolis: The Urbanized Northeastern Seaboard of the United States*. MIT Press, Cambridge, MA.

Hall, P., and K. Pain. 2006. *The Polycentric Metropolis: Learning from Mega-City Regions in Europe*. Earthscan, London.

Hershberg, T. 2001. Regional imperatives of global competition. In J. Barnett, ed. *Planning for a New Century: The Regional Agenda*. Island Press, Washington, D.C.

Levine, J. N. 2001. The role of economic theory in regional advocacy. *Journal of Planning Literature* 16(2).

Regional Plan Association. 2006. *America 2050: A Prospectus*. National Committee for America 2050, New York.

Salet, W., A. Thornley, and A. Kreukels. 2003. Institutional and spatial coordination in European metropolitan regions. In W. Salet, A. Thornley, and A. Kreukels, eds. *Metropolitan Governance and Spatial Planning Comparative Case Studies of European City-Regions*. Spon Press, London.

Scott, A., ed. 2001. *Global City-Regions: Trends, Theory, Policy*. Oxford University Press, New York.

Stone, Jr., B. 2008. Urban sprawl and air quality in large U.S. cities. *Journal of Environmental Management* 86:688–698.

Stone, Jr., B., and M. O. Rodgers. 2001. Urban form and thermal efficiency: How the design of cities influences the urban heat island effect. *Journal of the American Planning Association* 67(2):186–198.

U.S. Census Bureau. 2004. *U.S. Interim Projections by Age, Sex, Race, and Hispanic Origin.* Retrieved June 4, 2008 from www.census.gov/ipc/www/usinterimproj/.

Wheeler, S. M. 2002. The new regionalism: Key characteristics of an emerging movement. *Journal of the American Planning Association* 68(3):267–278.

2

The Megalopolis, the Blue Banana, and Global Economic Integration Zones in European Planning Thought

Andreas Faludi

"National planning in this country is widely believed to be an un-American activity, an exercise in bureaucratic hubris best left to the French," says Fishman (2007) in the opening sentence of a paper on the history of national planning in America. Subsequently he sets out to demonstrate that national planning is "as American as the family farm, the transcontinental railroads, the great hydroelectric dams of the South and West, and the interstate highway system." This chapter is about planning on a similar scale, which is that of the European Union (EU), strongly influenced as it is by French—and also Dutch—thinking. The reader needs to be aware that the EU is a much looser grouping of sovereign member states and with less of a common identity than the United States. In referring to planning on this scale, *national planning* would not be the right term to use. For planning efforts spanning the EU, this chapter uses the term *European spatial planning* as distinct from spatial planning at the level of the EU member states and their subdivisions, often called regions or provinces.

Indeed, European planners have formulated an overall vision as a framework for integrating various spatially relevant policies pursued by the EU or the member states and their regions. The outcome is the policy document called the European Spatial Development Perspective (ESDP) (Commission of the European Communities [CEC] 1999). The making and application of this document have aroused the interest of a small but lively academic community reflecting on the meaning and practical effectiveness of such an undertaking (Faludi and Water-hout 2002; Jensen and Richardson 2004; Waterhout 2008).

The ESDP has aroused interest in the United States too, with the Lincoln Institute of Land Policy sponsoring a course in 2001 and a publication, *European Spatial Development* (Faludi 2002). This has been a source of inspiration for taking steps toward "American Spatial Development and the New Megalopolis" (Carbonell and Yaro 2005). Later, this exercise became America 2050. By mid-century, the U.S. population is estimated to reach 440 million. One of the expected outcomes is growth concentrated in a few super cities or megaregions, also dubbed megalopolises (Gottmann 1961). The upshot of the engagement of planners from the United States with the European example has been to explore these huge areas of dynamic growth and their implications. Studies have explored what the expected population increase might mean for some of the megaregions, including one by the University of Pennsylvania Schools of Design (2005) on the archetypical megalopolis on the East Coast of the United States that was the object of Gottmann's study. Another one by Catherine L. Ross at Georgia Tech concerned the Piedmont Atlantic Megaregion (PAM) in the Southeast. As in Europe, the management of such megaregions includes spatial planning. As the report on PAM states, echoing the rationale for the whole America 2050 exercise,

> Our first century was founded on Thomas Jefferson's national plan calling for westward expansion, and the second century was stimulated by Theodore Roosevelt's vision for an improved and expanded energy and natural resource infrastructure designed to encourage and support industrial expansion. A Third Century Strategy is needed to contend with the expected population growth and the challenges of competing in an increasingly global economy. This third century of planning argues for a new national framework that supports spatial planning through policies and federal funding. (Ross 2006)

So the "takeaway idea for American planners was strategic development policy at the continental scale based on alternative spatial visions of core and periphery," explains Carbonell (2008) in the foreword of the third volume of a series published by the Lincoln Institute under the title *European Spatial Research and Planning* (Faludi 2008).

Europe is also faced with the opposite situation of that projected to exist in the United States in mid-century: population decline, estimated to be of the same magnitude as population growth in the United States. This means that the EU, as presently constituted by twenty-seven member states and many more inhabitants than the United States, will actually be less populous in 2050. In fact, in terms of its share of the world population, the EU has been able to hold its own only by admitting more and more new members. This process, called enlarge-ment, irks voters wary of countries such as Turkey, with whom accession nego-tiations are underway.

Population decline does not mean that there will be no more pressure of urban growth. Indeed, the European Environmental Agency (2006) recently voiced concern about the effects of urban sprawl on sustainability. This is one of the fiercely professed goals of the EU. However, when it comes to the European scale, population growth and the resulting pressures are not at the core of the de-bate. Rather, the unevenness of economic development is. This raises sensitive equity issues. The second volume published by the Lincoln Institute, *Territorial Cohesion and the European Model of Society* (Faludi 2007), describes a situation in which this unevenness has become particularly problematic. The EU has picked up ten additional member states, and the title highlights the aspiration for eq-uity across the newly enlarged European space. Equity translates into the idea of balanced spatial development. As will become evident to Europeans, the territory of the United States, with its megalopolises spread from California to the Mid-west, the eastern seaboard, and the Southeast, seems distinctly more balanced than that of the EU, so the effect of engagement across the Atlantic has been mu-tual. According to the successor document of the ESDP adopted by the planning ministers of the member states in May 2007 called the "Territorial Agenda of the European Union," so-called polycentric development is intended to help "secure better living conditions and quality of life with equal opportunities, oriented to-wards regional and local potentials, irrespective of where people live—whether in the European core area or in the periphery" (Territorial Agenda 2007). The EU is committed to this policy, which is being increasingly articulated under the flag of "territorial cohesion" (Faludi 2006). The statutory third cohesion report of the European Commission—a kind of executive of the EU—states the underlying rationale, which is that "people should not be disadvantaged by wherever they happen to live or work in the Union" (CEC 2004).

This would never have come up had there not been significant territorial dis-parities in Europe. Molle (2007) identifies three major aspects of such disparities: access to markets, access to know-how and innovation, and access to member state information. This third disparity focuses on "the problem that national bor-ders create to communication and the care for the environment and hence to a balanced development of the European space." Being crisscrossed by national bor-ders, these EU disparities are the result of geography and, in particular, history. The half-century partition of Europe into a prosperous west and rapidly catch-ing up south and a Central and Eastern Europe still recovering from their isola-tion has not created an equitable playing field. Disparities and the requisite regional cohesion policies, including policies to pursue territorial cohesion in Europe, existed before, but accepting new member states from these parts has rendered them more acute.

The wider context is the pursuit of what is called a European model of society. Indeed, Davoudi (2007) sees territorial cohesion as the "spatializing" of this model. The model offers greater protection than the American and Anglo-Saxon model—of the United Kingdom as the main exponent in the EU—against economic insecurity and inequality. "At the heart of both models lie century-old debates about the relations among the state, market, and civic society, between individual liberty and social responsibility, between economic efficiency and social equity, and between the state as provider and interventionist and the state as facilitator and enabler." Davoudi adds that the concept of territorial cohesion "brings a new dimension to these debates by extending the application of the principles of social models beyond individuals and social groups to places and territories."

As Carbonell (2008) observes, what this comes down to is that the European ideal of spatial equity is favoring "development in place over selective migration to locations of greater opportunity." The reason is that regional identity factors are extremely strong in Europe (Robert 2007), a fact also commented on by American Europe-watcher Rifkin (2004). Americans are said to be more footloose and to have fewer problems leaving the territory in which they have their roots. The one-time French chief planner Guigou (2001) has even described the people of North America as nomadic, to contrast them with Europeans. Indeed, as Huntington (2004) says, "manifestations of territorial identity are weak or missing in America."

European welfare states—and with them the EU—assume that policy can influence the distribution of development, and with it the incidence of disparities, so to bring the situation closer to the ideal of a European model of society. This model is a normative concept standing for moderating the pursuit of economic growth and competitiveness—otherwise at the core of the European integration project—with concerns for social welfare and equity, with sustainability and good governance being factored in for good measure. That there is a problem of reconciling these objectives can be taken as read. Inevitably, the balancing act that this implies must take place at the level of concrete decisions, where the outcomes are sure to vary from case to case.

Regional Policy and European Spatial Planning

The cradle of modest efforts at European spatial planning is the EU's regional policy addressing the issue of the balance of development, and with it the balance of life chances, in Europe. The objects of concern for regional policy are not only "least-favored regions" suffering from disparities (with the gross domestic product per capita being the most common indicator used; see Molle 2007) but also regions undergoing industrial restructuring and regions with a "geographic handicap." Mountain regions, islands, and thinly populated remote regions that are particularly affected by demographic decline represent this handicap. It is clear that the expected decline of Europe's population will add to concerns about the chances of such regions holding their own in global competition. Also, the core regions stand to benefit more from the "single market," which is shorthand for policies to remove barriers to trade and movement generally. So peripheral and otherwise disadvantaged regions receive aid from the EU to compensate them for their disadvantages, relative to core regions, on the level playing field that the EU wants to create. In fact, this can be seen as a kind of side payment to the member states concerned through their acquiescence not only to single market policies but also to the introduction of the common currency, the euro. The argument is that countries in the core of Europe stand to benefit more from such measures than those on the periphery.

Therefore, regional policy is the arena for discussing European spatial planning. However, the management of urban growth has not always been a secondary concern. Especially in the Netherlands, growth management has been a key issue for decades. Dutch planners have tried to control the growth of metropolitan areas consuming scarce open space. The country industrialized rapidly after World War II, with a growing population concentrating along the seaboard in the western Netherlands, known in the literature as the Randstad (Burke 1966; Hall 1984; Dieleman and Musterd 1992). With its seaports, the Randstad was the most favored location for heavy industry, and so the driver of urban growth was economic development, with the periphery losing out. At times, the planners were able to forge a coalition with regional economic policymakers. They succeeded in keeping development more balanced by distinguishing between industries that needed access to port facilities and those that did not. Those not needing port access could thus be diverted or persuaded by means of subsidies to stay in the periphery. Government supported this policy by decentralizing some of its services; for example, the Central Statistical Office finds itself on the periphery, where it was relocated to compensate for job losses caused by the closure of coal mines. In this way, Dutch planning achieved a synthesis between urban growth management and regional economic policy, but the relationship was never without its ups and downs. However, now the situation is the reverse. Regional economic policy favors development where investments are thought to bring greater returns so as to enhance the competitive position of the Dutch economy, and spatial planners follow this line too.

What the example of Dutch planning shows is that any such policy is contingent on a conceptualization of the territory overall. Identifying where the areas of high pressure are and which areas are losing out, which is what the America 2050 exercise has done based on population projections, is essential. In terms that border on political incorrectness, one of the government reports of the 1950s produced jointly by national and regional economic planners gave the answer in a report under the title "The West and the Rest of the Country." The equivalent in the United States would be the identification and labeling of the prairie states as being a chasm between the dynamic East and West of the continental United States. This chapter will discuss attempts at a similar conceptualization of the territory of the EU identifying winners and losers, the core and the periphery. In these attempts, the example of the megalopolis identified by Gottmann (1961) along the eastern seaboard of the United States was a source of inspiration.

This happened when Dutch planners started looking beyond the borders of their small country after World War II. They attempted to conceptualize the position of the Netherlands in a wider transnational and European context. They reckoned that identifying concerns that surpassed the local and regional scale would strengthen the position of planning. Inspired by the example of Gottmann's megalopolis, they presented their country as forming part of a similar configuration stretching from southeast England to northern Italy. Involving planners from other countries in reflecting about this development on the macro scale seemed natural. This resulted in a permanent Conference on Regional Planning in Northwest Europe that included planners from Germany. This was remarkable because Germany had occupied and subjugated the Netherlands from 1940 to 1945. In the late 1950s, Dutch planners had already put their faith in the emergent European Economic Community, hoping that it would address planning issues, particularly growth management. The practice of its predecessor, the European Coal and Steel Community, had already demonstrated that the enforced development of these key industrial sectors necessitated flanking measures, which of course coincided with the experience of Dutch national planners.

Dutch planners were not alone in expecting the European Economic Community to address their concerns. There was a lively discussion about how to achieve a better balance between the various parts of this new configuration. Seen from this angle, the issue is to identify which regions suffer disadvantages and which, because of their position in the European heartland, reap the benefits of what at that time was called the Common Market. However, the treaty, completed in March 1957 and establishing the European Economic Community, left no scope for accommodating such concerns. This was despite a number of proposals on the table for a common regional policy including the setting up of an investment fund. The signatories, the national governments of the member states, wanted none of this, though. The European Parliament (called the Parliamentary Assembly at the time) kept regional policy and planning on the agenda, but it did not have the right of initiative. Until the 1970s there was no real movement. Not until the 1980s did regional policy amount to more than distributing funds from the community coffers to member states to help finance their regional policies. And not until the 1990s were efforts undertaken to focus on priority issues of common concern and to factor in a form of planning.

With the rationale for EU regional policy being the existence of disparities considered to be unacceptable, what was needed was an operational definition. Since the late 1980s, this definition has remained roughly the same: Statistical regions with a per capita gross domestic product of less than 75 percent of the European Economic Community average adjusted for purchasing power parity receive investment funds.

From a planning point of view this is unsatisfactory. Planners would like policy to be based on spatial analysis and on the conceptualization of the situation overall, invoking spatial concepts. So this chapter looks at the role of the megalopolis and like concepts in shaping the conceptualization of European space. It shows that on this macro scale policymakers and planners turn naturally to such concepts. The example of the America 2050 exercise also bears this out. It, too, homes in on megaregions as the structuring devices for conceptualizing the North American situation.

Two conceptions of the European core were most influential: that of the Blue Banana and that of the pentagon (written with a lowercase *p* to distinguish it from the building in Washington, D.C.). The counterfactual was that of the European Bunch of Grapes, standing for a more polycentric Europe.

The Blue Banana

Before discussing the main ideas underlying this concept, one needs to look at the major planning traditions in Europe that were germane to the emergence of European spatial planning. In particular, the ESDP bears witness to the influence of two planning traditions. The first is French *aménagement du territoire*, a form of regional economic development policy informed by spatial analyses and spatial scenarios. A good example is "Le Scénario de l'Inacceptable" ("The Scenario of the Unacceptable"), published in 1971 (Avergne and Musso 2003). The second one relates to urban growth as practiced in the Netherlands and some other countries on the continent of Europe. Because, in ways that very much reflected French regional policy, the European Community already gave funding for regional development, a kind of French-style European spatial planning seemed unexceptional to its French proponents. Some representatives of the growth management school disagreed. The very idea of European spatial planning raised the hackles of member states fearing interference with their sovereign control over their territories. Such conflicts are typical of the ambiguity of European integration. Its members are benefiting from joining forces and removing barriers to internal trade. The same member states are jealous of the EU and its institutions for exercising control over what the member states can and cannot do, when these initiatives have been approved by their own representatives. In the case of the ESDP, this ambiguity has resulted in a murky compromise. The ESDP is the product of a voluntary form of intergovernmental cooperation but one that would have been impossible without the support of the European Commission. As the ESDP makes only too clear, in signing up to it the member states are not relinquishing any of their sovereign powers, nor are EU institutions bound by it.

This does not necessarily make the ESDP redundant. Making it has been a learning process for the better part of 10 years. With France, the Netherlands, Germany, and the European Commission as the main drivers, the ESDP has contributed to the Europeanization of planning at national, regional, and local levels. France and the Netherlands have been the initial proponents, with Germany as the main opponent of EU involvement. This debate, which has been resolved in favor of the German position, is of no immediate concern here. The conceptualizations of European space discussed here were influenced mainly by Dutch and, in particular, French thinking.

France started the ESDP in 1989 by calling a meeting of the twelve ministers of the European Community responsible for spatial planning and regional development of the member states (see Faludi and Waterhout 2002; Faludi 2002 for further discussion). The notion of a European core, or megalopolis, was at the heart of this French initiative, supported by the Dutch.

The French are good at geopolitics and are deeply concerned about the position of their country in Europe and the world. When the Iron Curtain fell in 1989, this was a shock. The French were forced to acknowledge that the center of gravity in Europe was about to move east, very much to the advantage of Germany. Containing Germany had been one geopolitical driver behind European integration, the other one having been the containment of the Soviet Union (Lieshout 1999). But Germany, already the European economic engine, became even more influential. The initiative of President Nicolas Sarkozy to form a Mediterranean Union illustrates this kind of thinking, which counterbalances the dominant concern of Central and Eastern Europe with a greater appreciation of the north–south dimension as a determinant of Europe's future (Grasland and Beckouche 2007).

In addition, the position of the institution responsible for French national planning, the Délégation à l'Aménagement du Territoire et à l'Action Régionale (DATAR, now called Délégation Interministérielle à l'Aménagement et à la Compétitivité des Territoires) had changed. Set up by President Charles De Gaulle in the early 1960s to promote the development of French regions as counterweights to Paris, DATAR had lost influence under Prime Minister Jacques Chirac, a former mayor of Paris who subsequently became French president. So DATAR was looking for a new rationale for its existence and found it in conceptualizing the situation of the French territory in the emergent European context. It is in this context that the so-called Blue Banana saw the light of day.

This came in the wake of a research project in which DATAR had commissioned a team of researchers at the University of Montpélier, with famous geographer Roger Brunet in charge (Brunet 1989). The aim was to study the French territory in its wider context. This study came out just in time to address the situation after the momentous fall of the Berlin Wall and the subsequent disappearance of the Iron Curtain dividing Europe. The DATAR study identified a European core area, which it called the *dorsale* ("backbone"). The message was that the *dorsale* no more than straddled the French territory and was bypassing Paris. So, from a European perspective, Paris, and even more so the French Atlantic Coast, were in danger of becoming marginalized.

How did the *dorsale* come to be called the Blue Banana? Apparently, the minister responsible, François Chérèque, who also happened to be the one who had called the first meeting of European planning ministers, visited DATAR to be presented with the results of the Brunet study. Upon entering the room that displayed the *dorsale* in blue on the wall, he asked, "What is this blue banana for?" A journalist from *Le Nouvel Observateur*, something like *Time* magazine, overheard this and published an article under this title (Alia 1989), and the name stuck. This article encapsulates the new spatial or territorial conceptualizations and fears of the time, and it is thus worth recalling the line of argument.

"Take a map of Europe and erase the borders. What remains? A new space," reads the opening sentence. What follows is the shocking news that *notre Hexagone* ("our Hexagon," the loving designation for France because of its shape), disappears from the map. The map in the Brunet study shows a banana reaching from London to northern Italy, "where the real heart of Europe beats." Paris itself does belong to what the article labels as the European megalopolis, but there is a problem. As indicated, the Banana straddles French territory only at Strasbourg in the east and Lille in the north. This Banana, the article warns, grows and blossoms "without us." To make things worse, it's in the Blue Banana, in the European core, where decisions are being made, where productive forces are concentrated, and where achievements are being registered. Indeed, as far as competitiveness is concerned, the Banana can hold its own in global competition, even against the megalopolis identified as Bos-Wash by Gottmann. (Indeed, the article refers to the Gottmann study.)

What is evident is the concern not only for regional balance but also for French competitiveness. The author asks why France has such a modest share of the Banana. In answering, the article touches on themes still being discussed in relation to competitiveness. One theme focuses on the centralization of political power in France that results in too much development in and around Paris. In contrast, the Blue Banana is polycentric, including many medium-size towns with a tradition of autonomous local government. It is relevant to note here that the way in which the Brunet team identified the Banana was by plotting all towns and cities with 200,000 inhabitants or more in the European Community of twelve (as it was then called), together with Switzerland and Austria.

So the prospects for the east of France, in the Alsace, were positive, more so because the Iron Curtain had just fallen. The south had good prospects too. There the researchers from Montpélier, a city located in the south, had discovered a sort of Sun Belt along the northern shore of the Mediterranean, called the Nord du Sud (the North of the South). However, France was under threat as a result of outdated administrative structures and the emptying out of its interior. A book published immediately after World War II had already identified this threat of the French regions being sucked empty, with the attraction of Paris as the culprit. It had come out under the telling title *Paris et le Desert Français* (*Paris and the French Desert*; Garnier 1947). However, echoing more recent thinking, the article warned that it would be wrong to put a brake on the growth of Paris. Paris needed to hold its own in global competition, in particular with regard to the other European world city of London. One of the themes in European regional policy and planning is how to maintain metropolitan growth engines while supporting a more polycentric form of development.

The Pentagon

The ESDP recast the Blue Banana into a "pentagon" consisting of London, Paris, Milan, Munich, and Hamburg, which it identified as the only "global economic integration zone" of the EU. Four such zones are alleged to exist in the United States, a fact that was thought to give the latter a competitive advantage. This pentagon covered 20 percent of the territory of the fifteen EU member states as constituted at the end of the 1990s. Within it, 40 percent of the population of the EU was producing 50 percent of its gross domestic product, which is why there was also talk of the "20–40–50 pentagon." (The boundaries were drawn deliberately so as to result in this easy-to-remember series of figures.)

In the face of such a concentration of economic activity, the policy of the ESDP was to promote a more polycentric form of development by encouraging the growth of global economic integration zones, each polycentric in itself, outside the pentagon. In European planning, polycentric development has thus become a "bridging concept" (Waterhout 2002) papering over the cracks between various aspirations.

A brief note on the substantive policies as announced in the ESDP is in order. In it, the member states of the EU and the Commission committed themselves to a "spatial approach" of coordinating various "spatial policies," or "spatially relevant policies," with a view to the EU goals of cohesion and sustainability and their territorial effects. This is a key difference between the aspirations of whatever continental-scale planning there is in America and in Europe. For the purpose of providing a framework, the ESDP lists three spatial development guidelines:

- Polycentric spatial development and new urban–rural partnership
- Parity of access to infrastructure and knowledge
- Wise management of the natural and cultural heritage

Under each guideline, the ESDP identifies policy aims and options. These options should be interpreted "according to the economic, social, and environmental situation of an area, in order to create balanced and sustainable development" (CEC 1999). This is why the application of these aims and options is discretionary. There is no community competence for this kind of policy, nor did the member states want to give the community a fresh mandate.

Only a few of the options relate to the EU territory as such. They come under the first of the spatial development guidelines, polycentric spatial development and urban–rural partnership. We find a cluster of options under the heading "Polycentric and Balanced Spatial Development in the EU." This cluster includes options for structuring the EU territory as a whole. A polycentric system of cities, also described as polycentric development, is indeed one of the key concepts in the ESDP. Several of the policy options invoke it, in particular Option 1, which recommends strengthening "several larger zones of global economic integration in the EU, equipped with high-quality, global functions and services, including the peripheral areas, through transnational spatial development strategies" (CEC 1999).

The ESDP clearly connects this recommendation to the issue of the competitiveness of Europe. The reader is reminded that the Blue Banana evoked concern for the competitiveness, or rather the lack thereof, of the French territory outside the area purported to be the economic powerhouse of Europe. In this context it is worth pointing out that the ESDP came out in 1999, before the Lisbon

Strategy of 2000 identified competitiveness as the Achilles' heel of Europe. The Lisbon Strategy was adopted by the European Council of Heads of State and Government when they set the EU goal of "becoming the most competitive and dynamic knowledge-based economy in the world" (European Council 2000). In March 2005, the European Council decided to accept the Barroso Commission's proposal to make a new start with this strategy. This is laid down in its communication *Working Together for Growth and Jobs* (CEC 2005). The ESDP was ahead of its time in focusing on competitiveness.

Naturally, given its character as a spatial planning document, the ESDP relates competitiveness to the spatial configuration of the EU territory. It points out that this territory "differs from that of the USA with its several outstanding economic integration zones on a global scale: West Coast (California), East Coast, Southwest (Texas), Mid West" (CEC 1999). In ESDP terms, the territory of the United States is thus more balanced—more polycentric—giving the United States a competitive advantage, or so it is suggested.

At the EU-wide level, polycentric development means promoting the development of global economic integration zones outside the only existing such zone in Europe: the pentagon. Although it housed many of the command centers of Europe, this is not why this area has been called the pentagon. Like the Blue Banana, the area owes its name to a coincidence. During the drafting of the final version of the ESDP, the presidency of the EU was held by Germany. The Germans described the formation consisting of London, Paris, Milan, Munich, and Hamburg as a *Städtefünfeck*. This was translated into English as "pentagon," which is correct but ignores the association that this term inevitably invokes. The French translator was savvy and translated the term into *le coeur de l'europe* ("the heart of Europe"), but the power of the term *pentagon* is so strong that it is used even in French texts.

Ten years before the publication of the ESDP, another definition of this core gained fame or notoriety, as the case may be, under the name "Blue Banana." Also, the European Commission conducted a study of the "Central Capital Cities" region of Europe (CEC 1996), which overlaps with the pentagon. Another study, also for the Commission, articulated the radically different concept of a "European Bunch of Grapes" (Kunzmann and Wegener 1991). The latter symbolized the notion of a more balanced European territory pursued by the ESDP (Waterhout 2002; see also Waterhout 2007).

Within this notion of a balanced Europe, the global economic integration zones form the counterweights to the pentagon. Just as in French planning, the *métropoles d'équilibre* (the "metropolises of balance") of the 1960s and 1970s were intended to form counterweights to Paris. The ESDP gives no definition of global economic integration zones. However, from the context it is obvious that these zones are to be regarded as assets in global competition and gateways to the rest of the world. There is no difference between the ambivalence with which the ESDP regards the pentagon—an asset when it comes to the global competitive position of Europe but a menace when it comes to internal balance—and the ambivalence with which the French, and later the rest of Europe, looked at the Blue Banana. Europe, having only one such zone, is seen as problematic. This is why the formation of more such zones

> has to be pursued, to ensure regionally balanced development, because the EU is becoming fully integrated in the global economy. Pursuit of this concept will help to avoid further excessive economic and demographic concentration in the core area of the EU. The economic potential of all regions of the EU can only be utilized through the further development of a more polycentric European settlement structure. The greater competitiveness of the EU on a global scale demands a stronger integration of the European regions into the global economy. (CEC 1999)

At this macro level, polycentric development is being promoted in ESDP follow-ups, starting with a document produced by the French in 2000 (French Presidency 2000). Accompanying this report was a parallel study (Baudelle et al. 2002; Baudelle and Guy 2004) commissioned by DATAR. Also, DATAR itself has formulated four spatial scenarios for France in 2020, one of which—the preferred one—is identified as "networked polycentrism" (*polycentrisme maillé*) (Guigou 2002). The study positions the French territory in a polycentric configuration of *petites europes,* or little Europes. Another follow-up by the Conference of Peripheral and Maritime Regions (2002) shows what a determined policy might achieve between now and 2020 in terms of a polycentric Europe. It points out opportunities for stimulating new growth areas.

So the key European strategy is for global economic integration zones to develop outside the pentagon, thereby increasing Europe's global competitiveness. However, purporting not to be a "masterplan" (Faludi and Waterhout 2002), the ESDP leaves the question of where such zones should develop hanging in the air. Cooperation and initiatives from below are the keys to formulating the requisite transnational development strategies. The policy of encouraging cooperation between stakeholders is more generally applicable:

> As well as city networks at regional level, the need for complementing cooperation also applies to city networks at interregional, transnational or even European level. . . . Promoting complementarity . . . means simultaneously building on the advantages and overcoming of disadvantages of economic competition. . . . However, complementarity should not be focused solely on eco-

nomic competition but be expanded to all urban functions, such as culture, education and knowledge, and social infrastructure. (CEC 1999)

Note that the policy envisaged is not about European funding for the development of would-be global economic integration zones. Rather, cities and regions aspiring to become part of a new global economic integration zone are encouraged to take requisite initiatives, like cities and regions in the North Sea area according to the spatial vision (NorVision 2000) or around the Irish Sea (Kidd et al. 2003). With the accession of the first twelve member states by 2007, most of them in Central and Eastern Europe, new potential global economic integration zones have come into the picture. One north–south axis zone, stretching from the Baltic Sea through Poland, the Czech Republic, Slovakia, and Hungary to the West Balkans, is being considered. There is also an initiative under the telling name *Centrope* that focuses on Central Europe, with Vienna as one of the initiators.

In emphasizing cooperation and initiative from below, the ESDP reflects the shift to what has been dubbed the contemporary paradigm of regional development (Polverari and Bachtler, 2005). In this and other respects, the ESDP foreshadows territorial cohesion thinking, which focuses, among other things, on governance issues.

Conclusions

The key concern in European spatial planning is not the management of urban growth, let alone that of the pentagon. In fact, there is no concern for the performance of the one and only European megalopolis, considered by many to be the economic engine of Europe. This is despite that fact that the policy of increasing Europe's competitiveness is a topic discussed with increasing urgency since the European Council of Heads of State and Government resolved to turn Europe into the most competitive region globally by 2010. True, a discussion is taking place as to whether regional policy, amounting to compensating peripheral regions and regions suffering from the effects of industrial restructuring, is the best policy, or whether Europe's competitiveness would not be better served by focusing on the winners, which happen to be found mostly in the already prosperous regions of Europe. There is recognition of the fact that there are poorly performing regions in the core of Europe and high performers on the periphery. Finland, home to Nokia and other companies, is an obvious example. However, this is not articulated in terms of the pentagon or in spatial or geographic terms. In fact, nobody is standing up for the pentagon, or the Blue Banana for that matter.

Of course, the management of urban growth, including a concern for sustainability, can be factored into this equation. A high-quality environment can contribute to competitiveness by attracting knowledge workers and the "creative class" (Florida 2004). Also, planners are seeking to address the possible effects of climate change and mounting energy prices. These were identified as key challenges in the "Territorial Agenda of the European Union" adopted by the member states in May 2007. In this respect, it is interesting to note the findings from the report *Urban Sprawl in Europe* (European Environmental Agency 2006) that highlight the threat to the EU's environment and its social and economic balance. Maybe this publication heralds a campaign orchestrated from EU environmental policy to table the issue of urban growth on the European agenda. The European concern for combating climate change could add to this campaign. This would amount to a return to themes the Dutch planning pioneers of the 1950s and 1960s articulated, which are also being discussed in the context of America 2050. However, the concern for balanced development, encapsulated in the notion of polycentric development, continues to dominate discussion in the EU. New transnational networks, aspiring to the status of global economic integration zones, are seen as the instruments for achieving a better balance of regional development in Europe. However, there is no clearly defined policy other than encouraging seed money for research, networking, and initiatives from below. Any more ambitious policy that would define and promote criteria to which would-be economic integration zones have to conform would exceed the possibilities of the fragile construct of the EU.

References

Alia, J. 1989, May 18–24. C'est le grand atout de l'Europe de demain: Le trésor de la banana bleue. *Le Nouvel Observateur* 46–48.

Avergne, C., and P. Musso. 2003. *Les Grands Textes de l'Aménagement du Territoire et de la Decentralization*. La Documentation Française, Paris.

Baudelle, G., and C. Guy. 2004. Quel devenir pour l'Union Européenne? Scénarios pour 2020. Pp. 99–109 in G. Baudelle and C. Guy, eds. *Le Project Européen*. Presses Universitaires de Rennes, Rennes, France.

Baudelle, G., C. Guy, and J. Ollivero. 2002. Les scénarios de l'espace européen. Pp. 107–158 in G. Baudelle and B. Castagnède, eds. *Le Polycentrisme en Europe*. DATAR/Editions de l'Aube, Paris.

Brunet, R. 1989. *Les Villes Européennes: Rapport pour la DATAR*. La Documentation Française, Paris.

Burke, G. L. 1966. *Greenheart Metropolis: Planning the Western Netherlands*. St. Martin's Press, New York.

Carbonell, A. 2008. Foreword. In A. Faludi, ed. *European Spatial Research and Planning*. Lincoln Institute of Land Policy, Cambridge, MA.

Carbonell, A., and R. D. Yaro. 2005. American spatial development and the New Megalopolis. *Land Lines*. Volume 17, Number 2.

Commission of the European Communities. 1996. *Prospects for the Development of the Central and Capital Cities and Regions*. Office for Official Publications of the European Communities, Luxembourg.

———. 1999. *European Spatial Development Perspective: Towards Balanced and Sustainable Development of the Territory of the EU*. Office for Official Publications of the European Communities, Luxembourg.

———. 2004. *A New Partnership for Cohesion: Convergence, Competitiveness, Cooperation—Third Report on Economic and Social Cohesion*. Office for Official Publications of the European Communities, Luxembourg.

———. 2005. *Working Together for Growth and Jobs: A New Start to the Lisbon Strategy*. Office for Official Publications of the European Communities, Luxembourg.

Conference of Peripheral and Maritime Regions. 2002. *Study on the Construction of a Polycentric and Balanced Development Model for the European Territory*. Paper presented at the Conference on Peripheral and Maritime Regions of Europe, Rennes, France.

Davoudi, S. 2007. The European social model and spatial policy research. Pp. 81–103 in A. Faludi, ed. *Territorial Cohesion and the European Model of Society*. Lincoln Institute of Land Policy, Cambridge, MA.

Dieleman, F., and S. Musterd, eds. 1992. *The Randstad: A Research and Policy Laboratory*. Kluwer, Dordrecht, The Netherlands.

European Council. 2000. *Presidency Conclusions: Lisbon European Council, 23 and 24 March*. Retrieved September 4, 2008 from ue.eu.int/ueDocs/cms_Data/docs/pressData/en/ec/00100-r1.en0.htm.

European Environmental Agency. 2006. *Urban Sprawl in Europe: The Ignored Challenge*. Office for Official Publications of the European Communities. Luxemburg.

Faludi, A., ed. 2002. *European Spatial Planning*. Lincoln Institute of Land Policy, Cambridge, MA.

———. 2006. From European spatial development to territorial cohesion policy. *Regional Studies* 40(6):667–678.

———, ed. 2007. *Territorial Cohesion and the European Model of Society*. Lincoln Institute of Land Policy, Cambridge, MA.

———, ed. 2008. *European Spatial Research and Planning*. Lincoln Institute of Land Policy, Cambridge, MA.

———, and B. Waterhout. 2002. *The Making of the European Spatial Development Perspective: No Masterplan*. Routledge, London.

Fishman, R. 2007. *1808–1908–2008: National Planning for America*. Paper presented at the Rockefeller Urban Summit. www.rpa.org/pdf/temp/America%202050%20Website/Fishman/%20National%20Planning%20Final.pdf, accessed 2007.

Florida, R. 2004. *The Flight of the Creative Class: The New Global Competition for Talent*. HarperCollins, New York.

French Presidency. 2000. *Spatial Development: Summary Report—Synthesis*.

Garnier, J.-F. 1947. *Paris et le Desert Français*. Le Portulan, Paris.

Gottmann, J. 1961. *Megalopolis: The Urbanized Northeastern Seaboard of the United States*. Twentieth Century Fund, New York.

Grasland, C., and P. Beckouche. 2007. *North–South Regionalism*. Unpublished working paper. HAL Archives Ouverts.

Guigou, J.-L. 2001. Europe and territorial planning. Pp. 3–4 in A. Bailly and A. Frémont, eds. *Europe and Its States: A Geography*. La Documentation Française, Paris.

———. 2002. *Aménager la France de 2020: Mettre les Territoires en Mouvement*. DATAR: La Documentation Française, Paris.

Hall, P. 1984. *The World Cities*, 2nd edition. Widenfeld and Nicholson, London.

Huntington, S. 2004. *Who Are We?: The Challenges to America's National Identity*: Simon & Schuster, New York.

Informal Ministerial Meeting on Urban Development and Territorial Cohesion. (2007). Territorial Agenda of the European Union. Leipzig.

Jensen, O. B., and T. Richardson. 2004. *Making European Space: Mobility, Power and Territorial Identity*. Routledge, London.

Kidd, S., D. Massey, and H. Davies. 2003. The ESDP and integrated coastal zone management: Implications for the integrated management of the Irish Sea. *Town Planning Review* 74(1):97–120.

Kunzmann, K. R., and M. Wegener. 1991. *The Pattern of Urbanisation in Western Europe 1960–1990*. Institut für Raumplanung, Universität Dortmund, Dortmund, Germany.

Lieshout, R. H. 1999. *The Struggle for the Organization of Europe: The Foundation of the European Union*. Edward Elgar, Cheltenham, UK.

Molle, W. 2007. *European Cohesion Policy*. Routledge, Abingdon, UK.

NorVision. 2000. *A Spatial Perspective for the North Sea Region*. Vision Working Group, PLANCO Consulting, Essen, Germany.

Polverari, L., and J. F. Bachtler. 2005. The contribution of European structural funds to territorial cohesion. *Town Planning Review* 76:1.

Rifkin, J. 2004. *The European Dream: How Europe's Vision of the Future Is Quietly Eclipsing the American Dream*. Polity, Cambridge.

Robert, J. 2007. The origins of territorial cohesion and the vagaries of its trajectory. In A. Faludi, ed. *Territorial Cohesion and the European Model of Society*. Lincoln Institute of Land Policy, Cambridge, MA.

Ross, C. 2006. *Emerging Megaregions: Studying the Southeastern United States*. Center for Quality Growth and Regional Development (CQGRD) Georgia Institute of Technology, Atlanta

University of Pennsylvania. 2005. *Reinventing the Megalopolis: The Northeast Megaregion*. School of Design, Department of City and Regional Planning, Philadelphia.

Waterhout, B. 2002. Polycentric development: What is behind it? In A. Faludi, ed. *European Spatial Planning*. Lincoln Institute of Land Policy, Cambridge, MA.

———. 2007. Territorial cohesion: The underlying discourses. Pp. 37–60 in A. Faludi, ed. *Territorial Cohesion and the European Model of Society*. Lincoln Institute of Land Policy, Cambridge, MA.

———. 2008. *The Institutionalization of European Spatial Planning*. Delft University of Technology, Delft.

3

Spatial Planning in Asia
Planning and Developing Megacities and Megaregions

Jiawen Yang

One important aspect that differentiates Asian countries such as India, China, and Japan from the United States is the higher population density. Compared with the United States, India and China have similar land sizes but much larger populations. India's population is more than three times, and China's more than four times, that of the United States. Japan has about half of the U.S. population but about one twenty-fifth the land area. Urbanization in these Asian countries has created many megacity regions, which are vast urban agglomerations with populations of more than 10 million people each. According to a report by the United Nations (2004), in 2000 the globe had eighteen such urban agglomerations, with ten of them located in East, South, and Southeast Asia. Those noted were Tokyo and Osaka–Kobe in Japan; Mumbai (Bombay), Delhi, and Kolkata (Calcutta) in India; Jakarta in Indonesia; Beijing and Shanghai in China; Dhaka in Bangladesh; and Karachi in Pakistan. The intense economic interaction in these megacity regions has resulted in significant challenges in providing housing, infrastructure, and social services. Megacity agglomeration has become an attractive element of geographic policymaking (Laquian 2005).

Another relevant issue is the planning needed to address the competitiveness of megaregions in the global economy. The word *globalization* was created when the East Asian territories of Japan, South Korean, Taiwan, Hong Kong, and Singapore rose in the global economy in the second half of the last century. Following their success, China started to open markets and liberalize its economy. The stories of how these Asian countries, and European and American countries, have tried to become more competitive and improve or preserve their quality of life in recent decades has been documented (Newman and Thornley 2005).

Of particular interest in this chapter is an explicit discussion of the spatial and territorial dimensions of policymaking in East Asian countries, including China, Japan, and South Korea. Governments in these countries have acted differently from those of many other nations around the world. This chapter reviews the Asian experience of megacity and megaregion planning mainly from the following three perspectives: the intergovernment relationship that makes spatial planning possible, the concentration and decentralization of power relevant to megacity development and planning, and the planning for functional regions at the megaregion scale.

Intergovernment Relationships and Spatial Planning

The Top-Down Planning System

East Asian countries differ from their counterparts in many other parts of the world in their attitude toward spatial planning. In the United States, for example, any debate over planning, including spatial planning, often takes on a deep ideological flavor. In China, Japan, and South Korea, spatial planning has become a widespread consensus between industry and the bureaucracy. Very little ideological debate has taken place, and spatial planning happens in a natural way, supported by existing intergovernment relationships.

Compared with the federal system in South Asia, East Asian countries have historically set up a centralized government that is gradually evolving toward democracy. For the discussion of spatial planning, Table 3.1 roughly outlines the administrative hierarchy in the United States, China, Japan, and Korea in a comparative geographic and functional scale. More details will be added in the sections that follow. Among the three East Asian countries, Japan has the longest history of democracy and a market economy. In addition, because of its small size, Japan's government is less complex than China's. Japan probably provides the most easily understood example for readers outside East Asia.

Under its national government, Japan has forty-seven prefecture-level governments (including one prefecture-level metropolitan government, the Tokyo Metropolitan Government). Under the prefectures, Japan has more than 3,000 municipalities (cities, towns, and villages) (Abe and Alden 1988). In Japan, strategic policymaking for urban development and planning generally happens at the national level. The national ministries then dispatch information to prefecture government officials at the department director level, who act as chief policy-

Table 3.1

Administrative hierarchy at comparable scales.

United States	China	Japan	Korea
Federal government	Central government	National government	National government
State	Province, province-level city, autonomous region	Prefecture, designated metropolis	Prefecture, prefecture-level city province
County	County, county-level city, urban district urban district	Subprefecture, designated city, Urban district, county, city	Core city, special city, city
Municipality (New England style), borough	Town, township, street committee	Town, township	Homeowner association
	Resident committee, village committee	Ward, town, village	Neighborhood, village

makers for the prefecture government in regard to urban development and planning. The majority of the municipalities do not have much planning capacity. They seek planning and development guidance from the prefecture-level governments (Jacobs 2003).

China and South Korea have a similar top-down planning system in terms of the concentration of power at the higher levels. These similarities are not surprising. All three countries are heavily influenced by the Confucian ideology, which emphasizes hierarchy and order in the society. This ideology is reflected in the planning system as the overriding power of the higher-level government in development issues at the local level. In all three countries, the higher-level government can approve or override local government plans depending on whether they meet higher-level goals. The shared cultural tradition underpins similar planning systems.

This concentration of planning and development power at the top has made a spatial perspective a practicable choice when these countries try to develop their national economies. For example, during the planning of its economy (1949–1980), the Chinese central government used a strong spatial development strategy. The central government moved manufacturing plants away from the developed coastal areas in favor of the less developed inner and western parts of the country for reasons such as national security. This strategy intentionally distorted the location advantage of different places. An explicit spatial argument has also been advanced in the design and implementation of more liberal economic policies. In the early 1980s, the Pearl River Delta was given development priority for its geographic proximity to Hong Kong and Macao, the two closest market economies (Lin 1999). In the 1990s, the Yangtze River Delta was granted development priority for its geographic centrality for the national economy. The central government has promoted this spatial strategy by allocating strategic investment resources and decentralizing decision making to the priority areas.

In Japan, the long-lasting market economy owes much to the authority held by the higher-level government. This configuration allows leaders of the local governments to easily join together to discuss region-wide issues. For example, in addition to making many regional plans, the prefecture-level governments have been generally successful in coordinating infrastructure and land development issues across multiple municipalities (Jacobs 2003).

The Spatial Coordination of Sector Policies

One major argument for spatial policies in these nations is the need to use the limited land more efficiently. Their capacity in spatial planning can be well represented by the institutional arrangement for national land agencies and various land plans. In Japan, after World War II the central government emphasized land planning knowing that limited land area is a big constraint for Japan's economic development. The relationship between the economic plans and the development plan began formally in 1962, when the first national land plan in Japan was developed.

The need to link spatial policy to the overall development goals of the state eventually led to the creation of Japan's national land agency in 1974. According to the National Land Use Planning Act of 1974, one of the roles of this agency is to coordinate the sector policies set by other central ministries. The land agency makes comprehensive national development plans by conducting research and analysis of national land development patterns, drawing up the draft plan, and consulting with related agencies. Following the first national land plan in 1962, more plans were developed in 1969, 1977, and 1998 (Tanimura and Edginton 2001).

Japan has also established a series of prefecture and local land use plans to ensure coordinated control of land use, economic development, and environmental conservation. The National Land Agency makes broad-brush national land use plans for five land use categories: urban, agricultural, forest, natural parks, and nature conservation. These plans are then spatially translated by each prefecture into prefecture land use plans, which broadly indicate on maps the location of the five land use categories.

Similar, if not stronger, institutional arrangements can be found in China and South Korea. China has land agencies at all levels of government. The higher-level land agency sets up the guidelines for the lower level to follow. The land agencies at one government level can override the city plan proposed by the same-level city planning agency if the land use impact of the city plan conflicts with the guidelines set by the land agency. In both Japan and China, land use plans by the national and prefecture governments are only indicative, not statutory. Only the detailed land use control administered by local governments is statutory. In South Korea, the story is slightly different. The national government keeps detailed land use control for land parcels in the specified greenbelts, which will be discussed more thoroughly in the next section.

The Financial Backbone of Spatial Policies

Spatial planning and policies would not be implemented effectively without supportive fiscal institutions. The higher the level of the plan, the more broad the plan is. In Japan and China, for example, spatial policies reflected in the land plans generally encompass only the orientation of economic policy. They do not describe in detail how the plans will be implemented or which policy instruments will be used. Those policy orientations are then taken by the ministry involved in public works for their own investment plans for sewage systems, roads, urban parks and housing, airports, harbors, and railways. The central government plays an oversight role as fund supplier rather than acting as the direct instigator or implementer. Local government is responsible primarily for implementing the various plans.

The result is that, in Japan, around 80 percent of all government spending takes place at the local level, compared with a little more than 50 percent in the United States. However, one cannot take the 80 percent as an indicator for high local fiscal autonomy. In Japan, local government's revenue (local taxes and service charges) is 30 percent of total revenue on average. As for total tax revenue, the central government collects about 60 percent taxes, and local government collects roughly 40 percent. Central government then gives about half of its revenue to local government. About half of the transfer is in the form of specific grants, usually for particular public works, the content of which is controlled by the central government ministries (Tanimura and Edginton 2001). Through these grants, central government steers local government expenditures.

Coming from a planning economy, China's spatial planning was implemented with command and control. Today, as the market plays more roles in resource allocation, China begins to share the major features of Japan's fiscal institutions. In China, business income tax is a major resource of government revenue. This tax is also divided into two parts: a local government part and a national government part. About 30 percent of the total tax goes directly to the local government, and about 70 percent goes to the central government (Wang and Li 2006). In less developed areas, local tax revenue is not enough for the everyday operation of the local governments. For example, in Yongzhou, a prefecture-level city in Hunan Province, local tax revenue covers only 40 percent of the government operating cost. The remaining 60 percent comes from the intergovernment transfers (Yang and Ross 2007). The average nationally is that the central government, through transfers, covers about half of the local expenditures.

However, China is different from Japan in grants. The transfer from the higher-level government targets the insufficiency in the general operation of the lower-level government, rather than being project specific. At the level of the central government, the China National Development and Reform Commission (NDRC) manages some project-specific grants, which cover only a small portion of the total government expenditure.

Chinese local government raises funds for local public works with land lease revenue. In China, the state owns urban land, and the city government represents the state as the actual landowner at each locality. The local government can lease land for a lump sum payment up front, which covers 30 to 70 years of land rent. The Chinese city governments use this land revenue to promote local infrastructure development and urbanization.

Viewed from this perspective, the financial system in Japan appears to give it a much stronger implementation of its spatial polices. The ability of its central government to promote economic development through a national coordinated economic plan has won it the title of a development state. In China, the high fiscal autonomy at the local level has resulted in the loss of control of urban development. For example, the central government's land agency established a general urban population density standard for urban development of 100 square meters for every urban person. However, the central government does not have a strong mechanism to enforce this standard because the city governments changed this standard into a game of numbers. Therefore, the central government has rolled back some already decentralized functions to achieve enforceable land use control by national standards.

The Balance of Power in Megacity Development

The Decentralization of Planning and Development Power

Economic development planning is a dominant theme in Asia. In contrast to the overall planning and fiscal systems that feature centralization, East Asian countries have decentralized power to metropolitan and megacity governments, aiming to best serve local economic development by granting flexibility in policymaking to the megacity government.

Many Asian megacities have comprehensive and unified megacity governments. In India, for example, the state governments hold the power to authorize the creation of a municipal corporation for each metropolitan area. These corporations are generally elected government bodies that provide a variety of public services. In China, as the urban economic region extends beyond the administrative boundary of the central city, suburban counties are generally encouraged or forced to be absorbed by the central city. The result is a comprehensive and unified metropolitan government that covers and even extends beyond a functional metropolitan region. In Japan's urban prefectures, the prefecture governments work as the metropolitan government. A typical example is the Tokyo Metropolitan Government.

As mentioned previously, Japan's city government generally has low local autonomy, which is evidenced by its low fiscal autonomy (30 percent of the total expenditure covered through local revenue). However, this low autonomy does not persist at the same level in cities of different size. Big cities generally have greater autonomy with their higher fiscal capacity and a higher institutional capacity to deal with local development and planning issues.

Japan's cities and municipalities can be classified in a four-tier hierarchy according to the population size. At the top level, cities with populations approaching or greater than 1 million are classified as government ordinance designated cities. These cities include Tokyo, Osaka, Yokihama, Nagoya, and Kobe. The second tier, core cities, includes those with populations greater than 300,000 people. These are considered regional employment centers. There were thirty-five core cities as of April 2003. The third tier, the special case cities, generally have populations of at least 200,000. All municipalities (towns and villages) with populations lower than 200,000 tend to be classified as the fourth tier. The lower the city in the hierarchy, the higher the reliance on the prefecture-level government for policy and planning guidance (Jacobs 2003).

Cities of the first tier, the government ordinance designated cities, can take charge of some duties that are normally handled by the prefecture. They can lead their own agencies for land development and transportation policy within their prefecture-delineated city planning areas, which cover not only the city's territories but also other adjacent municipalities. The city planning area is essentially a metropolitan area defined by urban functions. The implication of this purposeful decentralization of power to the big cities is not difficult to discern: Large cities and urban areas become more efficient by making infrastructure and public service decisions at more localized scales. By doing this, they can address the unique problems they face as a result of their size.

The decentralization of power to big cities has also been evidenced by the promotion of a city to a higher tier along the ladder of the administrative hierarchy. In China, cities can be promoted at the province level, the prefecture level, or a county level. In past years, many county-level cities have been promoted to prefecture-level cities, with the city administrative territory suddenly expanding outward. Leading cities in a province can be promoted to the province level (Beijing, Shanghai, Tianjin, and Chongqin) or semiprovince level (Qingdao and Shenzhen), gaining more flexibility in making development policies. Shenzhen was even granted some legislative rights in 1992, evidence of local autonomy higher than that of a typical Chinese province government. This decentralization process can also be observed in South Korea. The Local Autonomy Act, passed in 1995, released many central controls and decentralized the power to the local government. Big cities have split from their provinces and become province-level metropolitan cities. Examples include Seoul and Pusan.

These three East Asian countries are different from their South Asian neighbors, which have granted almost no planning and development power to the metropolitan or megacity government. In India, for example, the state government makes decisions on the power and resources for the municipal corporation, which is the megacity government there. Kolkata was the capital of India before 1911. The metropolitan government is called Kolkata Municipal Corporation. It provides various municipal services, including water supply, sewage and drainage, solid waste management, street construction, maintenance, cleaning, lighting, naming, and numbering. However, the planning and development power, which is central to metropolitan government, belongs to units outside the municipal corporation. The Kolkata metropolitan planning committee and the Kolkata metropolitan development authority are both state government units (Siddiqui 2004).

The decentralization of power to the metropolitan or megacity level in different countries is associated with different performances in economic development and infrastructure supply. In China and Japan, where megacity government can have significant power over urban development and planning at the mega scale, the infrastructure supply tends to be timely, and economic development performance is good. However, South Asian megacities differ in the quality of urban infrastructure and widespread urban poverty. These differences cannot be explained solely by power allocation and decision making at the megacity scale, but they appear to be relevant (Yang and Ross 2007).

Power Centralization for Fighting Growth Externality

Despite the significant decentralization of power to the megacity government, the need to preserve some power at the higher-level government is also illustrated through East Asian examples. The greenbelt plan in South Korea perhaps is the best example.

Greenbelt or development control zones have been used in many nations to preserve the natural environment in the growing megacities. London, Tokyo, Beijing, and many other Chinese cities have set up greenbelts in their master plans. Land use transition is generally regulated and enforced by the city government; in Beijing, Tokyo, and South Korea, greenbelt plans are enforced by the central government.

In 1966, Seoul, the capital of South Korea, introduced greenbelts in its master plan for the first time. The greenbelt was a 10-kilometer band 15 kilometers from city hall. According to Bae (2007), the major purpose of this greenbelt preservation was to slow down population growth and industrial concentration in Seoul, thus preventing contiguous metropolitan sprawl from merging Seoul with other adjacent cities. In addition, this would develop a large recreational zone by preserving regional open spaces such as national and regional parks and riverbanks.

A regime of severe land constraint faced tremendous pressures stemming from rapid population growth and economic expansion. In 1971, it began to set up a national greenbelt plan, which was initially managed by the relevant group of city governments. Enforcement was soon tightened. Changes in land use in the greenbelt required approval from the president's office at the central government. At its peak, the national greenbelt plan covered 5,397 square kilometers, or 5.4 percent of the nation's land.

This greenbelt plan has aroused a lot of complaints by landowners who have property in the protected belts. A survey indicates that 99 percent of Korean respondents object to the plan, or at least to some of the restrictions. The comparable number in the United Kingdom is 56 percent (Kim 1996). Despite strong opposition from the local community, the national government has enforced the plan. By 1990, 5,200 residents had been penalized for greenbelt violation. This preservation plan was not relaxed until 1999, when a Greenbelt Reform Committee was set up, long after South Korea passed its peak of urbanization (Bae 2007).

Compared with that of Japan and South Korea, China's urbanization is far behind. In 2003, 42.9 percent of China's population lived in urban areas. The corresponding numbers are 80.3 percent in South Korea and 65.4 percent in Japan (United Nations 2004). Today, greenbelt plans are made and enforced by city governments. However, the urbanization and land preservation pressure is pushing China's central government to strengthen its control on urban land. In the late 1990s, the central government decided to take away from the local government land leasing decisions that exceed 525 mu (a mu equals 666.66 square meters) of farmland or 1,050 mu of any other land (Lu 2006). However, the local governments have successfully circumvented these regulations by breaking down big land transactions into several smaller ones. In 2006, the central government announced its second wave effort. They set up seven regional land monitoring offices across the country. One of their major tasks is to check compliance by local governments in leasing land for industrial investment and implementation of the density standard, violation of which has resulted in low-density development in past decades.

Developing and Planning for Megaregions

The Status of Megaregion Planning

Like many other nations, these East Asian countries have no fixed or standard definition of regions for statistical purposes. In Japan, for example, the forty-seven prefectures are aggregated on a regional basis, depending on the nature of the issue involved. For regional development plans, the forty-seven prefectures are usually aggregated into ten regions, including three metropolitan regions and seven predominantly rural regions.

A number of regional development plans exists for each of Japan's eight regions. Some of them were established by national acts, including the National Capital Region Development Act of 1956, the Kinki Region Development Act of 1963, and the Chubu Region Development Act of 1966. Development plans also exist for other regions, formulated by the National Land Agency in consultation with the prefecture-level governments (Abe and Alden 1988). Those plans provide a framework for population growth and land use. They are merely statements of intent rather than definite plans with budgets and projects ready for implementation.

For national economic development plans, the vast territory of China is usually broadly divided into three parts: the coastal area, the middle part, and the western area. With continuous urbanization and the increasing linkage between different metropolitan cities, megaregions have been introduced as a new framework for national spatial development policies. About ten megaregions have been identified, without clear-cut boundaries. The leading three are the Pearl River Delta, the Yangtze River Delta, and the Capital Region, all in the coastal area. These three megaregions use 1.6 percent of national land but house 10.6 percent of national population. They produce 40 percent of national gross domestic product but use only 28 percent of national capital investment. These three regions account for 80 percent of national investment and 72 percent of the national import–export activities (NDRC 2005). No other area better represents the opening up of China's economy than these megaregions.

China's intention for megaregion development is apparent in scholarly research. Based on an international comparison, Gao and Zhang (2004) state that economic agglomeration in megaregions should continue. Megaregions produce

70 percent of the national gross domestic product in Japan and 67 percent in the United States, but only 40 percent in China. They also think leading cities in megaregions will continue to grow. New York produces 24 percent of the national economy, Tokyo produces 26 percent, and London produces 22 percent. In China, Beijing produces only 2.5 percent, Guangzhou produces 2 percent, and Shanghai produces 5 percent. Based on these comparative statistics, Chinese scholars have proposed an interesting future for China. In the future, megaregions should occupy about 20 percent of the national land, house 50 percent of the national population, and produce 80–90 percent of the national gross domestic product (Gao and Zhang 2004).

Policymakers share these views. The state council views economic integration at this scale as the driving force of the second wave of economic growth (NDRC 2005). This is equivalent in importance to the first wave of economic growth driven by the reform and liberalization of the economy starting in the early 1980s. In the national 11th Five Year Plan (2006–2010), NDRC identified megaregion development as a national strategy to maintain the momentum of economic growth and social development.

China has started regional planning for two megaregions: the Yangtze River Delta and the Capital Region. These plans will focus on industrial development, water pollution, transportation infrastructure investment, and so on. However, China lacks the legal framework for regional plans that cover multiple provinces. By working out regional plans for these two megaregions, the state council hopes to provide examples for other regions to follow and to provide insight into legalizing regional planning in China. In the next section, the Yangtze River Delta is used to illustrate what China has accomplished under the auspices of megaregion development and planning.

The Yangtze River Delta as an Example of the Megaregion Rationale

The Yangtze River Delta is the place where the Yangtze River, China's longest river, flows into the Pacific Ocean. It is located in the middle of the eastern coastline. It covers an area of about 80,000 square kilometers. It includes sixteen cities in three different provinces: Jiangsu, Zhejiang, and Shanghai. Shanghai, a megacity with more than 10 million residents, is the leading city in this region. By administrative hierarchy, Shanghai City is a province-level city. All other cities are of county or prefecture levels, belonging to Zhejiang Province or Jiangsu Province.

The establishment of a shared megaregion identity generally precedes megaregion planning. This megaregion identity can be traced back to the early 1900s, when Shanghai became the financial center of China's economy. At that time, Shanghai was the headquarters of the majority of China's banks. More than half of the borrowing and lending activities happened there. Its business connection with the Jiangsu and Zhejiang provinces was also significant, partially evidenced by the information flow. Rice, silk, and cloth producers in Wuxi and Suzhou adjusted their prices according to the market information from Shanghai.

The milepost for the development of this megaregion came in 1992, when China decided to open Pudong, one of Shanghai's suburbs, as one of the leading special economic development zones in China. Shanghai and other cities in the region got a big boost. The new economic forces soon wove the cities into the modern megaregion shown in Figure 3.1.

Industries in Shanghai are capital intensive, and those in Zhejiang and Jiangsu provinces are labor intensive. In expanding their production capacity, many of Shanghai's plants contract the labor-intensive processes to plants in other cities. In updating their production systems toward more capital-intensive processes, plants in Jiangsu and Zhejiang have sought expertise from Shanghai. They hired Shanghai's engineers to work in their plants full-time or part-time.

As state-owned and private enterprises grew bigger in the 1990s, they began to evolve toward a multilocation system. Domestic private enterprises viewed new offices in Shanghai as a sign of their market status. More than 5,000 enterprises moved their headquarters to or created R&D centers in Shanghai. Shanghai's enterprises also invested outside. More than 60 percent of the total outflow is to Jiangsu and Zhejiang provinces (Gao and Zhang 2004). The megaregion development is also reinforced by the inflow of foreign capital. Many businesses from Hong Kong, Taiwan, and foreign nations locate their regional headquarters in Shanghai and build manufacturing plants in other cities.

In 2000, 50 percent of Shanghai's manufacturing products were sold in Jiangsu and Zhejiang provinces. Approximately 30 percent of Jiangsu's products and 20 percent of Zhejiang's products were sold in Shanghai (Gao and Zhang 2004). Different parts of the delta are thus linked by flows of money, products, services, production chains, and product markets (Gao and Wu 2006).

In order to build a competitive region, the central government has tried to promote cooperation between local governments. In 1982, shortly after the introduction of its economic reform policies, the central government created a planning office for the Shanghai Economic Region. At that time the region was composed of ten cities and fifty-five counties. The objective was to create more cooperation between Shanghai's state-owned enterprises and those in other cities. This economic region largely overlaps today's Yangtze River Delta megaregion.

The wave of megaregion planning appears to be driven mainly by the coordi-

Figure 3.1 The Yangtze River Delta Megaregion.

nated efforts of the city and province governments. In 1992, the city government began its own coordination process by starting a Yangtze River Delta Regional Cooperation Forum. Fifteen cities have been involved from the very beginning. Each city created a Yangtze Region Cooperation Office. The director of each office has participated in the forum annually. The stated objective is to improve the regional economic competitiveness through cooperation. In 1997, a higher level of cooperation, the mayor's forum, was established. Fifteen mayors attend the annual meeting. Since 2001, the deputy governors of these three provinces began their own annual meeting, which is a third cooperation platform. In May 2003, the heads of the three provinces began meeting without a fixed schedule. The evolving path of government forums reflects an increased willingness of the local government to negotiate a win–win outcome for the whole megaregion. The efforts have led to more of a shared vision and concrete achievements.

During more than two decades of competition for industrial investment, the city governments finally acknowledged the importance of the shared development and shared prosperity in the megaregion. A well-integrated megaregion economy can result in much greater competitive strength than a spatially separated metropolitan economy. The government leaders are now more willing to act together to integrate regional transportation systems, eliminate institutional barriers to a free flow of input factors, preserve the natural environment, share market information, develop regional plans, and coordinate infrastructure investment. As a result of these efforts, the mayors have signed an agreement that aims to unify the tourist market through information sharing and free entry. The three provinces have worked out an arrangement to build a utility system of natural gas supply rather than build three systems separately, which suggests significant improvement in scale economy. The provinces and relevant cities have also worked out a unified transportation plan for the megaregion. This plan created, for the first time, coordinated infrastructure investment in the region.

One of the megaprojects coming out of the transportation plan is the 35-kilometer Hangzhou Bay Bridge. The private sector financed 50 percent of the project. However, the most significant aspect of this bridge is not its size but the megaregion rationale that makes it possible. In past decades, major transportation infrastructure has been oriented toward a better connection to the capital city in each province. The bridge is in Zhejiang Province. However, it does not shorten the travel time to Hangzhou, the capital of Zhejiang Province. Instead, it shortens travel time from part of Zhejiang Province to Shanghai, the center of the megaregion.

The fifteen cities are well on the road to building multimode and multicity transit systems. For example, the transit card in Shanghai can be used not only for various transit modes such as bus, subway, light rail, and ferry boat but also for taxis. The card can also be used in other cities in the Yangtze River Delta, such as Hangzhou and Wuxi.

There are some problems that cannot be resolved through negotiation between these competing metropolitan government units. Metropolitan governments still fight for business investment to stimulate local economic growth. In doing this, city governments have tried to invest in strategic infrastructure projects, such as airports and harbors, with the danger of significant overinvestment for the megaregion. Perhaps the ongoing Yangtze River Delta Regional Plan can help prevent overinvestment. China's State Committee of Development and Reform (CSDR) has involved leaders from relevant province governments and city governments in this process. Mutually agreed-upon development ideas and investment projects will be listed in the regional plan. Future projects not in the regional plan will not be approved by the central government in the near future.

Conclusions

The challenges at the megacity or megaregion scale are not unique in East Asia. They have also intrigued planners, officials, and businesses in North America, Europe, South America, and Africa (Regional Plan Association 2006; Salet et al. 2003; Mila and Stren 2001; Marques and Bichir 2003). However, the East Asian countries are special in their approaches to these challenges.

First, China, Japan, and South Korea share a common cultural tradition of Confucian ideology. This has only a limited impact in Southeast Asia and almost no impact in South Asia and other parts of the world. In the Confucian ideology, individuals are encouraged to sacrifice for the benefit of the community. Similarly, in the intergovernment relationship, sacrificing local interest for a regional benefit represents a high moral standard. Based on this cultural tradition, all three countries have created strong central governments that have created top-down planning systems and actively promoted spatial development and planning, regardless of the different levels of democracy.

The legal frameworks in these three countries generally make it convenient for the central government to have a strong influence on local events. When and where command and control does not apply, fiscal institutions carry incentives for the cooperation of the local government. Japan has already set up this system, and China appears to be moving in this direction.

Second, East Asian countries have created consolidated and comprehensive metropolitan governments for megacity development and planning. In China, this is done through the promotion of the central city upward toward the administrative hierarchy, which results in the expansion of the administrative boundary of the central city. In Japan, cities are assigned different levels of development and planning functions, according to the size of the city. This governing practice is different from that of many parts of the world, particularly the United States, where an ideology of local autonomy has resulted in many small governments in a single metropolitan region.

Third, in meeting the megaregion challenges, the East Asian countries have used a mixed approach of central government involvement with local negotiation.

A megaregion has a small number of metropolitan governments. This makes government forums a practical solution to the megaregion governance challenge. The history of planning for China's Yangtze River Delta shows great promise. In Japan, the prefecture-level governments have actively promoted coordinated development of municipalities. In addition, Japan's central government has legalized regional planning. China's central government is still experimenting with an agenda of legalizing regional planning.

The Asian system of spatial planning has been criticized. For example, the involvement of the higher-level government happens at the expense of a lack of public participation. In Japan, strong central control has been criticized as the major factor keeping local government from developing innovative policies and inspiring policymakers (Tanimura and Edgintton 2001).

However, the positive aspects of the system can also be identified easily. The strong involvement of the central government in local public works has resulted in almost uniform public service throughout Japan, with very little variation between rich (usually metropolitan) and poor (usually rural) prefectures. In China, the decentralization of the planning and development power to the megacity government surely contributed to the growth of the economy. In South Korea, the enforcement of greenbelts by the central government helped preserve green space in urban areas under tremendous development pressures.

As population growth and urbanization continue, the United States will have more megacities and megaregions. They will face economic and ecological challenges similar to those in East Asian nations, though maybe of a different magnitude. Can the Asian experiences possibly shed light on policymaking in the United States? This overview of how East Asian countries have tried to surmount development barriers with megacity and megaregion planning probably illustrates the importance of policymaking at the mega scale. In addition, intergovernment relations in East Asia, particularly in Japan, could provide some answers to the equity objective formulated by American scholar Jones (2007). Transportation investment in China's megacities and megaregions could provide examples for American counterparts. These Chinese regions have already developed multimodal, integrated public transportation systems viewed as ideal investment strategies by American scholar Todorovich (2007). The East Asian experiences therefore can be valuable laboratories where policymakers can observe development outcomes in relation to different institutional foundations for the urban society.

The United States might not be able to learn much planning implementation from the Asian experience. East Asian government systems and planning practices have grown out of a cultural soil entirely different from that of the West. In addition, power decentralization to the megacity level from the central government, as in East Asia, probably cannot be achieved without power concentration upward to the megacity level from small municipality, city, and county governments in America. Today, proposals on strong metropolitan governments and megaregion planning in the United States generally evoke ideological debates. Concerns about the impacts of regional planning on local autonomy still appear insurmountable. Americans are reluctant to add metropolitan governments and metropolitan planning. Megacity governance and megaregion planning certainly take more political will.

References

Abe, H., and J. D. Alden. 1988. Regional development planning in Japan. *Regional Studies* 22(5):429–438.

Bae, C.-H. 2007. *Land Use Issues in Korea.* Paper presented at the Smart Growth in China Symposium, Beijing.

China National Development and Reform Commission (NDRC). 2005. *The Trend of China's Economy and Regional Development During the 11th Five-Year Plan: Report of National Strength.* Asian LII, Beijing.

Gao, R., and X. Wu. 2006. *The Spatial and Functional Structure of the Greater Shanghai Megaregion.* Shanghai Shanlian Press, Shanghai.

Gao, R., and J. Zhang. 2004. *The Great Shanghai Megaregion.* Shanghai Social Science Academy Press, Shanghai.

Jacobs, A. J. 2003. Devolving authority and expanding autonomy in Japanese prefectures and municipalities. *Governance* 16(4):601–623.

Jones, C. 2007. *Economic and Equity Frameworks for Megaregions.* Regional Plan Association. Lincoln Institute of Land Policy, Cambridge, MA.

Kim, T.-B. 1996. *Comparative Study of Green Belts in the UK and Korea.* Paper presented at the International Symposium on Green Belt Policy: UK and Korea, Yokohama.

Laquian, A. 2005. *Beyond Metropolis: The Planning and Governance of Asia's Mega-Urban Regions.* Woodrow Wilson Center Press, Washington, D.C.

Lin, G. C. S. 1999. State policy and spatial restructuring in post-reform China, 1978–95. *International Journal of Urban and Regional Research* 23(4):670–696.

Lu, X. 2006. *Urban Land Management.* Science Press, Beijing.

Marques, E. C., and R. M. Bichir. 2003. Public policies, political cleavages and urban space: State infrastructure policies in São Paulo, Brazil, 1975–2000. *International Journal of Urban and Regional Research* 27(4):811–827.

Mila, F., and R. Stren, eds. 2001. *The Challenge of Urban Government: Policies and Practices.* World Bank Institute, Washington, D.C.

Newman, P., and A. Thornley. 2005. *Planning World Cities: Globalization and Urban Politics.* Palgrave Macmillan, London.

Regional Plan Association. 2006. *America 2050: A Prospectus.* Regional Plan Association, New York.

Salet, W., A. Thornley, and A. Kreu Kels, eds. 2003. *Metropolitan Governance and Spatial Planning: Comparative Studies of European City-Regions.* E and F Spon, London.

Siddiqui, K. 2004. *Megacity Governance in South Asia: A Comparative Study.* The University Press Limited, Dhaka, Bangladesh.

Tanimura, P., and D. Edginton. 2001. National-level economic planning and spatial planning in Japan. In R. Alterman, ed. *National Level Planning in Democratic Countries: An International Comparison of City and Regional Policy-Making.* Liverpool University Press, Liverpool.

Todorovich, P. 2007. *A Transportation Strategy for 21st Century America*. Regional Plan Association, New York.

United Nations Population Division. 2004. *World Urbanization Prospects, Data Tables and Highlights* (2003 revision). United Nations Department of Economic and Social Affairs. New York.

Wang, J., and W. Li. 2006. *Urban Finance and Social Welfare Programs*. The Capital University of Economic and Trade Press, Beijing.

Yang, J., and C. Ross. 2007. Implementing spatial planning in China's market economy. *Urban Planning Forum* 6.

4

Identifying Megaregions in the United States

Implications for Infrastructure Investment

Catherine L. Ross and Myungje Woo

The spatial and functional dimensions of economic and environmental issues, which are most vital to quality of life and dependent on infrastructure, transcend current political boundaries. For example, environmental issues of air quality, water quality, water supply, and preservation of natural resources do not respect traditional boundaries. Free trade markets and improved information technologies are erasing traditional boundaries of economies. As this process of debordering states intensifies, there should be a larger entity than currently exists within the metropolitan or state area to coordinate the planning of infrastructure, economic, and environmental issues. Why are megaregions so important in terms of transportation and infrastructure planning? Megaregions, networks of metropolitan centers and their areas of influence that have existing social, environmental, economic, and infrastructure relationships, are geographic areas that will contain two thirds of the nation's population by the mid-twenty-first century (Amekudzi et al. 2007). They represent a new and potentially fruitful context for American transportation planning and other decision making related to social and economic development. As megaregions expand and continue to attract significant amounts of the country's population, economic activity, and global connections, they struggle with intense traffic congestion, pressures on the natural environment, constraints on resources, and other negative externalities associated with sprawling urban growth. Given continued growth, it is important to consider how planners, elected officials, and policymakers should structure transportation and infrastructure investment in order to address the particular challenges and opportunities presented by megaregions.

Under the megaregion approach, an emerging question is how we define these regions to effectively incorporate and respond to transportation and infrastructure planning. There have been recent efforts to identify megaregions at the national or regional scale in the United States, including the Northeast, Midwest, Piedmont Atlantic, Florida, Gulf Coast, Texas Triangle, Sun Corridor, California, and Cascadia megaregions (Center for Quality Growth and Regional Development [CQGRD] 2008). However, most research used a threshold method with population-related variables and geographic information systems by which several theme maps were overlapped. In Europe, Karlsson and Olsson (2006) compare three approaches, including the local labor market, commuting zone, and accessibility approach, using labor market data to delineate functional regions in the Fyrstad region of Sweden. Bode (2008) uses land price in delineating metropolitan areas, arguing that previous methods using commuting data understate the actual size of metropolitan areas. However, these methods have emphasized only one aspect, integration of interactions, using a single variable, without considering the relationships between these core areas and their hinterlands.

Although *mega* means "large," the definition of megaregion must not be limited to its spatial size because a megaregion should be characterized by both a functional integration of the urban cores as population and employment centers and the adjacent areas of influence, composed of small cities, rural areas, and natural resources of the region. Defining megaregions should explain the benefits we can derive from planning beyond a metropolitan scale.

The next section of this chapter discusses transportation and infrastructure issues in the context of megaregions. Emerging megaregions and their identification methods are presented in the following section. Next, a conceptual framework to identify megaregions, considering transportation and infrastructure investment, is outlined. The following section suggests the methods of identifying megaregions with core areas and areas of influence. The final section summarizes our concept of megaregion planning.

Why We Need a Megaregion Approach to Transportation and Infrastructure Investment

The trend of global economic markets and increasing international trade puts new pressures on national transportation systems. The significant growth of international trade since 1980 has strained the capacities of U.S. ports and the transportation networks that serve them. Over the next 30 years, the increase of international trade via ports is expected to be much higher than before. Most major ports in the nation are located in megaregions, such as southern California, the Gulf Coast, and the Northeast (Lang and Dhavale 2005; Regional Plan Association [RPA] 2006). Figure 4.1 presents estimated densities[1] of trade volumes with foreign countries in 2035. Estimated trade volumes in 2035 are concentrated in emerging megaregions (identified by RPA 2006).

In addition, many goods from international trade will be moved between megaregions for consumption and to production centers. This implies that the increasing movement of freight will affect not only internal transportation networks of the coastal megaregions but also major interstate highways that connect to other centers of agglomeration.

Specifically, more than 77 percent of commodities were moved from megaregions to other domestic destinations by truck in 2002, and this share is estimated to grow to 80 percent by 2035. In 2002 less than 60 percent of commodities relied on trucking in non-megaregions, and that number is predicted to remain unchanged in 2035 (Table 4.1). All this equates to megaregions experiencing heavier freight traffic on highways than other non-megaregion areas.

The average distance covered by truck freight is shorter (485 miles) than air (973 miles), rail (902 miles), and coastwise water (1,269 miles). Moreover, more than 65 percent of the tonnage of freight movements by truck is estimated to move less than 100 miles (Puentes 2008). This short distance of trucking implies that a freight movement policy between metropolitan areas at the megaregion level would be useful in relieving congestion caused by truck traffic on highways and ensuring just-in-time delivery of goods (CQGRD 2008).

However, the existing structure and requirements guiding transportation planning and infrastructure investment do not reflect these trends. For example, the urbanized areas of megaregions have fewer miles of interstate highways and local roads per 1,000 people than non-megaregions. Specifically, miles of interstate highways and local roads per 1,000 people are 0.0567 and 2.629 for megaregions, respectively, but non-megaregions have 0.0998 and 3.457 miles, respectively, as of June 2004.[2] This implies that interstate highways of megaregions may be more congested than those of non-megaregions, with fewer miles per capita of interstate highways and local roads.

In addition, although many proposed high-speed railway (HSR) corridors connect existing metropolitan areas, each passenger rail route has been identified based on existing transportation patterns, infrastructure, and relevant studies (National Surface Transportation Policy and Revenue Study Commission 2007) without full consideration of future social and economic environments and the global economy. Table 4.2 shows that about 65.7 percent of the proposed mileage of sixty-four intercity corridors (Schwieterman and Scheidt 2007) is located

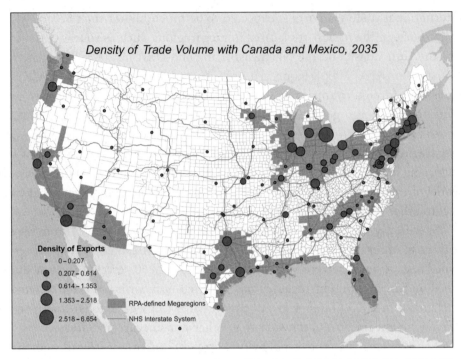

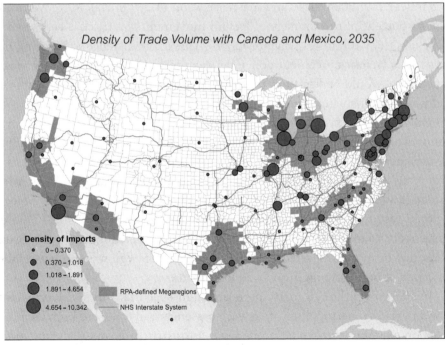

Figure 4.1 Density of Trade Volumes with Foreign Countries, 2035.

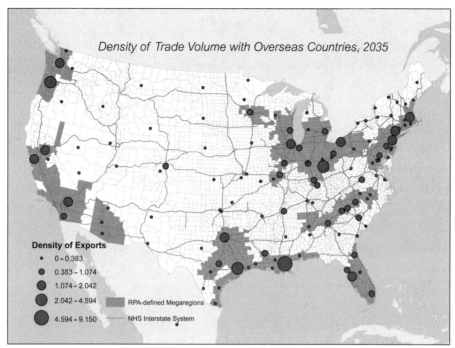

Density of Trade Volume with Overseas Countries, 2035

Density of Exports
- 0 – 0.383
- 0.383 – 1.074
- 1.074 – 2.042
- 2.042 – 4.594
- 4.594 – 9.150

RPA-defined Megaregions

NHS Interstate System

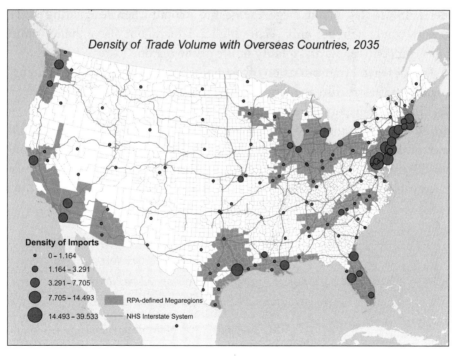

Density of Trade Volume with Overseas Countries, 2035

Density of Imports
- 0 – 1.164
- 1.164 – 3.291
- 3.291 – 7.705
- 7.705 – 14.493
- 14.493 – 39.533

RPA-defined Megaregions

NHS Interstate System

Table 4.1

Transportation modes for exporting goods to domestic destinations between megaregions and non-megaregions areas.

Modes	Megaregions		Non-Megaregions	
	2002 (%)	2035 (%)	2002 (%)	2035 (%)
Air and truck	0.02	0.04	0.01	0.02
Other intermodal	0.52	0.68	1.14	0.84
Pipeline and unknown	14.01	11.97	25.74	26.03
Rail	4.45	4.56	13.34	13.09
Truck	77.16	80.23	56.36	57.02
Truck and rail	0.19	0.2	0.21	0.22
Water	3.63	2.31	3.2	2.77

Source: CQGRD (2008).

within megaregions, and only 40.4 percent of them are formally designated as federal HSR routes. Taking megaregions into account when designating the HSR network would help not only secure higher demand but also enhance the economic competitiveness and quality of life of the region.

Recent federal transportation investments have focused on the maintenance of existing infrastructure in metropolitan areas. The 2005 Safe, Accountable, Flexible, Efficient Transportation Equity Act (SAFETEA-LU) is targeted at local transportation projects and does not coordinate at the regional level, even though much of the existing infrastructure in metropolitan areas was constructed more than 50 years ago and will need greater maintenance investment or an infusion of new capital (RPA 2006). As mentioned earlier, more than 70 percent of the na-

Table 4.2

Share of the proposed mileage of high-speed railway within megaregions and non-megaregions.

	Megaregions	Non-megaregions	Total
Federally designed routes	40.4%	20.1%	60.5%
Others	25.3%	14.2%	39.5%
Total	65.7%	34.3%	100.0%

Source: Derived from Schwieterman and Scheidt (2007).

tion's population and employment growth will be accommodated within megaregions by 2050 (Amekudzi et al. 2007; Ross et al. 2007; RPA 2006), meaning that the future economic success of the United States is directly related to the economic activities of these regions. Therefore, the investment in transportation connectivity and other improvements within and between megaregions is important to support their economic activity and roles as gateways to other parts of the nation (Meyer 2007). Also, an examination of international urban development and transportation infrastructure investment shows the benefits of such interjurisdictional approaches, which can include specializing infrastructure investment, sharing transport infrastructure, and diversifying economic activities (Glaeser 2007; Sassen 2007). Extending transportation and infrastructure planning to the level of the megaregion could deliver significant economic, social, and mobility benefits. This again raises the importance of delineation of boundaries.

Existing Methods of Defining Megaregions

This section describes current efforts to delineate megaregions. Whereas the Metropolitan Institute at Virginia Tech and the RPA have tried to define megaregions on a national scale, several institutions and local initiatives have identified regional-scale megaregions, such as the Piedmont Atlantic, Northeast, Northern California, Great Lakes, and Texas Triangle. These efforts are described here. In addition, we describe delineation approaches used by other countries.

Delineation Approaches in the United States

Since the Northeast Megalopolis, from the north of Boston to the south of Washington, D.C., was identified by Gottmann (1957), such megaregional agglomerations of population and economies have been taking place across the United States. The University of Pennsylvania and the Lincoln Institute of Land Policy have recently begun a national debate on megaregional geography, and researchers have commonly defined megaregions as interconnected large-scale regions beyond the traditional political boundaries. Specifically, the University of Pennsylvania (UPenn) School of Design (2004) defines Supercities, a concept of megaregions, as "extended networks of metropolitan centers linked by interstate highway and rail corridors." The Great Lakes Megaregion plan (Delgado et al. 2006) similarly defines its megaregion as "a set of interconnected metropolitan areas," and the Northeast Megaregion plan from UPenn (2006) defines its megaregion as "large, connected networks of metropolitan regions that are driving an increasing share of global production and trade."

For purposes of discussion, the existing practices of defining megaregions in the United States are divided into two geographic levels: national and regional.

National-Scale Delineation Approach

Among these efforts, the recent approaches by the UPenn School of Design (2004), the Metropolitan Institute at Virginia Tech (Lang and Dhavale 2005), and the RPA (2006) are notable at the national scale, providing criteria to identify megaregions and drawing the boundaries using the county as a basic analysis unit.

Virginia Tech's Metropolitan Institute defines "megapolitan areas" as clusters of counties with more than two metropolitan areas combined and a total population of more than 10 million by 2040. As seen in Figure 4.2, they identified ten megapolitan areas using diverse criteria. The focus was on the functional relationships between counties based on the criteria by which the Census Bureau—defined statistical areas. Metropolitan areas, micropolitan areas, and combined statistical areas (CSAs) are delineated. Thus, the criteria for identifying initial megapolitan areas relies on the contiguity and connectivity of existing core-based statistical areas (CBSAs), between CBSAs and CSAs, and between CSAs, defined by population size and commuting patterns. Such megapolitan areas were determined by other criteria, including cultural and historical geography, transportation networks, and development trends.

RPA (2006) identifies ten megaregions (Figure 4.3), with boundaries not identical to those of megapolitan areas, identified by Virginia Tech's Metropolitan Institute (Figure 4.2), perhaps because of differences in criteria and method

Figure 4.2 Ten Megapolitan Areas Identified by the Metropolitan Institute at Virginia Tech.

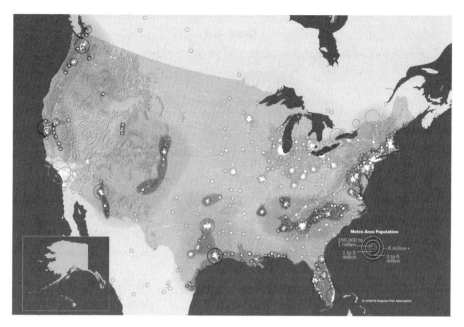

Figure 4.3 Ten Megaregions Identified by the Regional Plan Association.

(Table 4.3). Although their specific methods have not been published, they are based on the common interest of the following five categories of relationships: environmental systems and topography, infrastructure systems, economic linkages, settlement patterns and land use, and shared culture and history.

Table 4.4 compares the results of the megapolitan and megaregion approaches by describing which metropolitan areas are contained in each. The Metropolitan Institute includes Oklahoma City and Tulsa, Oklahoma as megapolitans, focusing on the Interstate 35 corridor, and includes Houston in the Gulf Coast Megapolitan. However, RPA excludes those Oklahoma metropolitan areas from megaregions and identifies a triangular form of metropolitan areas within Texas. The Metropolitan Institute identifies a broader area as the Northeast megaregion, including Richmond, whereas RPA's region stretches south to the Washington, D.C. metropolitan area. However, the Metropolitan Institute delineates a smaller area for the Midwest megaregion, whereas RPA identifies a broader area including Minneapolis, Minnesota and Buffalo, New York. In addition, RPA excludes Knoxville, Tennessee from the Piedmont Atlantic Megaregion, and the Metropolitan Institute excludes Jacksonville from the Florida megaregion.

Although they identified ten similar megaregions, the differences are critical. Such differences result from the inclusion or exclusion of some metropolitan areas that are core areas in the regions, rather than hinterlands. At this time,

Table 4.3

Comparison of delineation criteria of megaregions in the United States (at the national scale).

	Metropolitan Institute	Regional Plan Association
Analysis unit	County	County
Requirement of megaregions	More than 2 metropolitan areas and 10 million population by 2040	NA
Analysis criteria	Population size	Environmental systems and topography
	Contiguity	Infrastructure system
	Cultural and historical geography	Economic linkage
	Physical environment	Settlement patterns and land use
	Links of large centers	Shared culture and history
	Growth projections	
	Goods and service flows	

Source: CQGRD (2008), derived from Metropolitan Institute and Regional Plan Association reports.

it is hard to tell why the results are different because RPA's method has not been published. It should be noted that the criteria for identifying core areas must be comprehensive to fully explain their relationships.

REGIONAL-SCALE DELINEATION APPROACH

Although there have been some discussions about nationwide megaregions in the United States since Gottmann identified the Northeast Megalopolis, regional-scale efforts to identify megaregions have been identified as Northeast by UPenn, Piedmont Atlantic by Georgia Institute of Technology (Georgia Tech), Northern California by San Francisco Planning and Urban Research (SPUR), Great Lakes by the University of Michigan, and Texas Triangle by the University of Texas, Austin.

The criteria used in delineating regional-scale megaregions can be categorized into Census Bureau–defined criteria for statistical areas, transportation and economy, environments, and political environments (Table 4.5). Because most of the Census Bureau–defined criteria are used in five megaregions, except for "commuting" with the Great Lakes[3] and the Texas Triangle, these criteria play a key role in identifying megaregions. The reason why population, contiguity, and

Table 4.4

Comparison of identified megaregions and megapolitan areas in the United States.

Metropolitan Institute (10 megaregions)	Regional Plan Association (10 megaregions)
1. Northeast (including Richmond, VA)	1. Northeast (excluding Richmond, VA and Virginia Beach, VA of Chesapeake)
2. Midwest (including Chicago, IL; Detroit, MI; Indianapolis, IN; Cincinnati, OH; Columbus, OH; Pittsburgh, PA; and Cleveland, OH)	2. Great Lakes (including Minneapolis, MN; Chicago, IL; St. Louis, MO; Indianapolis, IN; Louisville, KY; Cincinnati, OH; Columbus, OH; Cleveland, OH; Detroit, MI; Pittsburgh, PA; and Buffalo, NY)
3. Piedmont (including Knoxville, TN)	3. Piedmont Atlantic (excluding Knoxville, TN)
4. Peninsula (excluding Jacksonville, FL)	4. Florida (including Jacksonville, FL)
5. Gulf Coast (including coast areas of Louisiana, Mississippi, Alabama, Texas, and Florida)	5. Gulf Coast (including coast areas of Louisiana, Mississippi, Alabama, Texas, and Florida)
6. I-35 Corridor (including Tulsa and Oklahoma City, OK; Dallas–Fort Worth, San Antonio, and Austin, TX)	6. Texas Triangle (including Dallas–Fort Worth, Houston, San Antonio, and Austin, TX)
7. Valley of the Sun	7. Arizona Sun Corridor
8. Cascadia	8. Cascadia
9. NorCal	9. Northern California
10. Southland	10. Southern California

Source: CQGRD (2008), derived from Metropolitan Institute and Regional Plan Association reports.

commuting flows are used as primary criteria is that most plans have attempted to identify core metropolitan areas as population and employment centers in the region and to analyze their relationships.

Other criteria, including transportation, economy, physical environment, and political environment, were used to complement the primary criteria or to delineate the boundaries of hinterlands of core areas. Some specific criteria, such as an industrial history, were used only for the Great Lakes because this region has historically shared industrial activities, specifically manufacturing. Freight movement and transportation networks were considered in two studies to measure the connectivity between regions.

Environmental issues have taken on significance in delineating megaregions. For example, all studies emphasize the conservation of environmentally sensitive areas. Other environmental resources, such as open space, recreation resources, and watersheds were considered. Geographic characteristics, including

Table 4.5

Delineation criteria of selected megaregions at a regional scale in the United States.

		Piedmont Atlantic	North-east	Northern California	Great Lakes	Texas Triangle
Census-defined criteria of statistical areas	Population	•	•	•	•	•
	Contiguity	•	•	•	•	•
	Commuting	•	•	•	•	
Transportation and economy	Freight movement	•				•
	Transportation network	•			•	•
	Industrial history				•	
Environments	Geography	•		•		
	Environmentally sensitive area	•	•	•	•	•
	Open space and recreation resources		•		•	
	Watershed	•	•			
Political environments	Regional groups			•		

Source: CQGRD (2008).

oceans, rivers, and mountains, were considered as obstacles that prevent connectivity within and between the different regions.

In addition, the Northern California megaregion considers existing government-defined regional groupings. Because megaregional planning does not mean creating a new megaregional government, it would be useful to review the scope of government entities in delineating megaregions.

Delineation Approaches from Abroad

Table 4.6 shows different delineation criteria that are used in selected foreign countries. Because European and East Asian countries (except China) are small, some megaregions are transnational. As a result, these transnational megaregions are more focused on the connectivity between major cities and countries via infrastructure, such as a high-speed railway system and undersea canals, rather than the delineation of boundaries of hinterlands.

The functional urban regions of the Randstad, in the Netherlands, include a core and a hinterland. A core area consists of municipalities that have a total of at least 20,000 jobs and a job density of seven jobs per hectare (17.29 jobs per acre). Commuting data are used to identify hinterland areas. Similar to the con-

Table 4.6

Delineation criteria of foreign megaregions.

	Randstad (the Netherlands)	NUTS (European Union)	Zhujiang Delta (China)	Northeast Asian Megaregions
Analysis unit	City	City	—	City
Analysis criteria	*Core*	*NUTS*	*Physical geography*	*International interaction*
	Employment density	Population size	Flood zones	Air passenger traffic
	Population size		Coastal lines	Flow of information
		Non-administrative units	River basins	International labor migration
	Hinterlands	Continuity		
	Commuting flows	Geography		
		Socioeconomics		
		History		
		Culture		
		Environment		

NUTS, Nomenclature of Territorial Units for Statistics.
Source: CQGRD (2008).

cept of employment interchange measure of the U.S. Census, municipalities that send more than 10 percent of commuters to the core areas are assigned to the hinterlands. Twenty-five functional urban regions are identified in the Randstad area (Lambregts et al. 2006).

The European Union (EU) divides member states into three regions. The Nomenclature of Territorial Units for Statistics (NUTS) is used to designate administrative divisions of the member states for statistical purposes. The NUTS is a hierarchical classification of areas because it subdivides the member states into NUTS 1, NUTS 2, and NUTS 3 (Figure 4.4). The NUTS 1 regions are subdivided into other NUTS administrative divisions. The EU defines territorial units using normative criteria: population size and geographic areas (existing administrative units). The NUTS are similar to the system of the U.S. statistical boundaries, such as the Metropolitan Statistical Areas (MSAs) in their delineation criteria and uses. Although they are not directly applicable to megaregions, useful information can be drawn from their decision criteria.

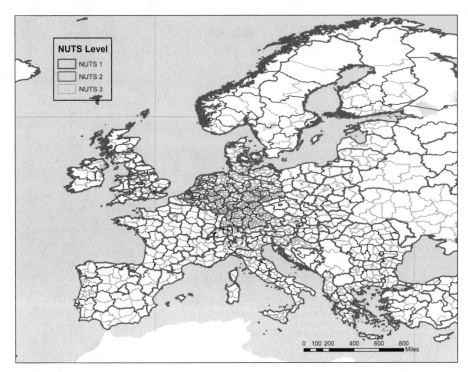

Figure 4.4 Nomenclature of Territorial Units for Statistics Levels of the European Union. Data Source: ESRI, 2006.

Table 4.7 presents the thresholds of the average population size to divide the regions into NUTS 1, NUTS 2, and NUTS 3. However, if there are no administrative units in these population scales in a member state, a new geographic unit (nonadministrative unit), which constitutes existing small administrative units, can be aggregated considering such relevant characteristics as contiguity, geography, socioeconomy, history, culture, or environment (The European Parliament and the Council of the European Union 2003). For example, the entire territory of the Republic of Croatia, which is one of three official candidate countries of the EU, corresponds to NUTS 1. However, although existing counties represent NUTS 3, there are no administrative units for the NUTS 2 based on the population threshold. Because the NUTS level 2 is an important framework for implementing regional policies in Croatia, there was an effort to form statistical regions at the NUTS2 level by combining counties (Bakaric 2006).

In a study of Southeast Asia, Macleod and McGee (1996) divide urban regions into three regions: urban core, metropolitan areas, and extended metropolitan regions, which are later called mega-urban regions. The extended metropolitan regions are similar to hinterlands of the U.S. megaregions, while authors do not specify the boundaries of the region (Douglass 2000). Chu (1996)

Table 4.7

The minimum and maximum thresholds for the average population size of the NUTS regions.

	Minimum	Maximum
NUTS 1	3,000,000	7,000,000
NUTS 2	800,000	3,000,000
NUTS 3	150,000	800,000

NUTS, Nomenclature of Territorial Units for Statistics.
Source: Article 2 of the Regulation (EC) No. 1059/2003 of the European Parliament and of the Council of 26 May 2003 on the establishment of a common classification of territorial units for statistics.

describes one Chinese megaregion, the Hong Kong–Zhujiang Delta, in a framework of the world city system. The region is defined by physical characteristics, such as flood zones, coastal lines, and river basins, and includes seven municipalities and twenty-one xians (counties) with a total area of 42,600 square kilometers (16,448 square miles).

Since the Cold War era, policymakers in China, Japan, and Korea have increasingly emphasized the three countries' mutual political and economic

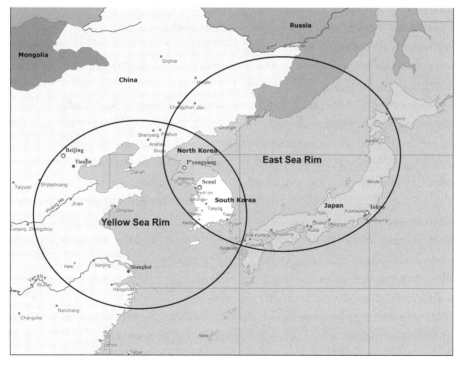

Figure 4.5 The Yellow Sea Rim and the East Sea Rim in Northeast Asia (Choe, 1996).

relationships. Choe (1996) presents two emerging Northeast Asian megaregions: the Yellow Sea Rim and the East Sea Rim (Figure 4.5). Without the issue of specific boundaries of the megaregions, he identifies transnational interactions between major cities using several criteria, such as air passenger traffic, the flow of information (the volume of international telephone calls), and international labor migration.

Conceptual Framework for Identifying Megaregions

Structure of Megaregions: Core Areas and Areas of Influence

A region is categorized into a uniform region and a functional (or nodal) region (Cadwallader 1996). A uniform region is an area that has homogeneity of certain characteristics, such as history, culture, environment, and industry. A functional region is characterized by a high degree of social and economic interaction. Healey's (2004) relational approach emphasizes the relationships of places that are located in particular relational networks. In addition, Healey describes an essentialist approach as a traditional approach in which physical proximity is important and specific boundaries of regions or settlements are identified. In this approach, regions are divided into several zones, such as core areas informed by higher value-generating activities and its area of influence by lower ones. However, the areas of influence support the core areas by providing complementary functions. In this case, these two spatial areas, including a core area and its areas of influence, are assumed to generate "vertical synergy"[4] resulting from the performance of different economic roles and the host of complementary activities, residential offerings, and environments.

We propose that megaregions should include core areas, which are highly agglomerated and interact with each other via certain types of networks, and their areas of influence, which support the functions of the core areas and are characterized by the shared characteristics of history, culture, and environmental corridors. Furthermore, the enhancement of economic competitiveness, the preservation of environments, and the growth management against excessive spatial expansion indicate that defining megaregions entails both the identification of interactions between core metropolitan areas and the delineation of areas of influence where environmentally sensitive zones are threatened by uncontrolled and sprawling development patterns. Also, as Sassen (2007) mentions the rural enterprise zones require megaregional investment to provide low-wage jobs to play a more complete role in the global economy, the areas of influence would include potential areas for future industrial use to support the economic vitality of core areas in a global market. Such areas should be taken into account for future transportation and infrastructure planning.

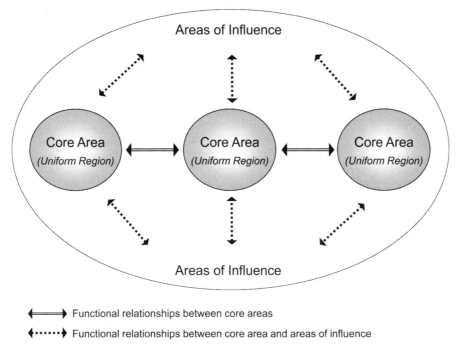

Core Area
(Uniform Region)

Core Area
(Uniform Region)

Core Area
(Uniform Region)

Areas of Influence

Areas of Influence

◄────► Functional relationships between core areas

◄┄┄┄► Functional relationships between core area and areas of influence

Figure 4.6 Spatial Structure of Megaregions.

Whereas each core area and area of influence is a uniform region, the spatial structure of megaregions, where core areas and areas of influence interact, forms a functional region. In other words, the spatial structure of megaregions, which are divided into core areas and their areas of influence, represents an essentialist approach, whereas the megaregion itself forms a functional region because several core areas and their areas of influence have their own functions and generate certain types of synergy. The relationship between several core areas within a megaregion would be identified by a relational approach. Areas of influence, characterized by uniform regions, are also identified by a relational approach (Figure 4.6). However, some essentialist criteria are commonly used in identifying both core areas and areas of influence. For example, proximity and contiguity are significant throughout the process of identifying both core areas and areas of influence.

Criteria for Identifying Megaregions

The criteria used in the previous studies can be categorized into essentialist criteria and relational criteria, as Healey (2004) presents. Essentialist geography is a traditional approach in which the relationship between places is hierarchically determined by their activities. Proximity and contiguity are important factors that characterize their relationship. On the other hand, the relational approach

Table 4.8

Criteria for identifying core areas and areas of influence.

	Major Categories	Criteria	Methods
Core areas	Essentialist approach	Agglomeration	Population
			Employment
		Economic activity	Economic product
			Globalization
			Greenhouse gas emissions
		Geographic relationships	Contiguity and proximity (distance)
	Relational approach	Economic interaction	Movement of commodities Spatial autocorrelation statistics
		Movement of information and financial capital	Graph theory approach
			Industrial structure
		Social interaction	Migration
			Commuting
			Travel frequencies
		Infrastructure networks	Transportation networks
			High-bandwidth networks
		Socioeconomic characteristics	Historical and cultural relationship
Areas of influence	Essentialist approach	Natural environment	Environmentally sensitive areas (watershed, forest, and farmland)
		Physical environment	Geographic obstacles (e.g., mountains, rivers, flood zones, oceans)
			Green infrastructure (open space and recreation resources)
		Political environment	Regional groups
			Voting patterns
		Geographic relationships	Contiguity and proximity (distance)
	Essentialist–relational approaches	Socioeconomic characteristics	Population
		Employment	Density functions
		Land price	Multivariate analysis method

Table 4.8 *continued*

Major Categories	Criteria	Methods
	Historical characteristics	Mapping method
		Cultural characteristics
		Future growth
Relational approach	Social interaction	Migration
		Commuting
	Economic interaction	Movement of commodities
	and financial capital	Movement of information
		Industrial structure

Source: CQGRD (2008).

emphasizes that spatial effects cannot be determined by physical proximities because the effects may occur from a distance as well as nearby. In addition, specific territories do not necessarily bound a place, and the nodes and borders are continually changing according to their relationship with others.

In the megaregion studies, several criteria including proximity, contiguity, population growth, settlement patterns, and political boundaries expressed as essentialist criteria were used to identify candidate megaregions. In addition, relational criteria such as commuting patterns, labor migration, and industrial flows have been analyzed to examine interactions between regions. In a spatial context, although the relational approach is important to understanding broad economic issues in a national and global economy, the traditional (essentialist) approach is useful in policy implementation. For example, specific boundaries of regions are needed for effective physical infrastructure planning and implementation. In addition, such boundaries and distance criteria are useful to designate and protect environmentally sensitive areas. Thus, a desirable approach should incorporate the advantages of both essentialist and relational approaches.

There is no doubt that population and employment concentrations are among the most important criteria in defining megaregions. As seen in Table 4.8, each core area can be defined by the criteria of population, employment, economic product, globalization, greenhouse gas emissions, contiguity, and proximity. The interactions of core areas of the region can be measured by the movement of commodities, financial capital, information, and people; by the transportation and high-tech infrastructure networks; and by the industrial structure and historical and cultural relationships.

Although areas of influence normally are established as a buffer zone outside core areas, they are important to frame spatial planning so that the future growth of population, economy, and infrastructure is accommodated. It is necessary to take into account the preservation of environmentally sensitive areas from the threat of rapid urban growth, physical environments, and socioeconomic and political environments that can be used to draw a uniform region. In addition, socioeconomic and economic relational criteria should be used to measure the relationship between core areas and areas of influence.

Procedures for Delineating Megaregions

The procedure for delineating megaregions could include several stages: identifying core areas, delineating the boundaries of areas of influence, applying local characteristics, and finalizing the boundaries (Figure 4.7). After the initial delineation of core areas and areas of influence, the most important components of the procedure, local characteristics are used to revise the boundaries. The boundaries of megaregions are reviewed periodically to reflect changes in impacts on natural environments, regional growth, and demands for infrastructure in a global marketplace.

Although some different criteria were applied for delineating regional megaregions, most previous studies relied on overlapping maps created by geographic information systems and tabulating the information using a descriptive analysis for both core areas and areas of influence. Although a mapping method and a descriptive analysis sometimes provide clear distinctions between spatial units, it is difficult to distinguish subtle differences between areas. More elaborate methods suggest that the spatial elements of the point[5] (usually the centroid of polygon) and network patterns, described by Unwin (1981),[6] would be used in identifying core areas and measuring the agglomerations and interactions between regions. Surfaces and regions would be used for areas of influence by identifying homogeneous areas that share common criteria.

Identifying Core Areas

Most megaregion studies use existing Census Bureau–defined MSAs as core areas. Although MSAs explicitly represent the concentration of population, they are defined by population threshold and commuting ties and fail to incorporate economic activities and the interaction of other characteristics between regions. Here, we suggest specific procedures and methods of identifying core areas.

- Measuring agglomerations of population and employment, economic activities, and geographic relationships, using essentialist criteria (identifying hub areas and other core areas). A spatial autocorrelation statistic, such as Moran's I,[7] can be used to find a peak area.

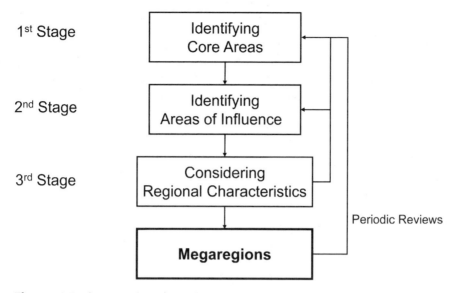

1st Stage

2nd Stage

3rd Stage

Identifying
Core Areas

Identifying
Areas of Influence

Considering
Regional Characteristics

Megaregions

Periodic Reviews

Figure 4.7 The Procedure for Delineating Megaregions.

- Identifying candidate core areas by contiguity and proximity. Large areas that cover multiple core areas would be considered to test their relationships.
- Measuring the extent of interactions between hubs and candidate core areas using relational criteria, such as social and economic interactions and infrastructure networks. Graph theory and Markov chain approaches are applicable for those diverse criteria to identify a hierarchy system of the region.
- Determining hub areas and other relevant core areas.

Besides a threshold method, mathematical models, such as graph analysis and Markov chains, have been used to measure the relationships between regions.

Since Nystuen and Dacey (1961) pioneered the graph theory approach in urban systems, this concept has been broadly used in grouping or ranking regions based on commuting flows, commodity flows, telephone flows, and migration flows. The direct and indirect associations measured by these flows, between city or region pairs, are quantified and the strongest networks are identified (Nystuen and Dacey 1961; Campbell 1972; Dietvorst and Wever 1977; Puebla 1987). In this approach, a spatial unit is represented by a point, and the relationship between spatial units is represented by a line. The measured flows form an origin and destination matrix where each place I sends its largest flows to place J, which is larger than place I. Place J is defined as the central place or nodal point. This network of nodal points and largest flows is the frame of the urban hierarchy with urban cores and their subordinate cities in the entire region. This method is useful to draw spatial structures for each megaregion where functional relationships between central counties and their outlying counties, or between metropolitan areas, can be measured.

Whereas the graph theory approach captures only the present situation of the relationships in the urban system, the Markov chain approach reflects the process of change in the system (Dietvorst and Wever 1977). This method is based on acceptance of the interaction matrix itself as representing the structure of the interaction phenomenon without implying any causal structure and on computation of the probabilities (P_{ij}) calculated by dividing the observed flow from I to J by the corresponding row sum of interaction from I to J. This probability matrix is converted into a limiting matrix calculated by the successive **n** powering of the probability matrix until each row becomes identical. The mean first passage time (MFPT) matrix is calculated as $MFPT_{ij} = \sum_{n=1}^{\cdot} nf_{ij}^{(n)}$. The element of this matrix corresponds to a nonspatial measure of proximity or functional distance between places I and J, meaning that the lesser value is the greater level of interaction. The average (MFPT) ($MFPT_j = \sum_i MFPT_{ij}$) for a given destination J is regarded as a summary measure of its overall accessibility and centrality in the urban hierarchy (Hirst 1975). Thus, clustering destinations, based on the MFPT, provides a delineation of functional regions and a regional hierarchy.

Identifying Areas of Influence

Identifying the areas of influence of core areas is more complex because regional characteristics are based on diverse criteria from physical environments to socioeconomic characteristics. The following procedure is suggested:

1. Identifying candidate areas of influence with density functions. The candidate areas of influence are tested by density gradients of demographic and economic factors. Geographically weighted regression analysis, or other econometrics, can be used to estimate density gradients of each spatial unit (e.g., county) and displayed on the map to find the spatial extent of influences of core areas.

2. Incorporating shared natural amenities. Natural and physical environments can be analyzed by a mapping method, as applied in previous studies. In addition, multivariate analysis methods, such as cluster analysis, would be applicable to group homogeneous areas using environmental data, including water area, topographic variation, temperature, and humidity.

3. Incorporating shared socioeconomic characteristics and projected growth areas. In a similar way, a mapping method and multivariate analysis method can be used.

Several multivariate analysis methods, such as factor analysis, principal component analysis, and cluster analysis have been increasingly used in delineating the boundaries of diverse regions. Similar origin and destination matrices in the graph theory and Markov chain approaches have been used in this analysis. For example, Illeris and Pedersen (1968) use factor analysis with interregional telephone flows to delineate places with a high degree of centrality in Denmark, Davies and Musson (1978) use commuting flows, and Roepke et al. (1974) use an input–output table of Ontario, Canada. Clark (1973) and Clayton (1980) use telephone flows to delineate urban linkage patterns and the major organizing nodes, respectively. Harrigan (1982) uses input–output flows to identify industrial and spatial clusters, and Slater (1981) uses them to analyze college student international flows. Although many researchers have used a single variable of flows in their analyses, multivariate analysis is useful because several variables can be used in the model. For example, Kim and Woo (2000) use both factor and cluster analyses with transportation flows, population and employment densities, office building areas, and a number of cultural facilities to delineate subcenters in Seoul, Korea.

Density functions have also been used to analyze spatial structure, noting that the urban core, which has significantly larger population and employment densities than surrounding locations, has a significant effect on the overall density function, with an assumption that population and employment density declines with distance from the core. Although this monocentric concept is well explained by a traditional negative exponential model, researchers have developed models— a cubic spline density function, a nonparametric estimation procedure, and a geographically weighted regression analysis—which can be used to analyze a polycentric spatial pattern. In a cubic spline function, the relationship between density and distance is modeled with piecewise and continuous polynomials. The x-axis is divided into several segments, and the points linking segments are called knots. If there are four knots denoted by X_0, X_1, X_2, X_3, X_0 and X_3 and are the minimum and maximum values of the x-axis, respectively. Muniz et al. (2003) use cubic spline density functions to delimitate the density effect of satellite cities in Barcelona's metropolitan area. However, regressions including multiple variables denoting distances to employment centers might have the problem of multicollinearity. Alternatively, McMillen and McDonald (1997) use a nonparametric estimation procedure, locally weighted regression, to reduce the misspecification bias of the locations and multicollinearity. In order to identify subcenters, McMillen (2001) propose a two-stage nonparametric procedure and apply the method for identification of subcenters to a variety of cities. Craig and Ng (2001) also use a nonparametric procedure to identify employment subcenters using quantile smoothing splines for Houston. The common idea of all these nonparametric procedures is to find local rises in the density function by comparing the gradients of the fitted employment density functions with what would be expected without an employment subcenter. In addition, Fotheringham et al. (1998) suggest that geographically weighted regression can be used to examine the spatial variability of regression results over space and the presence of spatial nonstationarity. It assumes that a relationship might vary over space and that parameter estimates might exhibit significant spatial variations in some cases. If spatial variations of employment can be mapped from these methods, it would be a useful technique to identify subcenters and to investigate the urban spatial structure of a metropolitan area.

In fact, these methods, including graph theory, Markov chains, multivariate analysis, and density functions, have been applied for a metropolitan-level spatial analysis and have not been used in megaregion analysis in the United States. Because urban hierarchical systems are also applied to megaregions, these methods are useful to identify urban cores and to delineate the boundaries of their hinterlands.

Although this procedure can draw emerging megaregions on a national scale, different weights on specific criteria should be given at the regional level because each region has its own economic, social, historical, and cultural characteristics. These regional characteristics and the relationships between the core areas and the areas of influence should be considered in the final delineation of megaregions. In addition, the boundaries of megaregions and delineation criteria should be reviewed periodically to inform future changes.

Conclusions

Economic and social interactions are increasingly taking place at the megaregion scale beyond the traditional political boundaries. More population and economic activities are expected to be concentrated in emerging megaregions. In this context, megaregion planning has been discussed as an approach capable of responding to challenges presented by debordering, increased global competition, the rising significance of regions, environmental resource planning and management (including climate change), transportation planning, and infrastructure investment in a global economy.

One of the key issues in megaregion planning is how we define and identify megaregions. In order to compete with foreign megaregions, the United States needs to increase economic competitiveness while maintaining the quality of life in the region. The megaregion should include both core areas, which are interconnected agglomerations via transportation networks, and their areas of influence, which support the functions of the core areas while expanding economic opportunities throughout the megaregion and resolving environmental issues.

Census Bureau–defined statistical areas that most previous studies used as basic units in their delineation methods provide a basic picture of the large-scale region at the national level. However, simple population thresholds have defined their core areas, and the interaction between core areas and outlying communities or between CBSAs has been measured by only commuting ties and proximity. Although simple methods can be easily applied for broader areas such as the United States, they normally fail to incorporate complex relationships between the regions.

Most previous megaregion studies used a mapping method and a descriptive analysis with diverse criteria including population, contiguity, commuting patterns, freight movement, transportation networks, and environmental characteristics. Although a mapping method and a descriptive analysis present a more systematic procedure than those for Census Bureau–defined statistical areas, a high degree of social and economic interactions between core areas and between core areas and the areas of influence are too complex to be captured by these methods.

We apply the essentialist and relational approaches presented by Healey (2004) for spatial planning to identify megaregions. We suggest a functional spatial structure of megaregions with core areas and areas of influence based on an essentialist approach. Each core area and area of influence forms a uniform region itself. However, three-stage systematic procedures for identifying megaregions are performed mostly by a relational approach. In the first stage, core areas are identified through a combination of spatial autocorrelation statistics, graph theory methods, and Markov chains. In the second stage, the areas of influence are delineated by density functions, multivariate analysis methods, and mapping methods. Finally, the core areas and the areas of influence are reexamined in terms of regional characteristics and the relationship between these two areas.

Notes

1. The densities were calculated by dividing the estimated weights of commodities in 2035 between the United States and foreign countries by areas of regions using the data from the U.S. Federal Highway Administration's Freight Analysis Framework (FHWA 2006). The unit of density is thousands of short tons per square mile.
2. These data are reorganized from the table of miles and daily vehicle-miles of travel in FHWA (2006), and Regional Plan Association–defined megaregions are used as tentative megaregion locations in this analysis.
3. Although an extensive analysis with commuting sheds was conducted in the Great Lakes plan, this criterion does not have weight in defining the Great Lakes megaregion because the au-

thors conclude that commuting shed analysis has little meaning in such a large-scale geographic area (Delgado et al. 2006).

4. On the other hand, "horizontal synergy" can be achieved when each area has similar characteristics and generates economies of scale. Meijers (2005) examines the synergetic effects for the Randstad region in the Netherlands.

5. Spatial units, such as cities, counties, and metropolitan areas, are recognized as points when the relationships between those units are analyzed.

6. Unwin (1981; cited by Cadwallader 1996) explains spatial distribution with four major elements: points, lines, surfaces, and regions. A point pattern is used to represent the distribution of spots that are of interest. A line pattern is used to describe a pattern of networks, such as roads and railroads. Surfaces are represented by isolines where points of equal value are connected.

7. Moran's *I* is a weighted correlation used to detect departures from spatial randomness. Han (2005) uses this method to delineate spatial clustering of condominium property values in Singapore.

References

Amekudzi, A., L. Thomas-Mobley, and C. Ross. 2007. Transportation planning and infrastructure delivery in major cities and megacities. *Transportation Research Record* No. 1997: 17–23.

Bakaric, I. R. 2006. *Methods of Multivariate Analysis to Uncover Socio-Economic Differences Among Spatial-Economics Entities*. ERSA Conference Papers ersa06p56. European Regional Science Association. Louvain-la-Neuve (UCL)

Bode, E. 2008. Delineating metropolitan areas using land prices. *Journal of Regional Science* 40(1):131–163.

Cadwallader, M. 1996. *Urban Geography: An Analytical Approach*. Prentice Hall, Upper Saddle River, NJ.

Campbell, J. 1972. Growth pole theory, digraph analysis, and interindustry relationships. *Tijdschrift voor Economische en Sociale Geografie* 63:79–87.

Center for Quality Growth and Regional Development (CQGRD), Georgia Institute of Technology. 2008. *Megaregions: Literature Review of the Implications for U.S. Infrastructure Investment and Transportation Planning*. U.S. Department of Transportation, Federal Highway Administration, Atlanta.

Choe, S.-C. 1996. The evolving urban system in North-East Asia. In F.-C. Lo and Y.-M. Yeung, eds. *Emerging World Cities in Pacific Asia*. United Nations University Press, New York.

Chu, D. K. Y. 1996. The Hong Kong–Zhujiang Delta and the world city system. In F.-C. Lo and Y.-M. Yeung, eds. *Emerging World Cities in Pacific Asia*. United Nations University Press, New York.

Clark, D. 1973. Urban linkages and regional structure in Wales: An analysis of change, 1958–68. *Transactions of the Institute of British Geographers* 53:41–58.

Clayton, C. 1980. Interdependence in urban system and its applications to political reorganization. *Geografiska Annaler* 62B(1):11–20.

Craig, S. G., and P. T. Ng. 2001. Using quantile smoothing splines to identify employment subcenters in a multicentric urban area. *Journal of Urban Economics* 49:100–120.

Davies, W. K. D., and T. C. Musson. 1978. Spatial patterns of commuting in South Wales, 1951–1971: A factor analysis definition. *Regional Studies* 12(3):353–366.

Delgado, E., D. Epstein, Y. Joo, R. Mann, S. Moon, C. Raleigh, E. Rhodes, and D. Rutzick. 2006. *Methods for Planning the Great Lakes Megaregion*. Urban and Regional Planning Program, University of Michigan, Ann Arbor.

Dietvorst, A. G. J., and E. Wever. 1977. Changes in the pattern of information exchange in the Netherlands, 1967–1974. *Tijdschrift voor Economische en Sociale Geografie* 68:72–82.

Douglass, M. 2000. Mega-urban regions and world city formation: Globalization, the economic crisis and urban policy issues in Pacific Asia. *Urban Studies* 37:2315–2335.

The European Parliament and the Council of the European Union. 2003. Regulation (EC) no. 1059/2003 of the European Parliament and of the Council of 26 May 2003 on the establishment of a common classification of territorial units for statistics (NUTS). *Official Journal L* 154:1–41.

Federal Highway Administration (FHWA). 2006. The Freight Analysis Framework (FAF) Commodity Origin–Destination database.

Fotheringham, A. S., C. Brunsdon, and M. Charlton. 1998. Geographically weighted regression: A natural evolution of the expansion method for spatial data analysis. *Environment and Planning A* 30:1905–1927.

Glaeser, E. 2007. Do regional economies need regional coordination? In K. S. Goldfeld, ed. *The Economic Geography of Megaregions*. The Policy Research Institute for the Region, Princeton University, Princeton, NJ.

Gottmann, J. 1957. Megalopolis or the urbanization of the northeastern seaboard. *Economic Geography* 33:189–200.

Han, S. S. 2005. Polycentric urban development and spatial clustering of condominium property values: Singapore in the 1990s. *Environment and Planning A* 37:463–481.

Harrigan, F. J. 1982. The relationship between industrial and geographic linkages: A case study of the United Kingdom. *Journal of Regional Science* 22(1):19–31.

Healey, P. 2004. The treatment of space and place in the new strategic spatial planning in Europe. *International Journal of Urban and Regional Research* 28(1):45–67.

Hirst, M. A. 1975. Telephone transactions, regional inequality and urban growth in East Africa. *Tijdschrift voor Economische en Sociale Geografie* 66(5):277–293.

Illeris, S., and P. O. Pedersen. 1968. *Central Places and Functional Regions in Denmark: Factor Analysis of Telephone Traffic*. Lund Studies in Geography, Series B, No. 311. Department of Geography, The Royal University of Lund, Sweden.

Karlsson, C., and M. Olsson. 2006. The identification of functional regions: Theory, methods, and applications. *Ann Reg Sci* 40:1–18.

Kim, C. S., and M. Woo. 2000. The hierarchy of centers and their characteristics in Seoul. *The Journal of Korea Planners Association* 35:17–29.

Lambregts, B., R. C. Kloosterman, M. van der Werff, and E. R. Röling. 2006. Randstad Holland: Multiple faces of a polycentric role model. In P. Hall and K. Pain, eds. *The Polycentric Metropolis: Learning from Mega-City Regions in Europe*. Earthscan, London.

Lang, R. E., and D. Dhavale. 2005. Beyond megalopolis: Exploring America's new "megapolitan" geography. In *Metropolitan Institute Census Report Series*. Metropolitan Institute Census Report Series, Alexandria, VA.

Macleod, S., and T. G. McGee. 1996. The Singapore–Johore–Riau growth triangle: An emerging extended metropolitan region. In F.-C. Lo and Y.-M. Yeung, eds. *Emerging World Cities in Pacific Asia*. United Nations University Press, New York.

McMillen, D. P. 2001. Nonparametric employment subcenter identification. *Journal of Urban Economics* 50:448–473.

———, and J. F. McDonald. 1997. A nonparametric analysis of employment density in a polycentric city. *Journal of Regional Science* 37(4):591–612.

Meijers, E. 2005. Polycentric urban regions and the quest for synergy: Is a network of cities more than the sum of the parts? *Urban Studies* 42(4):765–781.

Meyer, M. D. 2007. Toward a vision for the nation's surface transportation system: Policies to transcend boundaries and transition to a new era. Pp. 7–18 in *The National Roundtable on Surface Transportation*. Regional Plan Association and Lincoln Institute of Land Policy, Tarrytown, NY.

Muniz, I., A. Galindo, and M. A. Garcia. 2003. Cubic spline population density functions and satellite city delimitation: The case of Barcelona. *Urban Studies* 40(7):1303–1321.

National Surface Transportation Policy and Revenue Study Commission. 2007. *Transportation for Tomorrow*.Washington, D.C. National Surface Transportation Policy and Revenue Study Commission

Nystuen, J. D., and M. F. Dacey. 1961. A graph theory interpretation of nodal region. *Papers and Proceedings of the Regional Science Association* 17:29–42.

Puebla, J. G. 1987. Spatial structure of network flows: A graph theoretical approach. *Transportation Research B* 21B(6):489–502.

Puentes, R. 2008. *A Bridge to Somewhere: Rethinking American Transportation for the 21st Century*. Metropolitan Policy Program at the Brookings Institution.Washington D.C. Regional Plan Association (RPA). 2006. *America 2050: A Prospectus*. New York.

Regional Plan Association. 2006. *America 2050: A Prospectus*. Regional Plan Association, New York.

Roepke, H., D. Adams, and R. Wiseman. 1974. A new approach to the identification of industrial complexes using input–output data. *Journal of Regional Science* 14(1):15–29.

Ross, C. L., A. Amekudzi, and J. R. Barringer. 2007. *Mobility in the Megaregion*. In 2007 Association of Collegiate Schools of Planning Conference, Milwaukee, WI.

Sassen, S. 2007. Megaregions: Benefits beyond sharing trains and parking lots? In K. S. Goldfeld, ed. *The Economic Geography of Megaregions*. The Policy Research Institute for the Region, Princeton University, Princeton, NJ.

Schwieterman, J. P., and J. Scheidt. 2007. Survey of current high-speed rail planning efforts in the United States. *Transportation Research Record* 1995:27–34.

Slater, P. B. 1981. Comparisons of aggregation procedures for interaction data: An illustration using a college student international flow table. *Socio-Economic Planning Science* 15:1–8.

University of Pennsylvania. 2006. *Uniting People, Places & System: Megalopolis Unbound*. School of Design, Department of City and Regional Planning. Philadelphia, PA.

University of Pennsylvania School of Design City Planning Studio. 2004. *Toward an American Spatial Development Perspective*. Philadelphia, PA.

Unwin, D. 1981. *Introductory Spatial Analysis*. Methuen, New York.

Part II

PLANNING AND DESIGNING FOR LIVABLE MEGAREGIONS

5

Megaregions or Megasprawls?
Issues of Density, Urban Design, and Quality Growth

Tridib Banerjee

Almost 50 years ago, a Greek planner named Constantin Doxiadis imagined a whole new scale of viewing urbanization of the world beyond the notion of megalopolis, made famous by Jean Gottmann's (1961) well-known work on the urbanization of the Atlantic seaboard. He called it ecumenopolis—or a system of continuous urbanized regions—which would come to represent the future pattern of global urbanization, not unlike what we see today in the night light images of the globe sent by orbiting satellites. Many of his other ideas, such as "dynapolis"[1] (a continuous lineally growing city and its core) and "ekistics" (a new science of human settlements), proved a bit romantic for the contemporary world. But he was prescient in his images of emerging patterns of urbanization worldwide, considering that world population was only about 35 percent urbanized at that time. Now we hear that Chinese policymakers are considering their future urbanization challenges met by nine or ten megaregions of some 50 million people each.[2] The BeSoTo (Beijing–Seoul–Tokyo) region spanning seas separated by a few hours' flight time is now a conceptual reality. And in the United States we are talking about ten megaregions containing some 80 percent of the urban population by 2050 (Regional Plan Association 2006).

The growing corpus of symposia, reports, and writings on the definition, dimensions, and distribution of megaregions have enlightened us about the megaregion trend and begun to define the challenges and opportunities that lie ahead. The question now is, "What's next?" Are megaregions destined to be megasprawls of one kind or another? What are the necessary imperatives for planning and public policy? What are the social, economic, environmental, and livability consequences of such growth? To draw from the title of Britton Harris' (1960) article "Plan or Projection?" we now have the projection, but what is the plan? Does the plan have a normative vision, or is it just a projection of the present? Although Doxiadis (1974) was upbeat about the future growth of cities and the emergence of the "ecumenopolis," he was much less specific about the human consequences of this scenario. He had very little to say about the impact of urbanization on the immediate environment, much less global warming, issues of economic growth, or the enduring concerns about poverty and social justice. His normative vision, if there was one, was overwhelmed by his enthusiasm for the projected urban growth worldwide.

My goal for this chapter is to explore the normative dimensions for the unfolding future of these megaregions in terms of density, design, and livability issues. I intend to organize this discussion in three parts. In the first part I review the previous normative visions involving development of large regions and the relevant concepts and predilections about the spatial form of regions at the metropolitan scale, including the recent literature on megaregions. In the second part, I propose that megaregions should be seen as systems of places and present an organizing construct for grouping them. I argue that this construct is consistent with the political economy of metropolitan and regional governance and therefore is appropriate for analytical and policy purposes. In developing this construct I suggest a typology for looking at the ten megaregions identified by the Regional Plan Association's (2006) *America 2050* report and the attendant institutional challenges for planning and governance. In the third part of the chapter I specifically consider the issues of density, design, and livability, drawing from the Southern California megaregion—the Los Angeles County to be specific—as a case in point. In the final concluding section I discuss the alternative possibilities for shaping the emerging forms of megaregions under the current constraints of governance and the normative principles that must guide such actions.

Forms of Megaregions

There are at least two major related and normative precedents of planning at the scale of larger regions.[3] One of those is Benton Mackaye's plans for the Appalachian region and the open space system for the eastern seaboard (Spreiregen 1965). The other example is that of Mumford and colleagues' regional vision embedded in the proposals of the Regional Plan Association in the 1920s, described by Carl Sussman (1976) as the "planning the fourth migration." Concerned about the unprecedented urban growth in the first half of the last century, Mumford clearly wanted decentralization of jobs and population from the urban core and envisioned a regional development that would allow open spaces to be abundantly available in the urban fabric, making it possible for the public to easily access open space and enjoy nature. It is interesting to note that today we are revisiting the cause for open spaces from an active living perspective. However, the forms of regional growth that would allow such "communion with nature" probably would be classified as urban sprawl today and score high on any of the dimensions of a sprawl index (Ewing et al. 2002). Indeed, the Regional Plan Association's second plan in the late 1960s already had to confront the urban sprawl that resulted from the policies of the earlier plan (Calthorpe and Fulton 2001).

In retrospect it seems that many of the normative visions of the American metropolitan development had indirectly prescribed urban sprawl by emphasizing lower-density development in their antipathy for higher-density urban living and associated anti-urbanist bias typical of the turn of the century (see White and White 1962). Consider Frank Lloyd Wright's "Broadacre City" concept. Although not conceptualized at the regional scale, the individualistic and pastoral values implicit in Wright's prescription for low-density urbanization presaged urban sprawl as its obvious outcome. Similarly, economist Jack Lessinger's (1962) case for "scatteration" (or planned leapfrog development) on the grounds of adaptability and resiliency in future urban growth was blatant advocacy for urban sprawl. In recent years other economists, especially of the libertarian or marketist bent, have celebrated sprawl as a market outcome and an expression of consumer sovereignty and personal liberty. Although presented as a positivist argument, the position of market determinism is also deeply ideological and romantically normative (Bruegmann 2005; Gordon and Richardson 1997; Ewing 1997).

Indeed, low-density urban growth—something we would characterize as urban sprawl—was the recommendation for future urban growth offered by Ian McHarg (1969), a staunch environmentalist, who placed ecological values above economic values. McHarg's recommendations usually were based on multidimensional analyses of the site or a region that defined the density and land use options. Often these analyses suggested very low-density urban development as the best option for urbanization given the ecological constraints of the region. But this deterministic position often was remiss about the higher-order consequences of such low-density development. Such issues as sustainability, increase in vehicle miles of travel, waste disposal, energy costs of such development or their ecological footprint, global warming, and the coming crisis of water availability were not included in McHarg's reckoning.

More than 40 years ago Friedmann and Miller (1965) argued that the emerging spatial structure of American urbanization comprised metropolitan core

regions and "intermetropolitan peripheries," a spatial order derived from technological choices and consumer preferences. They imagined that soon the cores and
peripheries would be unified within a single matrix, which they conceptualized as
an "urban field," where territorial identities of urban settlements are diffused or
absent as the urbanized space becomes continuous and unbroken, not unlike Doxiadis's notion of "ecumenopolis," or the prospects of megaregions we are facing
today. This is a classic scenario of deconcentration, decentralization, and diffusion of urban functions made possible by a high degree of auto-mobility and low-
density living, or what Fishman (2005) calls "bourgeois utopia." Clearly the
"urban field" scenario was inspired by the urban pattern of Los Angeles in its
earlier incarnation but also later in other metropolitan areas, as captured by Garreau's (1991) characterization of edge cities. All these writings were in a way an
endorsement of Mel Webber's (1964) earlier arguments about the emerging
order of the "non-place urban realm," ironically paralleling Kunstler's (1993)
characterization of much of the American landscape as a "nowhere" land.

In his search for performance characteristics of good city form, Kevin Lynch
(1990) talked about the most common patterns (actual, imagined, or idealized) of
urban and metropolitan form. All these patterns, in various combinations, can be
used to define, anticipate, or even desire the emerging form of the megaregions.
Three patterns are noteworthy. First is the notion of "galaxy," which suggests an
absence of hierarchy among the urban places, but with a hint of separation and
identity. It is interesting to note that in a recent report Lang and Dhavale (2005)
identify the Piedmont Atlantic megaregion as a "galaxy" of cities and a prime
example of one of the poles of their galaxy–corridor continuum in which they
locate various megaregions.

The best example of the galactic form of megaregion is the Ruhrgebeit in
Germany, at least the way it looked in the mid-twentieth century. Subsequently
a collective planning effort envisaged a regional open space system that would
be easily accessible to the communities of the region—very much in a Mum-
fordian sense—and would augment the separation and identity of various cities.
In recent years, however, despite some impressive accomplishments in convert-
ing industrial brownfield sites to productive cultural and recreational facilities,
much of Ruhrgebeit is beginning to look like American-style urban sprawl as the
regional open space compact is steadily eroded in favor of freeways and peripheral low-density suburban developments.

Lynch also spoke of a pattern he called a dispersed sheet, clearly referring to
the Los Angeles urban form of the 1960s, but today metropolitan areas of
Phoenix and Las Vegas will be the more appropriate candidates. He deplored the
faceless, shapeless form of contemporary metropolises, which lacked identity,
structure, and legibility—some of the themes of his earlier study of city images

(Lynch 1960). (Years later Frederic Jameson [1991] suggested that Lynch's findings of a lack of imageability of urban areas were a sign of alienation of the public with the immediate built environment of late capitalist societies.) Years later, as the Los Angeles urban region is morphing into a higher-density and ethnically polyglot metropolis with distinct place identities, *dispersed sheet* may not be an appropriate descriptor. Today the region may be better described as a polycentric net, another form prototype suggested by Lynch. Indeed, the image of a polycentric net underlies some of my own arguments for the mosaic and net representation of megaregions for analytical and policy purposes.

The point of this review is that there is a body of literature spanning almost three quarters of a century that looked at the possible forms and urbanization options of large regions. Some of these ideas were visionary and normative. Others were merely descriptive and taxonomic, in the positivist tradition of social sciences. Still others, in recent years, are speculative and certainly provocative. But one thing is clear. Whether visionary and normative or scientific and positivist, the intellectual tradition in the American planning culture has implicitly accepted or endorsed urban sprawl, as defined by low-density urban development. Some of this can be traced to the anti-urban sentiments of American intellectuals at the turn of the twentieth century (see White and White 1962, for example). Others come out of the belief in individual liberty and the deep faith in the market processes.

But few of these earlier visions or positions were analytic or based on solid empirical evidence. Furthermore, there is little in the way of policy guidance or institutional implications for implementing some of these ideas. For example, we don't know whether one form is more just and fair than the other or, from a utilitarian point of view, whether any of these candidate normative patterns is Pareto superior to the other ones and, more importantly, what might be the relevant criteria for evaluating their Pareto optimality or superiority, the guiding principles of decision making in Western liberal democracies. With these vexing questions in mind, I turn to some propositions for looking at the form of megaregions more analytically in order to develop a framework for normative thinking about the megaregion as a system of places.

Megaregions as Systems of Places

Much of the previous literature related to the definitions of megaregions has been dominated by census data and their necessary spatial containers, such as standard metropolitan statistical areas (SMSAs), primary metropolitan statistical areas (PMSAs), and combined metropolitan statistical areas (CMSAs). The discussions have been driven by trends and projections of population and employment growth and decline, but not necessarily with the experience of places and communities in transition or the livability aspects of such change. Here I propose that we think of megaregions as systems of places different from the artifacts of census data. I use the term *places* advisedly because not all populations of urbanized spaces are contained within the incorporated boundaries of cities. The notion of "systems of places" has the ring of "systems of cities" studies conducted by urban geographers (see Berry and Garrison 1955 for example), which typically focused on the dynamics of size and spatial distribution of urban settlements.

The main point of thinking of megaregions as systems of places is that it allows us to systematically examine the dynamics of change in the settlement patterns through such well-established techniques as rank–size distribution or similar measures of concentration and deconcentration. It could tell us whether a megaregion in question is evolving from a unipolar or primate distribution to a multipolar and nonhierarchical distribution, as in the galactic formation we considered earlier. The dynamics of rank–size distribution could tell us whether the Pareto coefficient is approaching the value of 1, indicating a well-articulated system that suggests the optimal condition of diffusion of economic development or innovation throughout the megaregion. Conversely, if the rank–size analysis shows an increase in the Pareto coefficient leading to a primate or dual-primate distribution, it would suggest growing inequality and polarization within the megaregion, resulting from declining or stagnant lower-order urban places that may need policy intervention. Such primate tendencies might also suggest a case of what Sites (2003) calls "primitive globalization," in which exogenous forces of global capital work in collaboration with local governments to produce significant urban change. Similar exogenous effects may also explain the swelling ranks of the migrant population, which further contributes to primacy and distortions in existing urban hierarchy.

In megaregions such as Southern California, where more than 90 percent of the urban population lives in cities, analytically thinking of them as a system of cities may make sense. In the Piedmont or Gulf megaregions, where a much larger share of urban populations is distributed among the peripheral unincorporated areas—in areas that could best be described by the term *desa-kota* (literally meaning "country and city"), which McGee (1991) uses to describe peripheral urbanization in Indonesia and other developing countries—counties might be the appropriate unit of analysis in examining the structure and organization of systems of places.

In our discussion of the future of megaregions, the notion of a system of places also has normative implications without privileging any particular form or pattern. The mission of restoring a sense of place and creating place identities in the midst of nonplace urban realities and the pervasive sense of placelessness (Relph 1976; Arefi 1999) should remain the major imperative for design and policy intervention at different scales within megaregions (Calthorpe and Fulton 2001).

Whether there is such a thing as regional identity, or whether the public is aware of such identity, is an important question to consider in the context of planning megaregions. Some observers believe that there are climatic, cultural, environmental, geographic, and historical determinants of regional identity and that the public is aware of such identities (Lynch 1990). Casey (2002), for example, offers the following definition of a region:

> By "region" I mean a group of closely concatenated places that are (1) spatially contiguous with each other (i.e., between which there is no void space); (2) temporally coexistent and thus cohistorical—that is, possessing a shared history, whether or not this is recorded by human beings. . . . In the practice of landscape painting region is a privileged, nonsubsumable domain in which natural presences, things and people and place, coinhere. It is privileged and nonsubsumable inasmuch as it is a primary way in which natural world organizes itself in our experience. Whether as wild or as cultivated, this world presents itself to us as always already regionalized.

Casey's definition further endorses the argument for looking at megaregions as systems of places, with a shared history defined by a nonsubsumable domain of nature. Of course this definition begs the question as to whether megaregions currently defined would satisfy such criteria.

An important consideration in defining the system of places, as is true in defining any concept of system, is how to delineate the boundaries of the system. Should it be based on natural regions or ecosystems such as valleys and watersheds? Or should it be based on economic linkages or drawn around political boundaries? Dewar and Epstein (2007) point out that models of regional definition often rely on three types of measurements: linkages, gradients, and boundedness, with respective emphases on flows and connections between points, fluctuations or continuums between phenomena or locations, and spatial units of political action or data inventory.

However, the regional reality may still elude these different approaches to regional definitions. Thus the southern boundary of the Southern California region conveniently stops at the international border, lately reinforced by a wall and increased border patrol. But San Diego and Tijuana are integral parts of the same ecosystem (cf. Lynch and Appleyard 1990), as San Diego residents are occasionally reminded when untreated sewage from the Tijuana River washes up the beaches of Coronado.

Analysis of the physical form of a megaregion must begin with an inventory of the natural setting and the ecosystem and the cultural adaptation of the landscape, including the uses of nature services in the development of the regional economy (cf. Cronon 1991). The McHargian approach to regional ecosystem analysis should serve as a model for such studies of regional ecosystems. If we look at the physical form of the megaregions we have identified to date, it should be clear that nature—coastlines of lakes, bays, and oceans, ranges of mountains, systems of rivers and streams, fertile valleys and watersheds, prairies and forestland, desert landscapes—have all played a role in shaping the landscape of megaregions and the pattern of urbanization. The examination of the built environment and settlement form should focus on their edges and interstices as well as on the natural landscape that has been adapted to make these settlement forms possible. Topography, drainage, aquifer recharge areas, ground and surface water sources, possible sites for waste disposal, and the like must be parts of such larger analysis of the systems of megaregions. Preservation of the natural landscape and ecosystem must be the first and most obvious step in defining the future form of megaregions.

The functions and organization of the existing settlements and their historical evolution must be examined and understood. This should necessarily involve understanding the economic functions and specializations of the settlements, distribution of employment centers, commuting patterns, residential mobility, and so forth. Analyses of this sort should inform us about the degree of specialization and location constraints or opportunities within the system of places.

The institutional and spatial organization of a megaregion as a system of places can be conceptualized at two levels: as an interconnected network of places that serves as a component of a regional "growth machine" (cf. Molotch 1976 and Castells 1996) and as a mosaic of autonomous political spaces created to exercise the sovereignty of "public choice" but with an exclusionary and inegalitarian outcome. Whereas the former construct has to do primarily with the nature of economic linkages and hierarchies within a megaregion, the latter is mainly about institutions and governance.

System of Places as a Net

The construct of a net may draw from Manuel Castells's (1996) characterization of emerging patterns of urban agglomeration in different parts of the world as an outcome of the increasing role of the information and communication technology in shaping urban patterns. He points to the constellation of cities in the Guangzhou–Hong Kong–Shenzhen megaregion and the infrastructure links between these cities. Boyer's (2000) recent essay on the future of urbanism and urban form in cyberspace—the world of Web sites, hyperlinks, and databases—

echoes some of Castells's arguments. The question remains as to whether or how we must be thinking of the form of megaregions inextricably linked to the "network" society and its digital divide and how we might engender "spaces of places" in the ubiquity of "spaces of flow" (see Castells 2005).

Of course, the existing infrastructure network is an important determinant of the spatial organization of the system of places. As Lang and Dhavale (2005) point out, the interstate highway system has played a major role in defining the linear organization of settlements within various megaregions in the second half of the twentieth century. Concentration of future growth at a higher density and with mixed use along infrastructure corridors or nodes remains a favorite scenario for the smart growth or new urbanist advocates. Transportation networks are likely to play a critical role in shaping the spatial organization of the settlement system.

Future improvements and possibilities of technological innovations and communication networks must be considered in this analysis along with the infrastructure capacity of water and other utilities and waste disposal. It may prove that the infrastructure net is more like a semilattice rather than a hierarchical tree in which the nodes and links are not always coterminous, implying a level of intractability in the conceptualization of the megaregion (cf. Alexander 1965).

It is possible to think of the regional net as comprising the natural services of the region, as Casey's definition of suggests. Thus rivers and streams, irrigation channels, aquifer regimes, valleys and ridges, soil patterns, and plant and animal habitats can all be considered part of an elaborate natural network defining the "privileged and non-subsumable domain" of the region.[4]

System of Places as a Mosaic

Any comprehensive analysis of a megaregion as a system of places must also include an understanding of the social ecology of the system. Distributions of populations by their demographic characteristics, ethnicity, and socioeconomic status should tell us whether there are concentrations of the poor, the elderly, the working class, or certain ethnic or migrant populations and how such ghettoes or enclaves (see Varady 2006) will fare in the future, or whether there are examples of systematic and institutionalized segregation and social exclusion.

If the infrastructure network or net hints at the inherent intractability of grasping the policy challenges for shaping the future megaregion, it is brought to fore in the form of the fragmented political spaces of American local governance. The questions of future density, affordable housing, environmental justice, equality in educational opportunity, equity in access to open space and amenities for public life, improved mobility, equal promises and possibilities for healthy living, and the like are all inextricably linked to the structure and institutions of local governance in America. Most metropolitan areas have emerged as a "fragmented metropolis," a term originally used by historian Robert Fogelson (1993) to describe the political space of the Los Angeles metropolitan area. Referring to the same phenomenon, economist and public choice theorist Charles Tiebout (1956) and his colleagues (Ostrom et al. 1961) wrote about efficiency in municipality service provision in a fragmented political space, arguing that the fragmentation serves as a political marketplace for the provision of public goods. The rights of the local government to decide how they want to define the quality of community life have led to what economists call "Tiebout sorting," in which some municipalities function as clubs requiring hefty membership fees in the form of high property or rental values by controlling their land use portfolios. Many of these municipalities serve as de facto gated communities through exclusionary zoning, without creating actual walls or gates. Meanwhile, the older and larger cities in the metropolitan area that are not able to keep their land use portfolio as exclusive have seen the rise of actual gated communities at a "sub-Tieboutian" level (Banerjee 2007). Furthermore, the fragmented Tieboutian space of America's metropolitan landscape has created not only clubs for the rich but also soup kitchens or enclaves of the poor (Banerjee and Verma 2006).

Toward a Typology of Megaregions

Accordingly, the landscapes of megaregions must be conceptualized as mosaics (or crazy quilts) and nets, the former referring to the fragmented spaces of local governance and the latter to the grid or network of infrastructure that weaves through this crazy quilt.

These two major schemas of megaregional forms with variations in between may imply an embellishment to the corridor–galaxy continuum suggested by Lang and Dhavale (2005). On one hand. we can think of subregional mosaics of political space around the core as first-order metropolitan cities connected by nets of infrastructure. On the other hand, we may conceptualize the entire megaregion as a mosaic of large cities and counties interwoven by an infrastructure network.

It is possible to consider the current configurations of the ten American megaregions identified by the Region Plan Association and the U.S. Census Bureau in a framework defined by two conceptual axes: the galaxy–corridor dimension identified by Lang and Dhavale and the mosaic–net continuum I suggest here. I should note that at one level the net–mosaic dichotomy is more of an analytical distinction and not mutually exclusive. Thus the mosaic of the Southern California urban form, which represents continuous and contiguous urbanized political space, is at the same time served by a well-developed network of some 600 miles of freeways. Similarly, a netlike regional form typical of the

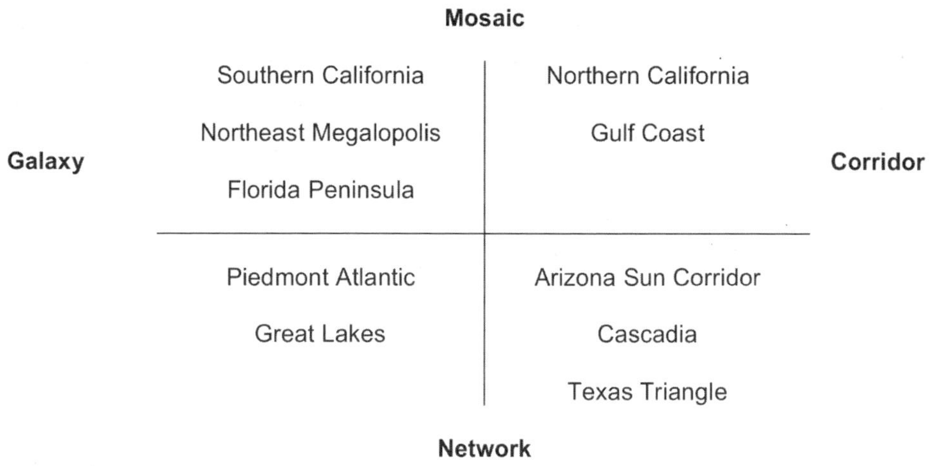

Mosaic

Galaxy	Southern California	Northern California	Corridor
	Northeast Megalopolis	Gulf Coast	
	Florida Peninsula		
	Piedmont Atlantic	Arizona Sun Corridor	
	Great Lakes	Cascadia	
		Texas Triangle	

Network

Figure 5.1 Classification of Ten Megaregions.

Piedmont Atlantic region also has clusters of mosaics around the major urban centers. Nevertheless, the schema presented in Figure 5.1 groups the ten megaregions by their similarities and differences. These differences are further illustrated by their institutional characteristics (Table 5.1).

Table 5.1

Selected characteristics of the Ten megaregions by form type.

Form Type[a]	Megaregion[b]	Number of Metropolitan Areas[c]	Percentage Urbanized[d]	Density[e]
Galaxy–mosaic	South Florida	12	92.0	397
	Southern California	6	98.2	352
	Northeast Megalopolis	31	89.3	265
Mosaic–corridor	Northern California	13	93.3	265
	Gulf Coast	16	83.0	146
Corridor–network	Texas Triangle*	12	83.5	193
	Cascadia	10	84.5	158
	Arizona Sun Corridor	2	94.1	93
Network–galaxy	Great Lakes	50	83.0	264
	Piedmont Atlantic	33	67.3	253

*The number of metropolitan areas and percentage urbanized are for the I-35 corridor only, which Lang and Dhavale (2005) use as a discrete megaregion. In their schema the Houston metropolitan area is included in the Gulf Coast megaregion.

Sources:[a]Lynch (1990); [b]Regional Plan Association (2006); [c,d]Lang and Dhavale (2005); and [e]Glaeser (2007).

It should be apparent that the planning for future population growth and development will have to account for the structural characteristics of the megaregions, their natural environments and economic predilections, and ultimately the institutional challenges of governance their specific circumstances present. The five cases of planning overtures at the megaregional level reviewed by Dewar and Epstein (2007) show wide variation in approaches and strategies based on local circumstances while maintaining several common policy themes. In the following section I focus on the Southern California megaregion and what we might learn from the current experiences here to think about density, design, and quality of life.

Density and Quality of Life

In an earlier study we examined the nature of the metropolitan mosaic in some depth by looking at the land use portfolios of some eighty-eight cities in the County of Los Angeles. These cities comprise 99 percent of the urban population in the county. Applying a cluster analysis of the 1993 land use data for the cities in Los Angeles County, we were able to obtain six distinctive clusters defined by their land use profiles.[5] The majority of the cities had membership in three main clusters, which we called edge cities, suburbia, and generic. The latter had a mixed portfolio without any specific land use specialization, hence the name *generic*. The other two were more specialized, representing older and newer suburbs, the latter being exclusively residential. In addition, three clusters with highly specialized land use, but with a shorter list of members, emerged. These were respectively called industrial, apartment, and greyfield cities, corresponding to their primary specialization. The last category is a special legacy of Southern California and includes cities with large extractive uses such as oilfields or rock quarries. Figure 5.2 summarizes the six clusters and their socioeconomic and temporal correlates. It is apparent from Figure 5.2 that the generic cities are the oldest and most diversified in land use and socioeconomic characteristics. The largest cities in the region—Los Angeles, Long Beach, Glendale, Pasadena, and the like—all belong to this cluster. They are also most likely to respond to the changing demands of population growth and globalization. This diagram also shows that land use specializations occur at two extremes. On one hand, we see three boutique clusters of smaller numbers of older cities that serve lower-income populations and industrial and commercial activities. On the other hand, we see two clusters of exclusive suburbs and edge cities, which are newer and serve upper-income and white populations.

This analysis is an example of some of the dimensions of Tiebout sorting and the resultant Tieboutian space that characterizes the metropolitan mosaic of Los Angeles County. Subsequent diagrams further illustrate how the inegalitarian Tieboutian space contributes to segregation, inequities in services, and environ-

Degree of Land Use Specialization	High	Industrial City Greyfield City Apartment City		Edge City Suburbia City
	Low		Generic City	
Race		Non-White	Mixed	White
Income		Lower Income	Mixed Income	Upper Income
Age of the City		Older	Oldest	Newer
Overall Tendencies				

Figure 5.2 Socioeconomic Characteristics of Clusters.

mental justice issues. Figure 5.3 shows the inherent relationship between residential exclusivity and density: The higher the exclusivity, the lower the density. Note also that because of the unique land use specializations of certain cities, density is low when the percentage of residential use is low. Figures 5.4 and 5.5 illustrate the predictable relationship between density and median income, the association being slightly stronger in the case of gross density. Figure 5.6 shows that immigrants tend to populate cities with higher densities, a fact related to the lower incomes of many immigrant groups. Finally, Figure 5.7 shows that supply of per capita open spaces and public facilities increases as one moves further from the center, again suggesting environmental inequities that are increasingly becoming a focus of active living research.

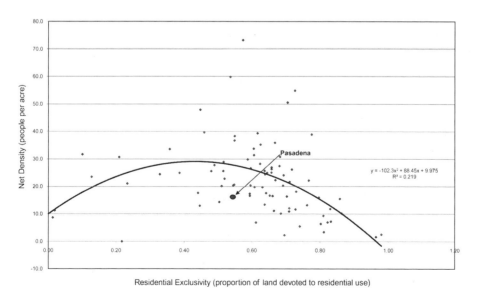

Figure 5.3 Density and Residential Exclusivity of the Municipalities, Los Angeles County.

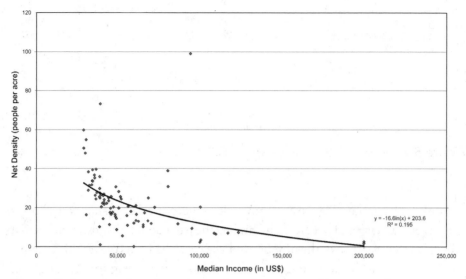

Figure 5.4 Net Residential Density and Median Income by Municipality, Los Angeles County.

Although the ten megaregions are expected to grow at different rates, all of them will have to hold a significantly larger population than they have now. The Southern California region will have to accommodate a population size of two Chicagos by 2025. The question of density and land use distribution will continue to remain a critical component of future policy choices.

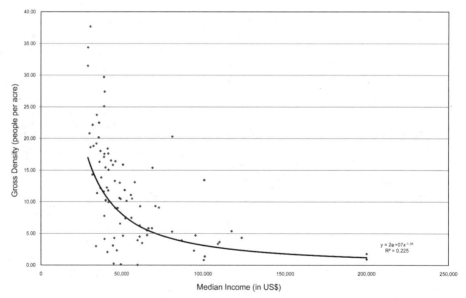

Figure 5.5 Gross Residential Density and Median Income by Municipality, Los Angeles County.

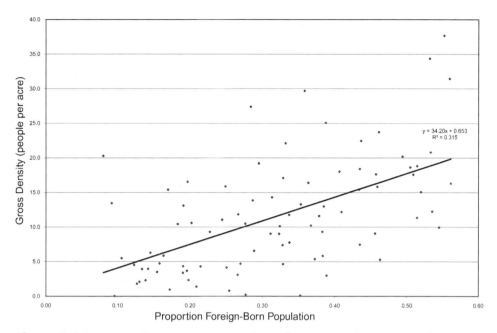

Figure 5.6 Density and Foreign-Born Population by Municipality, Los Angeles County.

Yet from all available accounts, single-family detached homes remain the dominant housing choice for the 70 percent of the American public. Even Andreas Duany, the champion of new urbanist design, concedes that it is only the remaining 30 percent of the American population who will remain the principal target for new urbanist design.[6]

Some observers hope that two demographic trends might trigger greater demand for higher-density housing. One trend that is likely to boost the market for higher-density housing is the coming retirement boom in the ranks of baby boomers and their cohort of "empty nesters," who might choose to leave their suburban homes for inner-city townhouses and condominiums.

The second trend, more of a hope actually, is that the growing number of immigrants from the developing world, who are used to living in higher-density housing and using public transit, will tend to choose inner-city, higher-density living. There are several studies on the imminent "Latino new urbanism" in the Los Angeles area, which should fulfill such hopes (see Irazábal and Gómez-Barris 2007, for example). But if past trends are any indication, it appears that even the immigrant population, especially those who can afford it, will choose suburban communities of single-family homes. Ultimately it is the economic and demographic fundamentals that are likely to change the trend rather than anticipated cultural preferences.

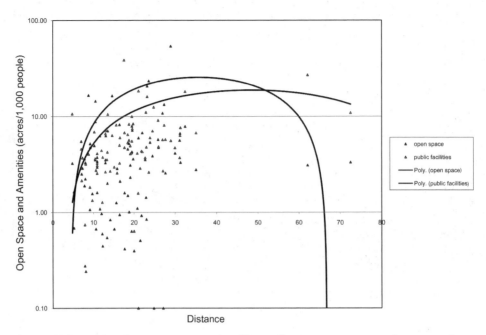

Figure 5.7 Supply of Open Spaces and Public Facilities as a Function of Distance from the Central City, Los Angeles County.

However, there is no question that a revival of the urban core of American cities has been underway for some time. Calling this phenomenon the fifth migration,[7] Fishman (2005) argues in a perceptive essay that a type of what he calls "reurbanism" is already underway, mainly because of the large number of immigrants who have refilled the previously decanted core of American cities. He expects that the reconcentration of the urban core will continue as the baby boomers begin to reach retirement age and move back to the city.

Some Thoughts on Megaregional Form and Design

In anticipating the future growth and planning of megaregions, it should be evident that the issues of global warming and climate change will play a major role. As Dewar and Epstein (2007) point out, megaregions are precisely the scale at which environmental risks and disasters (e.g., droughts, floods, hurricanes, forest fires, water availability, sustainability, energy efficiency, and carrying capacity) must be addressed. Current enthusiasm over smart growth, sustainable development, and alternative and decentralized energy systems will undoubtedly continue. How such initiatives will shape the form of megaregions remains an open question.

To prevent megaregions from becoming megasprawls, containment of exist-ing urbanized areas and preservation and protection of the regional landscape and natural resources must be the first order of business. The prospect of containing urban growth within limited space, which this policy would require, will un-doubtedly trigger the sprawl-versus-compact-cities debate, although this would be unnecessary in the megaregional context (see Ewing 1997, for example). Oth-ers will raise the issue of loss of liberty, economic decline, and distributive jus-tice. But all of these concerns could be allayed by demonstrating effective choices for concentration of density, efficient and mixed land use, transit-oriented de-velopment, infill housing, recycling of greyfield or brownfield sites, adaptive reuse of underused or obsolete building stock, and the like. Improving intra-urban and interurban access and mobility with public transportation, using ex-isting rail or freeway rights-of-way, will be another important priority for organizing the spatial structure of the megaregions.

Many initial efforts toward megaregional planning are considering such strategic approaches (see Dewar and Epstein 2007). In the past decade we have seen several large-scale visioning exercises; "Envision Utah" is the most notable one and has inspired other such initiatives. In the Southern California region, the Southern California Association of Government has undertaken such an ex-ercise successfully and produced a pithy strategic vision called the Compass Plan for the megaregion.[8] The plan simply requires all political jurisdictions to ac-commodate their prorated share of the regional population growth in 2 percent of the land, to be distributed only along transit corridors or transit nodes (Fig-ures 5.8 and 5.9). This approach protects existing single-family neighborhoods while distributing density, thus achieving, at least in theory, some distributive justice in access to shopping amenities, schools, parks, and open spaces.

The Southern California Association of Government Compass Plan is con-sistent with the vision of a de facto corridor city currently pursued in many cities of Southern California as an alternative to urban sprawl. Since the 1970s, when the Los Angeles City Council formally approved the idea, a "centers concept"—a polycentric form connected by transit lines—was the driving vision behind the planning and development of Los Angeles. Recently the adoption of a citywide ordinance known as Residential Accessory Services zoning seems to have em-braced the concept of the corridor city. This ordinance allows an increase in floor area ratio to 3.0 (from 1.0, previously prescribed) for new residential construc-tion in arterial corridors with a 50-foot height limit and ground-level retail. Driven by the imperatives of increasing housing supply while saving single-family neighborhoods, this policy also indirectly promotes transit ridership in the city. In a separate study Banerjee et al. (2005) explored the ridership and land use implications of what they called transit corridor developments along some

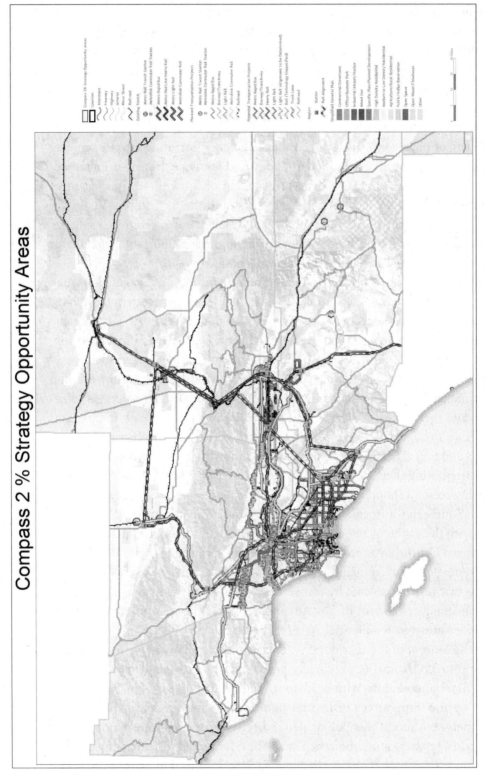

Figure 5.8 Results of a Regional Growth Visioning Exercise Conducted by the Southern California Association of Governments. Source: Southern California Association of Governments.

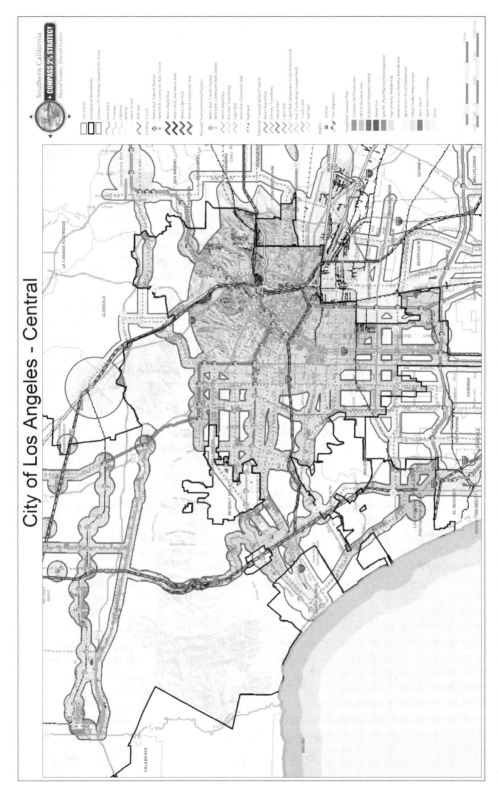

Figure 5.9 Visions of a Corridor City: Details of a Planned Growth Scenario for Central City Los Angeles. Source: Southern California Association of Governments.

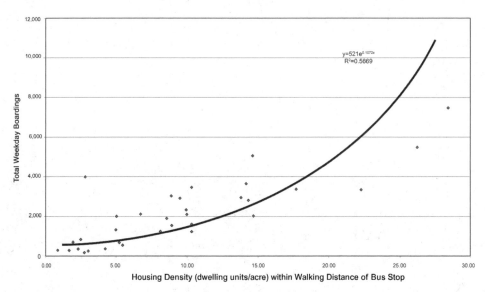

Figure 5.10 Rapid Bus Ridership along Ventura and Vermont Corridors and Housing Density within Walking Distance of Bus Stops, City of Los Angeles.

95 miles of Rapid Bus routes. The study of two major arterial corridors in the city of Los Angeles shows that increases in density along these corridors also lead to higher bus ridership, as one would expect (Figure 5.10), although the current density may have to be doubled or tripled to create a significant increase in ridership.

Obviously, in order for the corridor city scenario to take effect, a countywide adoption of the Residential Accessory Services type of zoning will be necessary, and indeed it may be in progress, driven by market forces.

It is also apparent that the growing shortfall in affordable housing stock can be met only through higher-density housing, although much of current housing construction around transit nodes of Southern California cities is not particularly affordable. Nevertheless, the corridor city may be the ideal scenario in which the interests of environmental advocacy, housing advocacy, and transit advocacy converge.

Although there might be cause to celebrate the vision of a corridor city where the interests of environmental advocates, housing advocates, and transit advocates converge, some caveats should be noted. There may remain several misgivings about the emergence of such a corridor city. First, one could argue that the linear distribution or "corridorization" of affordable housing may exacerbate environmental injustice as lower-income families and children are exposed to higher levels of air pollution, noise, traffic, and crime and are deprived of proximity to neighborhoods, parks, schools, and other community facilities. Second, this corridorization of affordable housing could lead to institutionalization of residential segregation, already in place through a "Tiebout-sorting" process. Third, one could argue that this outcome would presage continuing marginalization and isolation of the poor and immigrants. Fourth, there may be a negative impact on local businesses on successful commercial arterials as lower-income people move into those areas.

These are legitimate concerns. But given the exigencies of finding affordable housing, promises of the new initiatives cannot be overlooked. Furthermore, there is a long history of successful mixed-use and corridor city living in many cities in the United States and, of course, Europe. Social theorists such as Jane Jacobs (2002) and Richard Sennett (1971) discuss the positive urbanism of mixed-use street living. From the social ecology point of view these corridors may afford possibilities for a more positive and diverse social contact than that of isolated neighborhood enclaves (Banerjee and Baer 1984). Clearly, in order to mitigate environmental and distributive justice concerns, a new urban design vocabulary will have to be developed for these corridors. Recent works of Allan Jacobs (2002) should provide the inspiration for the future design of these arterials. We can imagine wide sidewalks, ample trees and landscaping, safe crossings and bus stops, small public spaces that encourage social life and contact, street markets and coffee shops that promote convivial public life, and the like. And of course there should be schools and parks within easy walking distance.

The availability of affordable housing ultimately will depend on not just identification of appropriate sites but also neighborhood- and street-scale design thinking. Urban design issues are as important as the location and design of the new housing.

Conclusions

I began this chapter with a review of both positive and normative interpretations of the forms and patterns of large-scale urbanization, looking for precedents for current challenges of megaregional planning. I have argued that in the American intellectual tradition, large-scale urban sprawl—or megasprawl—has been accepted or implicitly endorsed in both positive and normative narratives of regional growth. I have proposed that the emerging megaregions should be looked at as a system of places and have suggested the mosaic and net constructs for analytical and taxonomic purposes, in combination with the galaxy–corridor scenario advanced by others. Using these constructs as a framework, I have discussed the implications for density, design, and quality of life, drawing from the Southern California experience.

In an era of heightened consciousness about global warming and climate change, concession to megasprawl as an inexorable outcome is not acceptable.

Perhaps the most significant performance requirements for megaregional planning will be to contain the ecological footprint of the region while showing real growth in terms of green gross regional product per capita.

Finally, desired scenarios for density, design, and quality of life are not independent of the institutions of governance. Planning at the megaregional scale is essentially a problem of regional governance. We might imagine density, design, and conservation guidelines for the entire megaregion, but how such imperatives are implemented remains a governance challenge and calls for innovations in institutional arrangements.

Notes

1. It served as the organizing principle for his master plan proposal for Islamabad, Pakistan.
2. From my personal conversation with Manuel Castells, after his recent visit to China, also corroborated by the presentation of Jiawen Wang at the June 2007 meeting of the invited contributors in Atlanta to discuss megaregional research.
3. One could include the recent example of the California Coastal Zone Conservation Plan as an example of such megaregional planning, although it is less a product of visionary or normative initiatives.
4. I am grateful to Tom Luce for bringing this point to my attention at the June Atlanta meeting of invited contributors to this volume.
5. The findings of this study are reported in Banerjee and Verma (2006), without the related tables and graphs included here.
6. From an ABC *Nightline* special titled "America, the Ugly."
7. After Mumford's four migrations: the frontier pioneers who settled the continent, the labor movement from farms to factories, the migration to large cities and metropolitan areas, and the decentralization of large cites and the decanting of the core population. Fishman credits the term to Scott Campbell.
8. This plan does not extend to Las Vegas, which is considered part of the Southern California megaregion as conceptualized by the Regional Plan Association (2006).

References

Alexander, C. 1965. A city is not a tree. *Architectural Form* 122(1):58–61.

Arefi, M. 1999. Non-place and placelessness as narratives of loss: Rethinking the notion of place. *Journal of Urban Design* 4(2):179–193.

Banerjee, T. 2007. The Public Inc. and the conscience of planning. Pp. 107–127 in N. Verma, ed. *Institutions and Planning*. Elsevier, New York.

Banerjee, T., and W. C. Baer. 1984. *Beyond the Neighborhood Unit: Residential Environments and Public Policy*. Plenum, New York.

———, D. Myers, C. Irázabal, and D. Bahl. 2005. *Dynamics of Density, Land Use, and Population Growth*. USC/CSULB Metrans Transportation Center, Los Angeles.

———, and N. Verma. 2006. Sprawl and segregation: Another side of the Los Angeles debate. In D. Varady, ed. *Desegregating the City: Ghettos, Enclaves, and Inequality*. SUNY Press, Albany.

Berry, B. J. L., and W. L. Garrison. 1955. Alternate explanations of urban rank–size relationships. *Economic Development and Cultural Change* 3:196–198.

Boyer, M. C. 2000. Crossing cybercities: Boundary problems separating the regional space of the city from the matrix of cyberspace. Pp. 214–228 in R. Simmonds and G. Hack, eds. *Global City Regions: Their Emerging Forms*. Spon, London.

Bruegmann, R. 2005. *Sprawl: A Compact History*. University of Chicago Press, Chicago.

Calthorpe, P., and W. Fulton. 2001. *The Regional City: Planning for the End of Sprawl*. Island Press, Washington, D.C.

Casey, E. S. 2002. *Representing Place: Landscape Painting and Maps*. University of Minnesota Press, Minneapolis.

Castells, M. 1996. *The Rise of the Network Society*. Malden, MA: Blackwell.

———. 2005. Spaces of flow, spaces of places. In B. Snayal, ed. *Comparative Planning Cultures*. Routledge, New York.

Cronon, W. 1991. *Nature's Metropolis: Chicago and the Great West*. W.W. Norton, New York.

Dewar, M., and D. Epstein. 2007. Planning for "megaregions" in the United States. *Journal of Planning Literature* 22(2):108–124.

Doxiadis, C. 1974. *Anthropopolis: City for Human Development*. W.W. Norton, New York.

Ewing, R. 1997. Is Los Angeles–style sprawl desirable? *Journal of the American Planning Association* 63(1):107–126.

Ewing, R. H., R. Pendall, and D. D. T. Chen. 2002. *Measuring Sprawl and Its Impact*. Smart Growth America, Washington, D.C.

Fishman, R. 2005. The fifth migration. *Journal of the American Planning Association* 71(4):357–366.

Fogelson, R. M. 1993. *The Fragmented Metropolis: Los Angeles, 1850–1930*. University of California Press, Berkeley.

Friedmann, J., and J. Miller. 1965. The urban field. *Journal of the American Planning Association* 31(4):312–320.

Garreau, J. 1991. *Edge City: Life on the New Frontier*. Doubleday, New York.

Glaeser, E. 2007. Do regional economies need regional coordination? In K. S. Goldfeld, ed. *The Economic Geography of Megaregions*. The Policy Research Institute for the Region, Princeton University, Princeton, NJ.

Gordon, P., and H. W. Richardson. 1997. Are compact cities a desirable planning goal? *Journal of the American Planning Association* 63(1):95–106.

Gottmann, J. 1961. *Megalopolis: The Urbanized Northeastern Seaboard of the United States*. Twentieth Century Fund, New York.

Harris, B. 1960. Plan or projection? *Journal of the American Institute of Planners* 26(4):265–272.

Irazábal, C., and M. Gómez-Barris. 2007. *Diasporic Bounded Tourism: The Invention and Commodification of Traditions for Locally Bounded Mexicans in Plaza Mexico*. Paper presented at the Latin American Studies Association Conference, Montreal, Quebec.

Jacobs, A. 2002. *The Boulevard Book: History, Evolution, Design of Multiway Boulevards*. MIT Press, Cambridge, MA.

Jacobs, J. 2002. *The Death and Life of Great American Cities*. Random House, New York.

Jameson, F. 1991. *Postmodernism, or the Cultural Logic of Late Capitalism*. Duke University Press, Durham, NC.

Kunstler, J. H. 1993. *The Geography of Nowhere: The Rise and Decline of America's Man-Made Landscape*. Simon & Schuster, New York.

Lang, R. E., and D. Dhavale. 2005. *Beyond Megalopolis: Exploring America's New "Megapolitan" Geography* (Census Report No. 05:01). Metropolitan Institute, Alexandria, VA.

Lessinger, J. 1962. The case for "scatteration." *Journal of the American Institute of Planners* 28(3):159–169.

Lynch, K. 1960. *The Image of the City*. MIT Press, Cambridge, MA.

———. 1990. The pattern of the metropolis. Pp. 47–64 in T. Banerjee and M. Southworth, eds. *City Sense and City Design: Writings and Projects of Kevin Lynch*. MIT Press, Cambridge.

———, and D. Appleyard. 1990. Temporary paradise? A look at the special landscape of the San Diego region. Pp. 721–763 in T. Banerjee and M. Southworth, eds. *City Sense and City Design: Writings and Projects of Kevin Lynch*. MIT Press, Cambridge, MA.

McGee, T. G. 1991. The emergence of Desakota regions in Asia: Expanding a hypothesis. Pp. 3–26 in N. Ginsburg, B. Koppel, and T. G. McGee, eds. *The Extended Metropolis: Settlement Transition in Asia*. University of Hawaii Press, Honolulu.

McHarg, I. 1969. *Design with Nature*. Natural History Press for the American Museum of History, New York.

Molotch, H. 1976. The city as a growth machine: Toward a political economy of place. *American Journal of Sociology* 82(2):309.

Ostrom, V., C. M. Tiebout, and R. Warren. 1961. The organization of government in metropolitan areas: A theoretical inquiry. *American Political Science Review* 55(4):831–842.

Regional Plan Association. 2006. *America 2050: A Prospectus*. Regional Plan Association, New York.

Relph, E. C. 1976. *Place and Placelessness*. Pion, London.

Sennett, R. 1971. *The Uses of Disorder: Personal Identity and City Life*. Knopf, New York.

Sites, W. 2003. Remaking New York: Primitive Globalization and the Politics of the Urban Community. *International Journal of Urban and Regional Research* 29(4):1005–1007.

Spreiregen, P. 1965. *Urban Design: The Architecture of Towns and Cities*. McGraw-Hill, New York.

Sussman, C. 1976. *Planning the Fourth Migration: The Neglected Vision of the Regional Planning Association of America*. MIT Press, Cambridge.

Tiebout, C. M. 1956. A pure theory of local expenditures. *The Journal of Political Economy* 64(5):416.

Varady, D. 2006. *Desegregating the City: Ghettos, Enclaves, and Inequality*. State University of New York Press, Albany.

Webber, M. M. 1964. The urban place and the nonplace urban realm. In M. M. Webber, ed. *Explorations into Urban Structure*. University of Pennsylvania Press, Philadelphia.

White, M., and L. White. 1962. *Intellectuals Versus the City*. Mentor, New York.

6

Megapolitan America
Defining and Applying a New Geography

Robert E. Lang and Arthur C. Nelson

In this chapter we outline a new approach to defining America's metropolitan space around what we call megapolitan areas. We argue that multiple metropolitan areas are agglomerating into large, complex, and dynamic megaregions. We use the term *megapolitan* to characterize this trend. We begin with a review of where American has been and where it seems to be headed.

Over the past two and a half centuries, the United States has been one of the world's fastest-growing nations in percentage and real terms. From a base of 4 million in 1790, the United States eclipsed 300 million in 2006. Seemingly the envy of the stagnant or declining industrialized world, the United States will add 100 million new residents faster than any country on the planet except India and Pakistan (Nelson and Lang 2007).

To both conquer the continent—consistent with the manifest destiny views of the early nineteenth century—and create a nation, the United States facilitated impressive settlement tactics. The Homestead Acts awarded land across the West to those who would settle it for at least 5 years. To stitch the nation together through transportation and communication, the United States gave millions of acres of land to speculators who financed construction of railroads and, along

The authors acknowledge support received from the Lincoln Institute of Land Policy for research leading to and adapted for this chapter. The authors also acknowledge gratefully the assistance of Kelly A. Beavers of the Metropolitan Institute at Virginia Tech for data assembly and presentation.

their tracks, telegraph lines. To connect growing urban centers to each other, the United States launched a federal highway system culminating in the interstate highway system. As the nation grew in territory, population, and commerce, so did its urban areas. By 1920, most of the U.S. population lived in urban areas, and in 2000 nearly three quarters of all Americans lived in urban agglomerations called metropolitan areas.

We are witnessing the further agglomeration of the population into large-scale combinations of metropolitan areas. The Census Bureau has long recognized that multiple metropolitan areas are functionally integrated, usually through commuting patterns. Beginning with the 1980 census, the concept of consolidated metropolitan statistical areas has evolved into combined statistical areas (CSAs) based on the 2000 census. But the census does not so much look ahead as explain the past and present.

The purpose of this chapter is to present and apply a theory of agglomerations of human settlements into megapolitan regions and areas as viewed in about 2040. This is an important exercise because it may help recast parochial views into ones that are based at least on large, often multistate economic units, the individual parts of which affect the well-being of the whole, if not on a view that the nation is rapidly becoming a system of a few very large engines of economic influence.

The chapter has four sections. The first reviews evolving notions of how America's urbanization patterns can be characterized, based on literature emanating mostly from Jean Gottmann's megalopolis conceptualization more than 40 years ago. The second expands on the megalopolis idea to devise a construct we call megapolitan. The third uses census-derived methods to define the megapolitan areas in ways that allow them to be mapped reasonably objectively. The fourth illustrates the American megapolitan landscape in 2030 in demographic and economic terms. Research and policy implications conclude this chapter.

From Megalopolis to Megapolitan

> The Megapolitan concept seems to have popularized the idea that the modern cities are better reviewed not in isolation, as centers of a restricted area only, but rather as parts of "city-systems," as participants in urban networks revolving in widening orbits.
> —Jean Gottmann (1987)

Geographer Jean Gottmann, writing more than two decades after publishing his influential book *Megalopolis* (1961),[1] understood the impact his thinking had on urban theory. Today, a new trans-metropolitan geography is emerging that advances many of Gottmann's ideas. Researchers in the United States and Europe are proposing new methods for classifying and tracking the megalopolis (Faludi 2002; Yaro et al. 2004; Carbonell and Yaro 2005; Lang and Dhavale 2005; Lang and Nelson 2006). And although Gottmann was specifically referring to the northeastern United States, the latest round of research extends the concept to clusters of networked metropolitan areas around the world. For example, European researchers argue that large-scale urbanized areas are the primary geographic unit for integration into the world economy (Faludi 2002). The European Union (EU) currently has one well-defined "global integration zone," the area inside the "pentagon" demarcated by London, Hamburg, Munich, Milan, and Paris (Schon 2005).

This chapter expands Gottmann's megalopolis to current trends in American trans-metropolitan development.[2] Gottmann's original study of the Northeast's megalopolis (1961) held that the region was unique in several ways, including its large size and commercial inventiveness. By the time Gottmann revisited the megalopolis in the late 1980s (Gottmann 1987; Gottmann and Harper 1990), he acknowledged that several other U.S. regions could qualify as megapolitan. He noted especially the cases of the Midwest and West Coast but also saw a nascent megalopolis forming in the South around Atlanta. Our work has identified twenty megapolitan areas found in all regions of the country, not just in the Northeast.

Gottmann's work influenced academics but had no impact on the way the U.S. Census Bureau defines space, probably in part because at the time his work discussed a single, unique region. But the idea of a functional trans-metropolitan geography is one that warrants the Census Bureau's attention. Regional economies now clearly extend beyond an individual metro area. The megapolitan concept recognizes this fact and suggests a new geography to show which regional economies are linked.

When the Census Bureau formalizes a geographic concept, it gains power. Consider a recent example. Rural development advocates lobbied the Census Bureau for years to redefine more heavily settled rural areas as quasimetropolitan places (Lang and Dhavale 2005). In 2003, the U.S. Office of Management and Budget, which oversees the Census Bureau, responded with the designation *micropolitan area*. Now micropolitans are literally on the map. Businesses, government agencies, and planners have new geography to work with. Publications took notice; for example, *Site Selection Magazine* started a list of "Top Micropolitans" in which to locate businesses (Starner 2005).

Megapolitan areas (or "megas") have a similar potential. For example, the concept of megapolitan regions was the cover feature story of *Business 2.0* in November 2005. *Business 2.0* is part of the Forbes publishing group and is the nation's leading business monthly magazine. The November 2005 issue was its best-selling newsstand issue ever.

Once megapolitan areas are officially recognized, private industries and government agencies will embrace this new geography.[3] And there are clearly cases in which the megapolitan scale is the most logical one at which to address problems. Consider the recent debate over the fate of Amtrak. The Bush administration wanted to eliminate all Amtrak funding in the 2006 federal budget. Defending this action, former U.S. secretary of transportation Norman Mineta (2005) wrote in the *New York Times*, "The problem is not that Americans don't use trains; it is that Amtrak has failed to keep up with the times, stubbornly sticking to routes and services, even as they lose money and attract few users." Amtrak is a national rail system with a profitable line connecting big Northeastern cities that offsets losses on service to remote rural locales. Megapolitan areas have two qualities—concentrated populations and often corridor form—that make them excellent geographic units around which Amtrak could be reorganized.

The Evolving Megapolitan Idea

The concept of a large-scale, trans-metropolitan urban structure has been debated among planners since the early twentieth century. The idea can be traced to a famous exchange in the pages of the *New Republic* in the summer of 1932 between noted theorist and critic Lewis Mumford and Thomas Adams, director of the Region Plan of New York and Environs (now the Regional Plan Association [RPA]).[4] The debate pitted what Fishman (2000) calls "regionalists" (such as Mumford) against "metropolitanists" (such as Adams). Metropolitanists believed that twentieth-century cities would maintain their nineteenth-century form even as they grew to 10 or 20 million residents and extended 50 or more miles from the center (Thomas 2000). They also argued by extension that most investment should go to fixing the metropolitan core.

Regionalists saw a radical shift in metropolitan structure, away from a monocentric metropolis and toward a more dispersed network of cities and villages arrayed across a vast—although integrated—space they called the "urban region" (Fishman 2000). After the mid-twentieth century, most new urban growth occurred outside the regional core, which fueled the development of sprawling and often connected metropolitan areas. The proposed "urban region" concept is thus the progenitor of the megapolitan area.

In the year after the Mumford–Adams debate, urban sociologist R. D. McKenzie (1933) published *The Metropolitan Community*. This book formally laid out the regionalists' thinking. McKenzie argued that American metropolitan development

> is tending to concentrate more and more in large regional aggregates. In every such aggregate, the population tends to subdivide and become multinucleated in a complex of centers that are economically integrated into a larger unity.

According to Thomas (2000), Gottmann's megalopolis "effectively completed the analysis of metropolitan regionalism undertaken by R. D. McKenzie three decades earlier." Like McKenzie, Gottmann emphasized economic integration.

RPA's Second Regional Plan in the 1960s (the first appeared in the 1920s under Adams) produced a series of reports on growth patterns in the New York metropolitan area. One document titled *The Region's Growth* contained a section on what it called the Atlantic Urban Region (Shore 1967).[5] This region stretched from Virginia to Maine and covered essentially the same area as Gottmann's megalopolis.[6] The RPA report extended Gottmann's work by including new data analysis to show regional integration. It also projected the spread of urbanization to 2000 (which looks very similar to current patterns).[7] The RPA report featured an aerial photo portrait that documented variation in growth patterns from the cores to the edges of the region.

Interestingly, *The Region's Growth* appeared just before the explosion of suburban office development in the early 1970s (Garreau 1991; Lang 2003). For example, Dulles Airport and its accompanying access road through Fairfax County, Virginia are shown as the "metropolitan fringe" in the photo essay. Today, the "Dulles Corridor" anchors one of the nation's biggest and most important high-tech concentrations.[8]

The Region's Growth raised an important point: Is the Atlantic Urban Region a "super-city or a chain of cities?" The report found,

> The main difference between an urban area at the scale of the Atlantic Urban Region and the traditional metropolitan scale is that the emerging larger form has a multitude of major nodes whose areas are likely to be largely autonomous. Nevertheless, the individual urban centers benefit from mutual proximity, and there is bound to be increased integration. (Shore 1967)

The continuing spread and growing integration of large-scale urban space since 1967 now confirms the Northeast as a supercity.

Although Gottmann's and RPA's work was influential in the 1960s, and Gottmann's definition "continues to dominate dictionaries in geography," the megalopolis concept had little lasting impact outside academic geography (Baigent 2004). But that is starting to change. The current RPA president, Robert Yaro, has kept the idea of the megalopolis alive in recent years. Yaro advocates that Americans should do large-scale European-style "spatial planning" (Yaro et al. 2004; Yaro and Carbonell 2004). To that end, Yaro organized a meeting at the Rockefeller Brothers Foundation headquarters in Tarrytown, New York to begin a coordinated effort at advancing this idea. RPA's role in promoting the megalopolis makes sense. Greater New York is the nation's most populous metropolitan area, and it lies in the center of the oldest and largest megalopolis. RPA also has the longest history with the concept, which dates to the Adams–Mumford exchanges of the 1930s.

Megapolitan Areas Defined

We have undertaken theory building and analysis to advance the megapolitan concept (Lang and Dhavale 2005; Lang and Nelson 2006). Our work was the first to establish a transparent, data-driven approach to defining what constitutes a megapolitan area. Megapolitan areas are defined using multiple methods. The definition builds on prior attempts to determine trans-metropolitan clusters by adding new data, methods, and theory (Faludi 2002; Yaro and Carbonell 2004; Yaro et al. 2004; Carbonell and Yaro 2005). The current work on megapolitan development relies mostly on an analysis of spatial connectivity, which can be shown with tools such as satellite imagery. Such work focuses on the "space of places," or the physical distribution of the built environment. But there is also a "space of flows," or sets of connections that link places via transportation systems and business networks (Castells 1996). According to theory, the most complete geographic understanding emerges by looking at both the place and the flow of space (Taylor 2004). To their credit, the Census Bureau's metropolitan area definition combines both, making the definitions both useful and meaningful. Here, we expand this work to create an even larger unit of analysis, which is becoming increasingly necessary in today's global economy. The methods detailed here show how both place and flow determine megapolitan locations and boundaries.

The name *megapolitan* plays off the megalopolis concept by using the same prefix, *mega*. Interestingly, the name *megapolitan* was under consideration during the Census Bureau's last review of metropolitan area standards just before the 2000 census (*Federal Register* 1999; PRB 2000). As part of a redefinition proposal to categorize metropolitan areas by size, the catch-all "metropolitan" category was to be scrapped. In its place were to be "megapolitan" areas, where the central cities had more than 1 million residents, and "macropolitan" areas, or regions with central cities ranging from 50,000 to 999,999 residents.[9] Although this hierarchical system was not approved by the Office of Management and Budget, the Census Bureau clearly sees that American development patterns vary by scale.

The census seeks simple but definitive methods for defining and organizing space. Metropolitan areas were first officially designated in 1949 to show functional economic relationships (Anderson 1985). Commuting, which at that time mostly tied the edge to the core, was an easy proxy for this linkage. For instance, job losses in central cities would affect suburbs by lowering retail sales and depressing their housing markets. Thus the center and periphery existed as a single integrated unit, as shown by employment dependency. The Census Bureau wanted an easily measured and universal proxy for this relationship, and commuting best fit the model.

A direct functional relationship as indicated by commuting does not exist at the megapolitan scale (Shore 1967). The area is simply too big to make daily trips possible between distant sections. But commuting is just one—albeit key—way to show regional cohesion. Other integrating forces exist such as goods movement, business linkages, cultural commonality, and physical environment. A megapolitan area could represent a sales district for a branch office. Or, in the case of the Northeast or Florida, it can be a zone of fully integrated toll roads where a single "Easy Pass" or "Sun Pass" works across multiple metropolitan areas.

We have developed techniques that define a megapolitan area as follows:

- Combines at least two but may include dozens of existing metropolitan areas
- Totals more than 5 million projected residents by 2040[10]
- Derives from contiguous metropolitan and micropolitan areas, including relevant interstitial areas
- Occupies a roughly similar physical environment
- Links large centers through major transportation infrastructure within a range allowing same-day road travel to and from the most distant places (about 180 miles)
- Creates a usable geography that is suitable for large-scale regional planning
- Lies within the United States[11]
- Consists of counties as the most basic unit

Note that megapolitan—like metropolitan—space is not synonymous with the Census Bureau's "urbanized area." Urbanized areas indicate settlement at 1,000 people per square mile or more, which the Census Bureau uses to chart more intensely developed parts of metropolitan areas.[12] But all megapolitan and metropolitan areas include space that falls below this density threshold. The reason is that urbanized areas indicate a physical urban space, whereas megas and metros also factor in functional relationships at the county level. There are many counties in both megas and micros that are fully urbanized based on the census definition, but there are other less urbanized (sometimes barely urbanized) counties that link to metropolitan areas via commuting patterns. Similarly, counties in megapolitan areas maintain both physical and functional links.

Using counties as building blocks allows a detailed statistical analysis. County data extend back decades and are available in easy-to-read electronic formats (Katz et al. 2006). The Census Bureau reports long-form[13] data at the county level, which provides multiple demographic variables including information on race, income, mobility, housing, and education. All micropolitan and metropolitan area designations are based on counties. In fact, the Census Bureau established the metro and micro categories as a classification system in which to place counties. The Census Bureau determines where all 3,141 U.S. counties fit in the typology. There are three basic classes of counties: metropolitan, micropolitan, and non–core based (meaning neither metropolitan nor micropolitan).

Counties are also the most consistent U.S. unit of local governance. According to the National Association of Counties (2005), forty-eight of the fifty states have operational county governments. (Connecticut and Rhode Island are divided into geographic units called counties, but they lack governments.) Counties are charged by states to run both national and local elections. When counties are used as the most elemental unit, data on how megapolitan areas vote are available, including how they vote in presidential elections.

Megapolitan areas are an overlay category. A megapolitan area would not replace metropolitan or micropolitan areas. Instead it adds a larger unit of analysis by combining the metros and micros into a larger defined space. The Census Bureau already has such an overlay in its newly designated combined statistical areas (CSAs).[14] Once a county is determined to be either metropolitan or micropolitan, it is eligible to be in a CSA. Not all U.S. counties fall into CSAs, and likewise they not are labeled as megapolitan.

CSAs are the Census Bureau's first true trans-metropolitan category.[15] Metropolitan areas can combine with micropolitan areas to form larger-scale CSAs. Metros can also link with other metros, as micros can connect with other micros to make CSAs. Note that geography is not the sole determinant for the connection. Not all contiguous metros and micros are part of CSAs; there must be an economic, or functional, relationship. Currently, there are 120 CSAs. CSAs are important to the megapolitan definition because they show that the Census Bureau already grasps trans-metropolitan geography. They are also vital because CSAs serve as building blocks for the megas. Most of the megapolitan areas defined in this study begin with CSA-to-CSA links. With CSAs, the Census Bureau has moved along the path of defining megapolitan areas.

Megas are superregions that combine at least two, and often several, metropolitan areas. Megapolitan areas are big but not enormous and can easily be traversed round-trip by car in a day. Many of us sense that a large-scale metropolitan convergence is under way because we see metros that were once distinct places now merging into enormous urban complexes. Megas are defined here as having economic linkages, as demonstrated by commuter patterns. The anchor urban cores of megapolitans lie at least 50 miles but no more than 180 miles apart. The research examines ten representative megas, which are found in all corners of the United States.

The megas we identify are essentially the CSAs we project to 2040, derived by extending the census's current method several decades forward. Table 6.1

Table 6.1

The new regional hierarchy.

Type	Description	Examples
Metropolitan statistical area (MSA)	An "urbanized area" or "principal city" with at least 50,000 people plus surrounding counties with a 25% "employ-ment interchange measure" (EIM) in 2000	Pittsburgh Denver
Combined statistical area (CSA)	Two or more adjoining micropolitan and metro-politan areas that have an EIM of at least 15% in 2000	Washington–Baltimore Cleveland–Akron
Megapolitan area, (Phoenix–Tucson) defined by Virginia Tech Metropolitan Institute	Two or more metropolitan areas with anchor principal cities 50–200 miles apart that will have an EIM of 15% by 2040 based on projection	Sun Corridor Northern California (Bay Area–Sacramento)
Megaregion, defined by RPA and Lincoln Institute	Large, connected networks of metropolitan areas that maintain environmental, cultural, and functional linkages	Piedmont Texas Triangle

Source: Metropolitan Institute at Virginia Tech.

shows the relationship between metropolitan areas, CSAs, megapolitan areas, and megaregions.

The main criterion for a census-defined CSA is economic interdependence, as evidenced by overlapping commuting patterns. The same holds true for megapolitans. Based on projections of commuting patterns, the 2010 census could find that Phoenix–Tucson and Washington–Baltimore–Richmond qualify as CSAs. In 2020, several more metropolitan areas will pass this threshold, and at midcentury all the megapolitan areas we have identified should officially be CSAs.

Organizations such as the Lincoln Institute of Land Policy and the New York–based RPA are also developing new regional models and planning strate-gies to manage future metropolitan expansion (see Table 6.1). In 2006, those two organizations convened the National Committee for America 2050, a coalition of planners and civic leaders, to develop a national framework for America's rapid population growth and the emergence of what they call megaregions.

This new concept was explored during a University of Pennsylvania planning studio taught in 2005 by Armando Carbonell, chairman of the Lincoln Institute's department of planning and urban form, and Robert Yaro, president of the RPA. Although the Penn megaregions do not account for overlapping commuter sheds, they nonetheless describe networks of mostly contiguous metropolitan areas.

A Method to Define America's Metropolitan Geography

The key methodological questions in this study are, "Where are the megapolitan areas, what are their boundaries, how are the metro and micro areas within them connected, and what are the best names for these places?" Because megapolitan areas are defined primarily by physical space, the process of their creation begins with basic geography. As the Census Bureau does, this analysis essentially tests all U.S. counties to see whether they qualify as megapolitan based on the definition. After the possible counties that meet the geographic criteria are selected, other filters of cultural geography, environment, transportation networks, and future growth projections are overlaid to help delineate the final megapolitan boundaries. The population and demographic data used in this study come from the U.S. Bureau of the Census (2001, 2003). The geographic analysis was performed with ESRI's ArcGIS 8.3 software. This section outlines the steps we took to identify the ten megapolitan areas in the United States.

Mapping the Megapolitans

The first step in creating megapolitan areas involved producing a map of the micropolitan and metropolitan counties. To be considered as a candidate for megapolitan inclusion, an area must be a string of contiguous metropolitan and micropolitan counties, uninterrupted by non-metropolitan counties. Non-metropolitan counties can be defined as megapolitan only if metropolitan and micropolitan counties completely encircle them or if their borders are more than 60 percent contiguous with a metro or micro county.

Second, all counties were evaluated by their type of connectedness—micropolitan or metropolitan—to determine their eligibility as megapolitan. Potential megapolitan connections were given a priority based on their Census Bureau definitions. The highest priority was given to the CSA-to-CSA connection, followed by a metro-to-CSA, metro-to-metro, metro-to-micro, and micro-to-micro link.[16] For example, if two adjoining counties both belong to different

CSAs, then according to our definition their connection has the most strength and so would be included in the same megapolitan area. Conversely, two adjoining micropolitan counties represent a weak link and may not have enough gravitational pull to hold a megapolitan area together.

We have tested our analytic approach to defining megapolitan areas using a series of techniques. Chief among these were a series of maps to show major transportation networks and city locations for each megapolitan area, along with information on historical geography (Zelinsky 1973) and development trends (Yaro et al. 2004; Nelson 2004). Megapolitan edges were also determined by topographic elements that might constrain or redirect growth, as well as the boundaries of large-scale ecosystems (Meinig 2004). These additional considerations, or screens, smoothed the boundaries and helped to determine the fate of conflicted areas. At this point, the previous work by Gottmann (1961) and Yaro et al. (2004) was compared with the preliminary megapolitan areas. Adding these other filters ensured that the space that was defined initially by census-based criteria was not a statistical artifact but was instead a vibrant and real place. The data section that follows provides more insight into the local nature of megapolitan areas and how this information factored into determining boundaries.

The methodological rules we use are not the only basis for inclusion in a megapolitan area, although they are certainly the primary one. Just as the Census Bureau relies on local opinion and preference when determining geography, judgment calls based on local and regional information are an essential component of the definition process. A county may meet the criteria to be included in a mega but may not actually be a part of the area. Local knowledge is essential to determining compatibility. As this work continues, refinement to the megapolitan boundaries will be based partly on local input. Again, this mimics the vetting process that the Census Bureau itself uses in placing counties in metros, micros, and CSAs.

Finally, we do not carve the United States into spheres of influence based on a core–hinterland relationship. There are geographies that account for every inch of American space by showing various types of connections, including market areas or even the Federal Reserve Bank district to which a place belongs. Drawing such geographic boundaries is often a useful exercise, but it does not apply to our megapolitan area analysis. In our view, megapolitan areas should have discrete boundaries, as do metropolitan and micropolitan areas. The point is to show which counties belong to large-scale urban clusters and which ones do not. These analyses find a core and periphery to each mega, which may mean that most of the United States would fall within the sphere of influence of a megaregion. This work has led to the map of America's megapolitan areas shown in Figure 6.1.

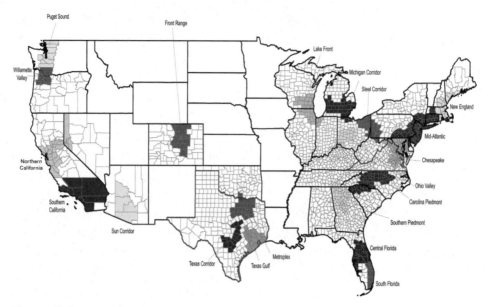

Figure 6.1 Megapolitan Area Map.

Megapolitan America circa 2030

Now that a megapolitan landscape has been defined, how does it illustrate America's demographic and economic conditions to 2030? This section compares the megapolitan areas and regions in 2000 and 2030 with one another and with the United States as a whole. It includes comparisons in terms of population, racial and ethnic diversity, and economic indicators.

Population

Table 6.2 shows the concentration of America's present and future growth nationally and among the megapolitan areas and regions. Megapolitan areas and regions occupy just 12 percent of the land area of the contiguous forty-eight states (where all the megas are found)—even accounting for the "San Bernardino effect"[17]—but account for about 60 percent of the current and projected population.

Diversity

A simple diversity index is constructed to illustrate the change in aggregate minority composition between the megas and with respect to the nation. The index is simply nonwhite population divided by total population using projections compiled by Woods & Poole Economics (2007). For the nation as a whole, the diversity index increases from 0.300 to 0.426, or by more than 40 percent. From 2000 to 2030, all diversity indexes for all megapolitans increase with the exception of

Table 6.2

Megapolitan areas and megaregions, 2000–2030.

Megaregion	2000 Population	2030 Population	Actual Change 2000–2030	Percentage Change 2000–2030
Megalopolis	**49,948,064**	**62,427,070**	**12,479,006**	**25.00%**
New England	8,133,219	9,873,668	1,740,449	21.40%
Mid-Atlantic	32,656,309	39,072,196	6,415,887	19.60%
Chesapeake	9,158,536	13,481,206	4,322,670	47.20%
Great Lakes	**33,641,220**	**39,536,775**	**5,895,555**	**17.50%**
Steel Corridor	7,140,287	7,434,689	294,402	4.10%
Ohio Valley	5,198,100	6,374,776	1,176,676	22.60%
Michigan Corridor	8,835,742	10,070,142	1,234,400	14.00%
Lake Front	12,467,091	15,657,168	3,190,077	25.60%
Piedmont	**12,633,926**	**19,096,474**	**6,462,548**	**51.20%**
Carolina Piedmont	6,460,338	9,431,809	2,971,471	46.00%
Southern Piedmont	6,173,588	9,664,665	3,491,077	56.50%
Florida	**12,474,423**	**20,312,554**	**7,838,131**	**62.80%**
Central Florida	6,975,772	11,352,506	4,376,734	62.70%
South Florida	5,498,651	8,960,048	3,461,397	62.90%
Texas Triangle	**16,525,203**	**25,598,697**	**9,073,494**	**54.90%**
Texas Gulf	5,699,704	8,535,961	2,836,257	49.80%
Texas Corridor	3,573,621	5,870,470	2,296,849	64.30%
Greater Metroplex	7,251,878	11,192,266	3,940,388	54.30%
Intermountain West	**7,878,204**	**13,434,396**	**5,556,192**	**70.50%**
Front Range	3,582,688	5,594,523	2,011,835	56.20%
Sun Corridor	4,295,516	7,839,873	3,544,357	82.50%
Cascadia	**6,901,160**	**9,927,217**	**3,026,057**	**43.80%**
Puget Sound	3,892,016	5,556,154	1,664,138	42.80%
Willamette Valley	3,009,144	4,371,063	1,361,919	45.30%
California	**31,115,430**	**42,854,619**	**11,739,189**	**37.70%**
Northern California	10,788,599	15,057,719	4,269,120	39.60%
Southern California	20,326,831	27,796,900	7,470,069	36.70%
Megapolitan Total	**171,117,630**	**233,187,802**	**62,070,172**	**36.30%**
U.S. Total	282,193,477	378,302,736	96,109,259	34.10%

Note: Megaregions are in bold.
Source: Metropolitan Institute at Virginia Tech, 7/1/00 population from U.S. Bureau of the Census and 7/1/30 projection based on data from Woods & Poole Economics, Inc.

Table 6.3

Diversity index.

Megapolitan Area	2000	2030	Change 2000–2030	Percentage Change 2000–2030
New England	0.257	0.459	0.202	78.60%
Mid-Atlantic	0.541	0.67	0.129	23.80%
Chesapeake	0.519	0.655	0.136	26.20%
Steel Corridor	0.256	0.34	0.084	32.80%
Ohio Valley	0.266	0.403	0.137	51.50%
Michigan Corridor	0.376	0.508	0.132	35.10%
Lakefront	0.423	0.581	0.158	37.40%
Carolina Piedmont	0.515	0.612	0.097	18.80%
Southern Piedmont	0.495	0.609	0.114	23.00%
Central Florida	0.389	0.598	0.209	53.70%
South Florida	0.636	0.668	0.032	5.00%
Texas Gulf	0.637	0.672	0.035	5.50%
Texas Corridor	0.552	0.644	0.092	16.70%
Greater Metroplex	0.588	0.627	0.039	6.60%
Front Range	0.41	0.564	0.154	37.60%
Sun Corridor	0.487	0.575	0.088	18.10%
Puget Sound	0.35	0.567	0.217	62.00%
Willamette Valley	0.275	0.501	0.226	82.20%
Northern California	0.618	0.686	0.068	11.00%
Southern California	0.649	0.636	−0.013	−2.00%

Source: U.S. Census, www.census.gov/population/cen2000/atlas/censr01-104.pdf, May 2007.

Southern California. Southern California has the highest level of diversity in 2000, so it actually experiences a decrease because of the extreme dominance of the 2000 Hispanic population. Its composition becomes more homogeneous as the black and Asian populations increase by 2030. New England experiences the greatest increase in diversity, from an index of 0.257 to 0.459. However, the diversity index in 2030 for New England is low among megas (the third lowest of all). The Steel Corridor is the least diverse megapolitan in 2030, a ranking it claims for 2000 as well. Table 6.3 presents diversity indexes for each megapolitan area.

Table 6.4 compares the minority and ethnic population changes of the United States with all megapolitan areas combined. This table shows that as a whole and

Table 6.4

Population by race and geography in the United States, 2000 and 2030.

Geography	White	Black	Native American	Asian	Hispanic
United States					
Population by race 2000	197,670	35,156	2,315	11,405	35,648
	70.0%	12.5%	0.8%	4.0%	12.6%
Population by race 2030	217,230	46,672	3,196	28,618	79,587
	57.4%	13.1%	0.8%	7.6%	21.0%
Megapolitan					
Population by race 2000	110,350	22,354	719	9,063	27,186
	65.0%	13.2%	0.0%	5.3%	16.0%
Population by race 2030	116,760	31,293	922	23,393	59,035
	50.5%	13.5%	0.0%	10.1%	25.5%

Source: Metropolitan Institute at Virginia Tech.

across all ethnic groups with the exception of Native Americans, megapolitan areas are more diverse than the United States in 2000 and become even more so by 2030 (Table 6.5).

Earnings and Gross Regional Product

The Mid-Atlantic has the highest gross regional product (GRP) among the megapolitan areas for 1990, 2000, and 2030. However, the Mid-Atlantic ranks lowest for GRP per capita, as illustrated by Table 6.6. By per capita measures, the Carolina Piedmont ranks highest, and the Front Range ranks second highest for

Table 6.5

Share of population change by race and geography, 2000–2030.

Geography	White	Black	Native American	Asian	Hispanic
Non-megapolitan	13,150	2,577	678	2,883	12,090
Share of change	41.9%	8.2%	2.2%	9.2%	38.5%
Megapolitan	6,410	8,939	203	14,330	31,849
Share of change	10.4%	14.5%	0.3%	23.2%	51.6%

Source: Metropolitan Institute at Virginia Tech.

Table 6.6

Regional product per capita, 2000–2030, megapolitan areas by rank in 2000 (figures in thousands of dollars).

Megapolitan Area	2000	2030	Change 2000–2030	Percentage Change 2000–2030
New England	$44	$66	$22	50.0%
Mid-Atlantic	$12	$15	$3	25.0%
Chesapeake	$103	$131	$28	27.2%
Steel Corridor	$39	$64	$25	64.1%
Ohio Valley	$72	$101	$29	40.3%
Michigan Corridor	$62	$75	$13	21.0%
Lakefront	$39	$52	$13	33.3%
Carolina Piedmont	$308	$353	$45	14.6%
Southern Piedmont	$46	$66	$20	43.5%
Central Florida	$125	$139	$14	11.2%
South Florida	$37	$45	$8	21.6%
Texas Gulf	$38	$50	$12	31.6%
Texas Corridor	$65	$84	$19	29.2%
Greater Metroplex	$99	$128	$29	29.3%
Front Range	$250	$286	$36	14.4%
Sun Corridor	$66	$95	$29	43.9%
Puget Sound	$82	$115	$33	40.2%
Willamette Valley	$53	$71	$18	34.0%
Northern California	$33	$45	$12	36.4%
Southern California	$15	$18	$3	20.0%

Source: Metropolitan Institute at Virginia Tech using data from Woods & Poole Economics, Inc.

Table 6.7

Share of change in gross regional product by geography, 2000–2030 (figure in trillions of 2006 dollars).

Geography	2000	2030	Change 2000–2030	Share
United States	$9,120	$17,254	$8,134	
Megapolitans	$6,191	$11,717	$5,526	68%
Non-megapolitans	$2,929	$5,537	$2,608	32%

Source: Metropolitan Institute at Virginia Tech using data from Woods & Poole Economics, Inc.

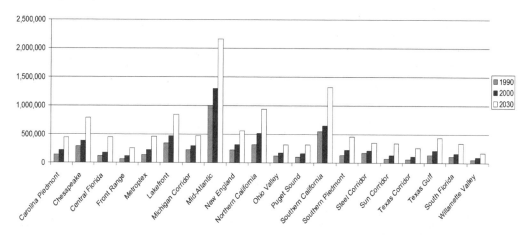

Figure 6.2 Gross Regional Product per Capita (US$) by Megapolitan Area, 1990, 2000, and 2030.

both 2000 and 2030. In 2000, the Florida Corridor ranks third highest, but by 2030 it is superseded by the Chesapeake and Metroplex areas.

Table 6.7 summarizes overall trends. Nearly 70 percent of the nation's growth in gross domestic product between 2000 and 2030—and beyond—will be concentrated in megapolitan areas and regions. Figure 6.2 compares gross regional product per capita by megapolitan area over time.

Research and Policy Implications

This chapter may have important implications for the policy movement advancing a new form of megaregional planning. Megapolitans are networks of metropolitan areas that group into larger but discrete geographic structures. Only deductive research has been done in the field. These studies start with an a priori geographic structure and seek empirical verification. This chapter presents a different approach. It uses both inductive and deductive methods that determine the nature of trans-metropolitan connectivity. It assumes that the megapolitan form can be shown by a census-based data analysis that reveals the commuter linkages between metropolitan areas. The results of this research will inform a growing audience of academics, planners, and policymakers who seek to improve land use practices on the trans-metropolitan scale. It remains to be seen whether this approach informs future research and, even more important, whether it helps shape future policymaking processes.

Notes

1. According to Baigent (2004:687) the term *megalopolis,* "meaning a large city, was in general press by the 1820s." The first scholarly use of *megalopolis* was by English urban planner

Patrick Geddes in 1927 (Thomas 2000). The word was originally meant as a pejorative to indicate overgrown cities.

2. Gottmann used the term *megapolitan* as an adjectival form of *megalopolis*, as he does in the quote at the start of this section.

3. Even if the Census Bureau does not designate megas in the short term, using existing census categories as basic building blocks creates a census-compatible geography that planning agencies could adopt.

4. The authors thank Robert Yaro, the current RPA president, for suggesting a history of megapolitan thinking and for providing guidance on the recent evolution of the idea.

5. Boris Pushkarev, RPA's chief planner in 1967, was the principal author of the Atlantic Urban Region section.

6. It covered a 150-county area that closely approximates the megapolitan region we identify in this chapter.

7. The RPA report significantly overestimated population growth in the Atlantic Urban Region, in part because the base it used for extrapolating growth trends included the peak of the baby boom. However, the current amount of settled area looks similar to what the RPA predicted. This indicates that the Atlantic Urban Region has thinned out because of fast growth at the low-density fringe.

8. The Corridor, sometimes called the "Silicon Dominion," played a vital role in starting the Internet.

9. At the bottom of the scaling were micropolitan areas, a concept that was adopted.

10. The megapolitan threshold requirement of more than 5 million residents by 2040 indicates a critical mass of people. The year 2040 was selected to show more than three decades of growth in megapolitan development. In 1970 a shift to more urbanized suburbs began in earnest. Lang et al. (2005) call this post-1970 style development a "new metropolis," of which megapolitans are one consequence. By 1880, the Atlantic Urban Region, or the Northeast Megapolitan Area, had almost 11 million residents (Shore 1967).

11. We stop at national borders for statistical purposes, but clearly some megapolitan areas extend into Mexico and Canada.

12. The Census Bureau also uses this statistic to identify core counties in a metropolitan area.

13. For a more detailed explanation of long-form data, see Berube et al. (2005).

14. According to Frey et al. (2006), just over half of all metropolitan areas are found in CSAs.

15. There were some earlier versions of trans-metropolitan areas. One such example is the Census Bureau's old consolidated metropolitan statistical areas (CMSAs), which occasionally captured two big regions, such as the Baltimore–Washington CMSA. But there were only eighteen CMSAs, of which just a handful made big metro linkages.

16. We are not the first researchers to use this method to identify megapolitan areas. Chute (1956) used contiguous census-defined metropolitan areas as the basis for urban regions.

17. The Census Bureau assigns whole counties to metropolitan areas despite their size and the extent to which the county is actually urbanized spatially. Many Western counties are larger than some Eastern states, with San Bernardino being the largest at 20,000 square miles. Future work will use Census Civil Divisions in selected large Western counties to craft more reasonable megapolitan maps.

References

Anderson, J. E. 1985. The changing structure of a city: Temporal changes in cubic spline urban density patterns. *Journal of Regional Science* 25(3):413.

Baigent, E. 2004. The geography of biography, the biography of geography: Rewriting the *Dictionary of National Biography*. *Journal of Historical Geography* 30(3):531–551.

Berube, A., B. Katz, and R. E. Lang. 2005. *Redefining Cities and Suburbs: Evidence from Census 2000*. Volume II. Brookings Institution Press, Washington, D.C.

Carbonell, A., and R. D. Yaro. 2005. American spatial development and the new megalopolis. *Land Lines* 17(2).

Castells, M. 1996. *The Rise of the Network Society.* Blackwell, Malden, MA.

Chute, C. F. 1956, June/July. Today's Urban Regions. *National Municipal Review* 45(6/7).

Faludi, A., ed. 2002. *European Spatial Planning.* Lincoln Institute of Land Policy, Cambridge, MA.

Federal Register. 1999. 64 FR 56628-56644.

Fishman, R. 2000. The death and life of American regional planning. Pp. 107–126 in *Reflections on Regionalism.* Brookings Institution Press, Washington, D.C.

Frey, W., J. H. Wilson, A. Berube, and A. Singer. 2006. Tracking metropolitan America into the 21st century: A field guide to the new metropolitan and micropolitan definitions. Pp. 191–234 in A. Berube, B. Katz, and R. E. Lang, eds. *Redefining Cities and Suburbs: Evidence from Census 2000* (Vol. 3). Brookings Institution Press, Washington, D.C.

Garreau, J. 1991. *Edge City: Life on the New Frontier.* Doubleday, New York.

Gottmann, J. 1961. *Megalopolis: The Urbanized Northeastern Seaboard of the United States.* Twentieth Century Fund, New York.

———. 1987. *Megalopolis Revisited: 25 Years Later.* University of Maryland Press, College Park.

Gottmann, J., and R. A. Harper. 1990. *Since Megalopolis.* Johns Hopkins University Press, Baltimore, MD.

Katz, B., R. Lang, and A. Berube. 2006. *Redefining Urban and Suburban America: Evidence from Census 2000.* Brookings Institution Press, Washington, D.C.

Lang, R. E. 2003. *Beyond Edge City: Office Sprawl in South Florida.* Brookings Institution Press, Washington, D.C.

Lang, R. E., and D. Dhavale. 2005. *Beyond Megalopolis: Exploring America's New "Megapolitan" Geography* (Census Report no. 05:01). Metropolitan Institute at Virginia Tech, Alexandria, VA.

Lang, R. E., E. J. Blakely, and M. Gough. 2005. "Keys to the New Metropolis: America's Big, Fast-Growing Suburban Counties." *Journal of the American Planning Association* 71(3): 381–391.

Lang, R. E., and A. C. Nelson. 2006. *Beyond the Metroplex: Examining Commuter Patterns at the "Megapolitan" Scale.* Lincoln Institute of Land Policy, Cambridge, MA.

McKenzie, R. D. 1997, originally published 1933. *The Metropolitan Community.* Routledge/Thoemmes, London.

Meinig, D. W. 2004. *The Shaping of America: A Geographical Perspective on 500 Years of History: Volume 4: Global America, 1915–2000 (Shaping of History).* Yale University Press, New Haven, CT.

Mineta, N. 2005. Starving Amtrak to save it. *New York Times,* February 23.

National Association of Counties. 2005. Facts about Counties. Accessed at: www.naco.org/Template.cfm?Section=About_Counties

Nelson, A. C. 2004. *Toward a New Metropolis: The Opportunity to Rebuild America.* Brookings Institution Press, Washington, D.C.

Nelson, A. C., and R. E. Lang. 2007. The next 100 million. *Planning* 73(1):4–6.

Population Reference Bureau. 2000. Goodbye "Metropolitan?" PRB On-Line: www.prb.org. April–June.

Schon, P. 2005. Territorial cohesion in Europe? *Planning Theory and Practice* 6(3).

Shore, W. B., ed. 1967. *The Region's Growth: A Report of the Second Regional Plan.* Regional Plan Association, New York.

Starner, R. 2005, March. Top micropolitans: Strength in numbers. *Site Selection Magazine.*

Taylor, P. J. 2004. *World City Network: A Global Urban Analysis.* Routledge, New York.

Thomas, J. L. 2000. Holding the Middle Ground. In R. Fishman (ed.), *The American Planning Tradition: Culture and Policy.* The Woodrow Wilson Center Press, Washington, D.C.

United States Bureau of the Census. 2001. Census 2000 Summary File One. Accessed from American FactFinder at http://factfinder.census.gov/servlet/BasicFactsServlet.

United States Bureau of the Census. 2003. Estimates and Projections Area Documentation Sub-county Total Population Estimates. Accessed at: http://eire.census.gov/popest/topic/method ology.

Woods & Poole Economics. 2007. Compiled projections provided to authors.

Yaro, R. D., and A. Carbonell. 2004. *Toward an American Spatial Development Perspective*. Lincoln Institute of Land Policy and Regional Plan Association, Cambridge, MA.

Yaro, R. D., A. Carbonell, and J. Barnett. 2004. Planning for America in a Global Economy. City Planning Studio Report. University of Pennsylvania School of Design, Philadelphia.

Zelinsky, W. 1973. *The Cultural Geography of the United States:* Prentice Hall, Upper Saddle River, NJ.

7

The Imperative of Growth, the Rhetoric of Sustainability

The Divergence of the Ecoregion and the Global Megaregion

Scott Campbell

Does the megaregional framework bring us closer to or further away from the sustainable region? Megaregions represent both a promising new analytical category of spatial research and a (still somewhat elusive) geographic district of planning and policy (Wheeler 2008; Zhang 2006; Yarwood 2006; Peirce 2006; Ooi 2006; Laquian 2005; John et al. 2005; Regional Plan Association 2006; Yaro and Carbonell 2004; Lang and Dhavale 2005). Although definitions vary, the U.S. discussion on megaregions emphasizes the shift from a traditional metropolitan framework (city, suburb, hinterland) to a large-scale, polycentric (or even non-centric) network of multiple adjacent metropolitan areas and their interstitial hinterlands.

The long-term utility of the megaregion as a distinct planning scale is still unproven. Does the megaregional approach confront or evade the core planning issues of equity, democracy, livability, economic vitality, and design excellence? If Jane Jacobs's old quip about a region being "an area safely larger than the last one to whose problems we found no solution" remains cogent, then the current interest in megaregions represents either a logical territorial scaling up to match the rapid expansion of regions or another attempt by stalwart regionalists to reassert (and update) the relevance of their old schema.

This chapter examines the implications of megaregion development on natural resources and the environment. How does the shift from a traditional, single-core metropolitan region to a megaregion alter the stand and discussion of regional environmentalism? Advocates of megaregions tout the benefits of the megaregion framework for sustainability, including its ability to "preserve large environmental (or 'green infrastructure') systems" (Regional Plan Association 2006). Megaregions are promoted as the more effective scale for environmental management than previous planning scales because the larger megaregion encompasses the holistic scale of environmental systems (e.g., watersheds, air basins, habitats) and thus allows integrated management of these systems within a coherent spatial planning framework. Implicitly, the push to make megaregions "the new competitive units in the global economy" (Regional Plan Association 2006) would indirectly benefit the natural environment as well: Efficient internal coordination of infrastructure construction, resource development, and land use at the megaregional scale would ostensibly reduce wasteful (i.e., unsustainable) transportation and land development practices. Development would be concentrated along clustered corridors and into urban cores of a polycentric megaregion. Furthermore, the push to be a competitive economic megaregion means providing quality-of-life amenities to attract the elite information and culture class, which in this postindustrial era translates into natural amenities (e.g., high-end outdoor recreation, appealing natural viewsheds, bike trails, preserves for second homes). In this optimistic framework, the megaregion represents the win–win situation of competitive, efficient, and sustainable territories.

My approach is not to take head-on the question of whether the megaregion truly represents a distinctively new pattern of human settlement. Nor do I take a descriptive inventory of natural resources in individual megaregions.[1] Instead, I examine how the introduction of the megaregion concept (as a spatial, analytical, and institution scale) is changing the way we approach planning. Specifically, how does the shift from a traditional metropolitan framework to a megaregion framework (a constellation of multiple metropolitan areas) shift our planning priorities? Do these shifts push planning efforts closer to or further away from the substantive priorities and values of environmental protection and ecological sustainability? And within the array of environmental priorities, does the megaregional framework work better for some aspects of environmental protection than others (e.g., watershed protection or air quality)?

The Concept of the Megaregion

The megaregion concept is a compelling but still fluid term and has several divergent interpretations. Differing accounts of megaregional structure and function will guide the analysis of the sustainable megaregion.

How to Conceive of the Shift from Region to Megaregion

There are two basic options:

The shift from a single metropolitan area to a network of multiple metropolises (mega = multiple metros)

The expansion of a single metropolitan area far into the hinterland (*mega* = sprawl, very large hinterland)

The shift from the region to the megaregion therefore can represent simply a scaling up or instead a more structural transformation. In practice, the megaregion is a hybrid of the two: a natural scaling up of regions with long-standing dynamics of regions still in play. However, one should avoid an essentialist view of megaregions. Contemporary regional dynamics have changed dramatically over the past 40 years, not simply because some intrinsic element of regions has changed but because many of the socioeconomic forces that play out in regions have themselves changed: the nature of trade, industrial relations, the relocation (and internationalization) of manufacturing, the changing landscape of housing markets and housing finance, migration policy, and so on.

Historical Roots and Contemporary Parallels of the Megaregional Idea

Although there are obvious overlaps between the phenomena of regions, megaregions, megacities, and global megaregions, there is a useful distinction between an international version of a strong-centered, primate megacity (e.g., megacities of Asia) and a typically U.S. version of a weak-centered, decentralized, or polycentric megaregion. The empirical question here is the demographic and economic (or functional) weight of the central city or cities relative to the larger regional settlements.

The contemporary megaregion debate is new, yet it has evident connections to both parallel and past literatures:

- An extension or scaling-up of metropolitan-based regionalism (Katz 2000; Orfield 2002; Benjamin and Nathan 2001)
- An update of midcentury regionalism as subnational planning (e.g., TVA, ARC)
- A reframing of the global cities view (Sassen 2001)
- An adaptation of the megacity idea to the American context
- Global city-regions (Scott 2001)
- A revisiting of the megalopolis idea (Gottmann 1961)

A Larger Layer on the Existing Map: Megaregions Both Erasing and Augmenting

The megaregion is both replacing the existing metropolitan structure and adding an additional layer to the existing metropolitan structure (i.e., substitutive and additive effects). In the past, regionalists defined regions based on several criteria, such as core (central city) plus hinterland (suburbs, rural areas); shared cultural, economic, or ecological characteristics; commute zones; watersheds; and industrial districts. The megaregion mapping efforts probably are changing the relative importance of these characteristics, often with greater emphasis on the infrastructure (highways, rail lines, airport sheds) that knit these megaregions together. The megaregional map is one of a network of nodes, corridors, and vast, low-density residential zones, surrounded by large buffer zones of reserve land (for either development or preservation). These characteristics of megaregions (boundaries, core, corridors, density, complexity, internal differentiation and disparities) will in turn shape environmental dynamics, including nature–urban boundaries (greenbelt, habitat corridors), energy systems, and commute distances.

Analysis, Idealism, and Institutions

The shift from region to megaregion represents a shift in three areas: geographic patterns of development, an analytical category (conceiving the territorial unit), and political boundaries and institutions. There is a danger in conflating these three, and one should not assume that these three shift simultaneously. Instead, there are temporal discrepancies (e.g., lag times) between these three. For example, megaregional patterns of development are arguably outpacing megaregional governance. (If so, this is nothing new in the history of urban development.) Differentiating between the three—unit of analysis, unit of governance, and scale of urbanization—would be a welcome step toward a more precise and nuanced discussion of megaregions. The megaregion therefore may be only a partially useful scale: Problems may appear at the region scale, but their causes—and also their solutions—may not necessarily be regional. Megaregional problems may not necessarily require megaregional governance.

A Megaregional Community?

What connects the various metropolitan components of a megaregion together? Can we speak of a megaregional community? The megaregional literature suggests several elements: infrastructure, land resources and major natural features, economic linkages, and shared airports and marine terminal networks. The residents (or at least the elites) in a megaregion are supposed to recognize that pooling resources, integrating infrastructure, and presenting a single voice to the global markets will improve the region's future economic prosperity. Whether these megaregions constitute a coherent community with shared megaregional environmental solidarity, identity, and collective self-interest is a harder question. Several megaregions share notable geophysical characteristics that can lend a shared identity: Cascadia is bounded by the Pacific Ocean and the Cascade Mountains, and the Great Lakes link the Midwestern megaregion. But these features are just one of several environmental challenges; for example, the Great Lakes are only a partial link for the Midwest but probably insufficient.

Internal and External Features

One traditional goal of regionalism has been to identify and redress regional differences. Regional differences include inequalities both within and between regions. Over time, regional development policy has shifted back and forth between the two. Although historically much of the measurable spatial disparity has been between U.S. regions (e.g., the former disparity between the industrial American North and the rural South), during the postwar period regional planning concerns shifted to an emergent urban–suburban inequality.

The contemporary megaregional emphasis seems to be shifting the emphasis back to the gap between regions, albeit in a reconfigured form (the booming New South and West, the declining Rustbelt) and with an explicit context of regions competing in a global economy. Although the megaregional framework ostensibly allows a focus on both intraregional and interregional inequality, there is a problematic tendency among contemporary megaregional writings to treat the megaregion as a homogeneous, unified whole (sublimating internal problems in order to present an external face as a unified player in a global competition between megaregional economic units), thereby neglecting the enormous disparities within the region.[2]

The Underlying Tension for Sustainable Megaregions: Growth Machine or Ecological Containment?

Underlying this chapter's analysis is an acknowledgment of urban planning's two seemingly contradictory impulses. On one hand, the field promotes expansion through urban growth coalitions, the expansion of jobs and tax revenues, the construction of infrastructure, and the push for more intensive land uses. On the other hand, planners often emphasize the importance of urban growth boundaries, sustainable development, "small is beautiful," and reducing our ecological footprint to mitigate the downsides of excessive materialism. This tension has a long history in planning, but it has renewed exigency in an era of climate change and global urbanization. This tension also complicates planning's current preoccupation with sustainable development, which is not readily compatible with the field's traditional emphasis on growth and expansion. This paradox between growth and conservation manifests itself in multiple contemporary planning situations and at many planning scales. And despite claims that the megaregional scale will promote reconciliation between the two forces, the tension between growth and preservation is at least as pronounced (if not more) at the megaregional scale.

Historically, the arguments for planning at the regional scale come from four corners: administrative efficiency (scale economies through sharing of resources and facilities), economic competitiveness (larger regions pull more weight in national and global markets), environmental protection, and social justice (e.g., overcoming urban–suburban inequalities in housing, schools, and job markets) (Campbell and D'Anieri 2001; Foster 2001). The political effectiveness of regional planning often depends on building coalitions across the administrative, business, environmental, social justice, and labor union movements that support each of these variants of regionalism. To understand the prospects of and obstacles to the sustainable megaregion, consider these four impulses in the world of megaregions. How does the megaregion change these traditional impulses toward regional planning? Which regional priorities are elevated, and which are demoted? And does environmental protection get easier or harder in the megaregion framework?

Will the Megaregion Growth Machine Trump the Ecoregion and the Social Justice Region?

The focus on creating a globally competitive megaregion with expanding boundaries (through infrastructural megaprojects such as high-speed rail, region-wide airports, and other trade hubs) will probably trump efforts to promote environmentally sustainable and geographically contained ecoregions (e.g., urban growth boundaries). The emphasis on megaregions will foreground some issues (e.g., economic competitiveness through larger-scale economies and large infrastructure networks) and push other issues into the shadows (e.g., traditional regional concerns for city–suburb social inequality). In this regard, the megaregionalists seem to have borrowed rhetoric from the global cities canon: Move up the hierarchy of major metro areas by becoming more competitive in the global economic networks.

Although some proponents view the megaregion as well suited to more efficient and compact land use (e.g., a kind of new urbanism on a superregional scale), the push toward the megaregion may instead exacerbate the sprawling polycentric (or noncentric) conurbation—the "semi-rustic megalopolis, hundreds of miles long . . . spreading across the Carolinas and other Southern states where bits and pieces of sprawl blend together along major freeways" (Tibbetts 2002–2003). Thus the bemoaned characteristics of the contemporary metropolitan region (auto dependent, land consumptive, intrusive to farmland, fragmenting habitat, not amenable to mass transit, radiating around the curvilinear highway rather than the central city) will take on even larger and more polycentric dimensions as megaregions grow.[3]

The implications for land conservation are troubling. Despite the potential for megaregions to offer a high-density, transit-oriented growth strategy, the push to megaregions may instead push more toward enormous, land-consuming sprawl. Some developers may embrace the megaregion framework as a means to build reurbanized, clustered developments. But many developers already view the megaregion as a vast new territory of developable land, the megaregion as real estate bonanza. Kaihla and Crawford (2005) responded to academic studies of megaregions with the title "The $25 Trillion Land Grab: Ten Megapolitans Are Poised for a Development Boom That, by 2030, Will Dwarf America's Post–World War II Buildout. Here's Our Treasure Map of Potential Opportunity." Looking at the Cascadia megaregion, the authors saw not the legacy of the urban growth boundary but instead simply lots of land to be bought and sold: "Vast quantities of cheap, prime greenfield surrounding Seattle, Portland, and Eugene give the Northwest megapolitan explosive growth potential" (Kaihla and Crawford 2005:97).

Here Myron Orfield may be right: Controlling infrastructure investment is crucial to controlling the direction of urbanization. The spatial structure of megaregions will be both shaped and reflected by its infrastructure networks. We know the historically critical and conflicting roles of infrastructure: It can knit together various metro zones into a larger, more competitive megaregion, and yet this same widespread infrastructural grid will exacerbate the loss of open space and habitat and elongates auto trips. This double-edged side of infrastructure, with both centripetal and centrifugal tendencies, is nothing new. But what is new with megaregions is not only the larger geographic scale—defined still at the regional and not national level—but also its more explicit role in connecting multiple metropolitan areas via linkages through the greenfield exurban and wilderness areas. To control the infrastructure may well be to control the direction of megaregions.

A Further Push away from Consolidated, Comprehensive, Multi-issue Regionalism

The greater scale and number of jurisdictions within megaregions will shift regional planning efforts even more toward collaboration (e.g., federated regionalism) and away from unitary government consolidation. This greater scale and complexity will also place greater emphasis on single-issue regionalism (e.g., transportation, water, technology development) rather than comprehensive, integrated regional planning. Regional efforts may target the low-hanging fruit of easy regionalism first (e.g., infrastructure) and neglect to move on to the greater challenges of hard regionalism (e.g., school equity, urban–suburban environmental inequality). Efforts to build broad-issue alliances at the megaregional scale (e.g., to tackle the harder social and environmental challenges on the coattails of the infrastructural and economic competitiveness issues) will give way to single-issue regionalism in the name of political expediency.

Increased Role of State Governments

This increased geographic scale (e.g., from single to multiple central cities, often including multiple states) will further highlight the critical role of state governments in regional efforts. (State governments have often been the driving force behind effective regional environmental efforts, as in Oregon, California, and New Jersey.) Efforts to develop multistate megaregions could lead to new forms of multistate agreements, including greater use of interstate compacts (e.g., the 1922 Colorado River compact between seven states, the Port Authority of New York and New Jersey, the Atlantic States Marine Fisheries Commission, and the Tahoe Regional Planning Agency) (Morrow 2005). This shift upward in scale also suggests a greater involvement at the federal level. This increase in state and federal participation could be beneficial for environmental efforts if effectively linked to state and federal legislation and regulations regarding the environment.

A Disconnect between Local Preservation and Megaregional Growth?

One already observes a tension at the regional scale: Residents often oppose growth at the neighborhood level but support growth region-wide (Fulton 2001). In the short term, this is a rational, self-interested response: It elevates local housing prices through both constrained local supply and expanded region-wide demand. But in the long run this behavior creates a kind of social trap or prisoner's dilemma (e.g., a tragedy of the commons) and a breakdown between local and regional environmental political movements. This discrepancy will probably get larger at the megaregional scale. At the regional scale, the megaregion growth machine will fuel land consumption at the fringes, with pockets of local environmental, antigrowth initiatives in a sea of growth and expansion. The resulting landscape resembles an archipelago of affluent green residential islands in a booming, dispersed, and denatured region. This is not a promising path to a sustainable region.

This local–regional disconnect presents a challenge to grassroots environmental organizing at the megaregional scale. Environmental planners will see in the megaregion both a promise and an obstacle: The megaregion will better encompass the holistic scale of environmental systems (e.g., watersheds, air basins, habitats), but the megaregion threatens to be a harder scale for environmental political organizing than the local or small-region scale. By extension, grassroots regionalism will become even more difficult (unless one can build megaregional coalitions of locally based groups).

Not All Megaregions Are Created Equal

Although the maps of megaregions seem to form a patchwork of solidarity across North America, great divides exist between the ten or more commonly identified U.S. megaregions (with their divergent commitments to environmentalism). Low-density, high-growth Sunbelt megaregions (e.g., the Arizona Sun Corridor, Florida, and Southern California) face challenges of water scarcity, rising summer temperatures, and rapid land consumption. By contrast, the Great Lakes megaregion has water (and the lakes moderate summer temperature extremes) but desperately need a revitalized economic base and updated industrial infrastructure. Cascadia (Seattle, Portland, and Vancouver) has both growth and remarkable natural features of water and mountains, but the former is threatening the latter. Emergent models of sustainability will vary greatly across these megaregions.

Green Megaregions (Ecoregions) as Branding

Megaregions (or subsets of megaregions) have the potential to market themselves as places with an emphasis on green building and high walking and bike usage, such as Cascadia (Toulon School of Urban Studies and Planning 2006). This is the selling not just of the natural environment but also of a regional culture of preserving and promoting the natural environment. The task of selling environmental protection is aided by the ability to sell nature as a marketable regional amenity rather than appeal to a more altruistic environmental ethos. Environmental benefits in this context consist of an expanding soft infrastructure of consumption-oriented recreation for the active living professional class. Although some deep ecologists decry nature-as-commodity environmentalism as short-sighted anthropomorphism, such an approach may be the most pragmatic initial strategy to preserve natural features within the megaregion.

Megaregions could reinforce this green branding with concrete policies such as megaregion-wide subsidy programs to reduce water and energy consumption and green building programs.

The Challenges of Measuring and Ensuring Megaregional Sustainability in a Large, Open System

Megaregions represent such open resource systems—especially given the megaregionalists' emphasis on participating in open global markets—that traditional measures of closed-system sustainability (e.g., territorial carrying capacity) don't readily apply. What are the new metrics of megaregion environments? The ecological footprint, allowing development impact to be measured in non-contiguous land units, offers more flexibility for open systems and is a good first step toward sustainable megaregion metrics. (One might expect greater variation of ecological footprints within megaregions than across megaregions, which suggests that no single megaregion might easily emerge as an ideal environmental prototype.) Perhaps one can envision the Leadership in Energy and Environmental Design for Neighborhood Development (U.S. Green Building Council) being ratcheted up to the megaregional level.

This open megaregion approach collides with the renewed interest in the social and environmental benefits of returning to more localized supply networks of goods and services (Pollan 2006; McKibben 2007; Shuman 2006). If one approach to environmental sustainability is greater local, small-scale provision of natural resources (e.g., food, water, energy), then the megaregion approach (with its more laissez-faire approach to national and global trade) would seem to make an orthodox model of self-sufficient ecoregionalism (Sale 1985) even more remote. One might envision a hybrid model that encourages greater consumption of goods and services produced within the megaregion itself (e.g., expanding Ebenezer Howard's greenbelt-feeds-its-garden-city model to the superregional scale).

Conclusions

Advocates of megaregions see the promise of this enlarged planning scale as bringing us closer to the ecoregion. Skeptics claim that megaregions will further foreground economic competitiveness over environmental protection. There is truth in both these positions. But both positions also run the risk of spatial scale determinism, presuming not just that the geographic scale of communities and planning can influence (along with many other factors) social priorities but that the spatial scale directly governs social behavior above all other factors.

The push toward the megaregional scale in itself will not bring us closer to or further away from the sustainable region. The megaregion offers opportunities for new kinds of environmental planning and protection, such as its inclusion of large areas of wilderness, watersheds, and habitats that the traditional metropolitan region cannot contain. Yet the same characteristics of the megaregion also present challenges to sustainable development because it will be tempting to fill in these greenfield interurban areas as part of a larger effort to knit together the megaregion with a decentralized infrastructural network. This applies not just to land but also to other natural resources: Residents and governments can either use the megaregional scale to preserve large freshwater watersheds or to exploit an even larger area for unsustainable ground and surface water extraction.[4]

Whether future urbanization mainstreams or marginalizes sustainable practices will not be primarily the result of an embrace or rejection of the megaregion (or of any alternative scale) but will instead be linked to social commitment to sustainability per se and to concrete tradeoffs between expansion and preservation. Although contemporary environmental and social problems may be expressed—and indeed embedded—in spatial relations at the megaregional scale, they are not easily corrected through spatial fixes. Whether a shift to the megaregional framework will tilt toward economic competitiveness, social justice, or environmental protection lies less in the innate characteristics of megaregions and more in the social and political movements that capture and define the megaregional movement.

In the end, the megaregion will highlight—and probably exacerbate—the core tension in planning between boosteristic growth and landscape conservation. Addressing these possible weaknesses of the megaregion in the early stages of the debate will both enrich the discussion and temper any unwarranted infatuation with this admittedly attractive concept.

Notes

1. This chapter also does not examine megaregions outside the United States, nor does it explicitly deal with transborder megaregions, although several U.S. megaregions (Southern California, the Great Lakes, Cascadia) are de facto transborder. The challenge of megaregions is certainly not limited to North America. The challenge of megacities is paralleled by—and perhaps even overshadowed by—the rise of megaregions in places such as the Yangtze River Delta (Laquian 2005; Leman 1998), Bangkok (Sintusingha 2006), and Beijing (Wu 1998).
2. An unequal "two-tier regionalism" might ensue: at the megaregion-wide scale, an elite federation of top-down metropolitan areas sharing a common goal of competing in global markets; at the smaller scale, the more traditional pattern of city–suburb regionalism with greater commitment to taking on the challenges of concentrated poverty, inequality, and environmental degradation.
3. Continued spatial segregation by race, income, and land use also presents barriers to sustainable land use patterns. The imbalance not just between jobs and housing but also between rich housing and poor housing will continue to encourage people to find housing far from places of employment and commerce, and the megaregional trend will probably make this even worse as the functional sizes of regional labor and housing markets expand (especially if the megaregion doesn't directly address class and fiscal segregation).
4. One can already see both a growing interest and apprehension in the possibilities of shipping water from wet to dry megaregions.

References

Benjamin, G. A., and R. P. Nathan. 2001. *Regionalism and Realism: A Study of Governments in the New York Metropolitan Area.* Brookings Institution Press, Washington, D.C.

Campbell, S., and P. D'Anieri. 2001. *Unpacking the Impetus for Regional Planning in the U.S.: Cooperation, Coercion and Self-Interest.* Paper presented at the Association of Collegiate Schools of Planning Annual Conference, Cleveland, OH.

Foster, K. A. 2001. *Regionalism on Purpose.* Lincoln Institute of Land Policy, Cambridge, MA.

Fulton, W. B. 2001. *The Reluctant Metropolis: The Politics of Urban Growth in Los Angeles.* Johns Hopkins University Press, Baltimore, MD.

Gottmann, J. 1961. *Megalopolis: The Urbanized Northeastern Seaboard of the United States.* Twentieth Century Fund, New York.

John, P., A. Tickell, and S. Musson. 2005. Governing the mega-region: Governance and networks across London and the South East of England. *New Political Economy* 10(1):91–106.

Kaihla, P., and K. Crawford. 2005. The $25 trillion land grab: Ten megapolitans are poised for a development boom that, by 2030, will dwarf America's post–World War II buildout. Here's our treasure map of potential opportunity. *Business 2.0* 6:97.

Katz, B., ed. 2000. *Reflections on Regionalism.* Brookings Institution Press, Washington, D.C.

Lang, R. E., and D. Dhavale. 2005. *Beyond Megalopolis: Exploring America's New "Megapolitan" Geography* (Census Report no. 05:01). Metropolitan Institute, Alexandria, VA.

Laquian, A. 2005. *Beyond Metropolis: The Planning and Governance of Asia's Mega-Urban Regions.* Woodrow Wilson Center Press, Washington, D.C.

Leman, E. 1998. The Yangtze Delta megalopolis. *Ekistics* 65(388–390):65–71.

McKibben, B. 2007. *Deep Economy: The Wealth of Communities and the Durable Future.* Times Books, New York.

Morrow, W. S. Jr. 2005. *The Case for an Interstate Compact APA (Interstate Compacts Projects).* Section of Administrative Law and Regulatory Practice, American Bar Association, Washington, D.C.

Ooi, G.-L. 2006. Beyond metropolis: The planning and governance of Asia's mega-urban regions, by Aprodicio A. Laquian. *ASEAN Economic Bulletin* 23(2):266.

Orfield, M. 2002. *American Metropolitics: The New Suburban Reality.* Brookings Institution Press, Washington, D.C.

Peirce, N. 2006. Stunning new prescription for America's Great Lakes megaregion. *Nation's Cities Weekly* 29:2.

Pollan, M. 2006. *The Omnivore's Dilemma: A Natural History of Four Meals.* Penguin, New York.

Regional Plan Association. 2006. *America 2050: A Prospectus.* Regional Plan Association, New York.

Sale, K. 1985. *Dwellers in the Land: The Bioregional Vision.* Sierra Club Books, San Francisco.

Sassen, S. 2001. *The Global City: New York, London, Tokyo* (2nd ed.). Princeton University Press, Princeton, NJ.

Scott, A., ed. 2001. *Global City-Regions: Trends, Theory, Prospects.* Oxford University Press, Oxford.

Shuman, M. 2006. *The Small-Mart Revolution: How Local Businesses Are Beating the Global Competition.* Berrett-Koehler, San Francisco.

Sintusingha, S. 2006. Sustainability and urban sprawl: Alternative scenarios for a Bangkok superblock. *Urban Design International* 11(3–4):151–172.

Tibbetts, J. H. 2002–2003. The freeway city. *Coastal Heritage* 17:3–12.

Toulon School of Urban Studies and Planning. 2006. *Cascadia Ecolopolis 2.0.* Portland State University, Portland.

Wheeler, S. 2008. Regions, megaregions, and sustainability. *Regional Studies.* Accessed at http://www.informaworld.com/smpp/content~content=a792757464~db=all on February 18, 2009.

Wu, L. 1998. Beijing at a crossroads: A new concept for Greater Beijing. *Ekistics* 65(388–390): 57–64.

Yaro, R. D., and A. Carbonell. 2004. *Toward an American Spatial Development Perspective.* Lincoln Institute of Land Policy and Regional Plan Association, Cambridge, MA.

Yarwood, J. R. 2006. *The Dublin–Belfast Development Corridor: Ireland's Mega-City Region?* Ashgate Publishing, Ashgate, UK.

Zhang, T. 2006. Beyond metropolis: The planning and governance of Asia's mega-urban regions. *Journal of Planning Education and Research* 25(3):333–334.

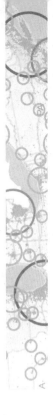

8

Mobility in the Megaregion

Catherine L. Ross, Jason Barringer, and
Adjo A. Amekudzi

The construction of the U.S. interstate system took place at a time when there was an extreme need for connectivity from our eastern to western borders. The system ensured greater mobility, continued economic development, and a basis for enhancing our national defense. The world that existed in the 1950s has changed dramatically. The institutions and infrastructure that have served us fairly well must now be reconfigured to meet current mobility and economic needs and provide a competitive advantage in the global economy. Once again, we must move forward with institutions, strategies, tools, and a vision of how we are going to maintain a competitive advantage and a high quality of life in a world where we will be increasingly called on to reduce our consumption of resources.

This chapter explores the practical implications of megaregions with respect to mobility and infrastructure investment. It outlines a functional approach to transportation planning in the megaregion, examines the Piedmont Atlantic Megaregion (PAM), and discusses infrastructure investment strategies to be considered at the level of the megaregion. Conclusions and observations are offered in regard to the contributions of megaregion planning.

Megaregions: Crossing Borders

The theoretical underpinning of megaregions is gleaned from a brief examination of the role of infrastructure in regional economic growth. Infrastructure is the skeleton linking neighborhoods, towns, and cities to regions, regions to megaregions, and megaregions and countries together. More explicitly, transportation and mobility hubs have historically proven to be advantageous to our cities and, by extension, regions (Fujita et al. 1999).

What role do mobility and transportation infrastructure play in the development and success of megaregions in the global context? Although the role of infrastructure in developing countries is a common topic, the use of infrastructure in highly developed countries and its role in expanding economic activity have not received the same amount of attention (Edgington et al. 2001). Infrastructure should be designed and created to support our global markets and provide the social infrastructure to sustain our lives, families, and communities. Numerous strategies and views have been put forward outlining the ability of regional planning to expand economic influence and the role of infrastructure in accomplishing that effectively (Edgington et al. 2001; Isard et al. 1998; Dreier et al. 2001).

Regions are characterized by numerous complex networks that deliver information, goods, and services. Each megaregion must be analyzed to understand its strengths and assess its current and future competitive advantage. What is the response of the United States to trends in globalization? How must it reorder priorities, reengineer institutions, and define a direction? In the United States, megaregions continue to outpace the growth of other spatial constructs of the nation and can be a primary tool for shaping redevelopment opportunities and fueling the renewal of our infrastructure. In 2030, approximately two thirds of the global population is expected to be urban (Cohen 2005), and similar conditions are expected in the United States. These trends will place increased demands on the nation's infrastructure that cannot be met by current planning and funding mechanisms. In order to compete and succeed in this global economic environment, we will have to fundamentally rethink the movement of goods and people both interregionally and intraregionally while identifying the cost of providing sustained improvements. A new planning and funding framework, expanded in geographic as well as temporal scope, is needed to inform decision making in order to improve domestic and global freight movement.

Freight Movement and Megaregions

The efficient movement of goods is essential because freight transportation significantly affects economic productivity (Jones 2007). The transportation infrastructure that connects metropolitan areas, allowing commodity movement by truck, rail, water, air, and other modes, is vital to the nation's competitiveness (Puentes 2008). A global economy and free trade will increase the demand for movement of goods and services. For example, the volume of shipments is projected to increase from 17.5 billion metric tons in 2002 to 33.7 billion metric tons in 2035 (Jones 2007). Trade between the United States and other countries is taking place in most megaregions. In 2005, approximately two thirds of the total U.S. global trade took place in the fifty largest metropolitan areas (Puentes 2008). To accommodate these future demands, we will need a freight transportation policy identifying the kind of transportation modes needed and directing sufficient investment to megaregions that are transporting large amounts of goods to global markets.

Transportation Modes of Freight Movement

Although the volume of shipments throughout the United States is projected to increase continuously, its effects on the transportation system vary depending on the transportation modes, the properties of transported goods, and the characteristics of geographic areas.

The freight transportation system is a complex network of land, water, and air. The Federal Highway Administration's 2006 Freight Analysis Framework includes seven modes of transportation: air and truck, other intermodal, pipeline and unknown, rail, truck, truck and rail, and water.[1]

Figures 8.1–8.3 show that more than half of exported goods were carried by truck to the ports of exit on the U.S. border. More than 60 percent of domestic commodity flows were moved by truck. On the other hand, the transportation modes of imported goods from foreign countries are distributed more evenly across several modes. For example, approximately 40 percent and 25 percent of imported goods from Canada and Mexico were carried by pipeline and rail, respectively, and 30 percent were moved by truck. The figures also show that megaregions relied more on trucks than non-megaregion areas for freight movements.

Domestic Commodity Flows

More than half of all commodities were carried by truck (64 percent) between domestic origins and destinations in 2002. Pipeline and unknown contributed 21 percent, rail 10 percent, and water 3 percent (Figure 8.1). Specifically, more than 77 percent of commodities from megaregions were moved to domestic destinations by truck in 2002, projected at 80 percent by 2035, whereas non-megaregion areas rely on less than 60 percent truck traffic in both 2002 and 2035 (Ross et al. 2008). This means that megaregions will experience heavier freight traffic on highways than non-megaregion areas. Approximately 4–5 percent of commodities are carried by rail in megaregions, compared with 13 percent rail usage in non-megaregion areas. Pipeline is highly used in non-megaregion areas, approximately 26 percent in 2002, compared with 4 percent in megaregions (Ross et al. 2008).

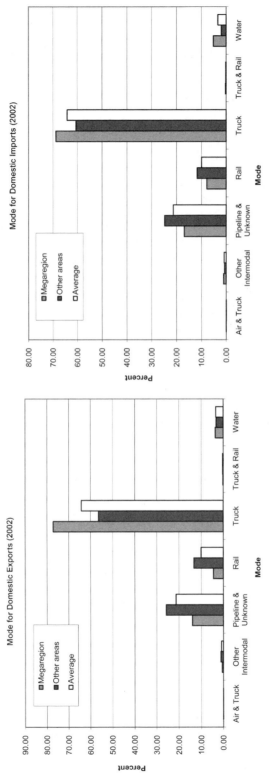

Figure 8.1 Transportation Modes for Domestic Trade Goods.

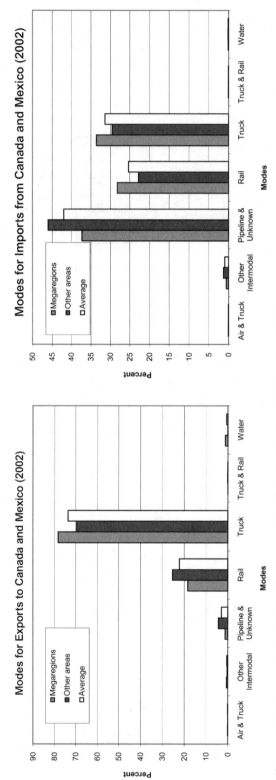

Figure 8.2 Transportation Modes for International Trade Goods with Canada and Mexico.

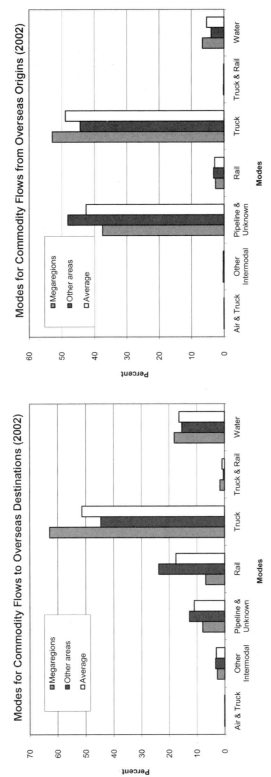

Figure 8.3 Transportation Modes for International Trade Goods with Overseas Countries.

Table 8.1

Comparison of growth rates of domestic commodity flows between megaregions and non-megaregion areas, 2002–2035.

Modes	Exports (%)		Imports (%)	
	Megaregions	Non-Megaregions	Megaregions	Non-Megaregions
Pipeline and unknown	68.7	88.5	68.9	91.6
Rail	102.3	82.9	84.5	87
Truck	105.3	88.5	99.1	93.5
Water	25.7	61.4	47.7	45.4
Total	97.5	86.4	89.3	91.5

Source: Derived from the Freight Analysis Framework Commodity Origin–Destination Database (FHA 2006).

Table 8.1 also shows that an increase in exporting commodity flows by truck and rail will take place in megaregions, whereas non-megaregion areas will increase their use of the pipeline and water modes by 2035. However, for importing goods from other domestic regions, there is no significant difference between megaregions and non-megaregions, except for the increase in pipeline usage in non-megaregions.

The average distance covered by truck freight is shorter (485 miles) than that of air (973 miles) and rail (902 miles). Moreover, more than 65 percent of the tonnage of freight movements by truck is estimated to move less than 100 miles (Puentes 2008). The short length of trucking implies that changes in freight movement policy between metropolitan areas at the megaregion level would be useful in relieving congestion caused by truck traffic on highways and ensuring just-in-time delivery of goods. Road and rail infrastructure throughout the nation is becoming increasingly taxed, with an expected price tag of hundreds of billions of dollars needed over the next 15 to 20 years just to cover maintenance and capacity enhancement (American Society of Civil Engineers 2005).

Commodity Flows from and to Overseas Countries

Table 8.2 shows how different transportation modes move export and import goods between origins, destinations, and ports. For export goods, the reliance on trucks in megaregions may increase from 63 to 74 percent between 2002 and 2035, whereas the reliance on water, rail, and pipeline may decrease. Although freight movement by truck will increase in non-megaregions as well, other trans-

Table 8.2

Transportation modes of commodity flows from and to foreign countries.

| | Exports (%) | | | | Imports (%) | | | |
| | Megaregions | | Non-Megaregions | | Megaregions | | Non-Megaregions | |
Mode	2002	2035	2002	2035	2002	2035	2002	2035
Air and truck	0.06	0.12	0.07	0.10	0.06	0.09	0.08	0.11
Other intermodal	2.33	2.99	3.23	2.83	0.30	0.57	0.28	0.59
Pipeline and unknown	7.93	4.49	12.68	7.50	37.48	21.44	48.14	37.96
Rail	6.81	5.35	23.71	19.77	2.60	2.48	3.19	5.21
Truck	62.88	73.71	44.55	53.50	52.87	71.81	44.32	53.16
Truck and rail	1.64	1.36	0.42	0.61	0.13	0.15	0.09	0.12
Water	18.03	11.98	15.30	15.69	6.57	3.47	3.90	2.85

Source: Derived from the Freight Analysis Framework Commodity Origin–Destination Database (FHA 2006).

portation modes, such as water (16 percent), rail (20 percent), and pipeline (8 percent), are expected to account for large proportions of freight movement in these regions.

For import goods, the pipeline and unknown mode plays a significant role next to truck in both megaregions and non-megaregion areas. For example, approximately 37 percent of commodities are moved by this mode in megaregions, and 48 percent in non-megaregion areas. This may be because of the characteristics of imported goods, such as oil and natural gas. However, the reliance on trucks may increase to 72 percent in megaregions by 2035, and the use of the pipeline and unknown mode may decrease from 37 to 21 percent during the same period (Table 8.3).

Policy Implications

As a result of the global economy and free trade, both international and domestic trade is taking place in megaregions. Although the freight transportation system includes a complex network of roads, rail, water, and air, more than half of the exported goods were moved by trucks in 2002. This trend is projected to continue over the next few decades. The reliance on trucking is higher in megaregions than non-megaregions. The congestion caused by truck traffic on highways limits economic productivity, increasing the cost of product transportation and generating problems for production schedules. Because these trends are estimated

Table 8.3

Comparison of growth rates of commodity flows from and to overseas countries between megaregions and non-megaregion areas, 2002–2035.

Mode	Exports (%)		Imports (%)	
	Megaregions	Non-Megaregions	Megaregions	Non-Megaregions
Pipeline and unknown	32.7	9.3	28.2	38.7
Rail	83.9	54.2	114.1	186.9
Truck	174.4	122	204.4	110.9
Water	55.6	89.6	18.4	28.6
Total	134.1	84.9	124.1	75.9

Source: Derived from the data of Freight Analysis Framework Commodity Origin–Destination Database (FHA 2006).

to continue, an opportunity exists to enhance freight transportation throughout megaregions by focusing on highway improvements and alternative modes such as rail.

In order to prepare a strategy to effectively address these challenges, we should study the demands of freight movements, the types of infrastructure that efficiently meet those needs, and the geographic areas where those demands will increase by analyzing the characteristics (e.g., commodity groups) of goods and their possible transportation modes for each megaregion. For example, approximately 75 and 23 percent of imports and exports (in value of millions of dollars) through the Detroit Combined Statistical Area in 2002 were moved by truck and rail, respectively, and 54 percent of these products were machinery, parts, and motorized and other vehicles (Yoder 2006). Thus, many export and import goods transported through the Detroit area (Midwest megaregion) are bulky goods. This implies that the efficient highway and rail system distributing those heavy goods from the port of entry or exit is critical to the economic vitality of the region. Importantly, it begs the issue of what kind of conveyance might be more efficient in reducing emissions.

Highway Systems and Megaregions

Most urban areas within megaregions are served by or close to interstate highways. However, the capacity and load of roads and streets are different between megaregions and non-megaregions. For example, Table 8.4 shows that urbanized

Table 8.4

Miles of interstate highways and local roads of federal aid urbanized areas, 2006.

Total Miles/1,000 People

	Interstate	Local
Urbanized areas of megaregions	0.0586	2.6949
Urbanized areas of non-megaregions	0.1075	3.8068

Note: A federal aid urbanized area is an area with more than 50,000 people that encompasses the census-defined urbanized areas (FHA 2001).
Source: Reorganized from the table of miles and daily vehicle miles of travel in FHA (2006).

areas of megaregions have fewer miles of interstate highway and local roads than non-megaregions. Specifically, miles of interstate highways and local roads per 1,000 people are 0.06 and 2.69 for megaregions, but non-megaregions have 0.11 and 3.81 miles, respectively.

Although congressional high-priority corridors have increased from twenty-one to eighty since 1991, some routes within megaregions have not been designated as high-priority corridors. They include the routes between Dallas–Fort Worth and Houston (I-45) (Zhang et al. 2007; FHA 2001) and San Antonio and Houston (I-10) in the Texas Triangle; the route between Houston, New Orleans, and the Gulf Coast (I-10); the interstate system of central and west Florida (I-75, 4); and the route between Washington, D.C. and New York (I-95). Additionally, routes that connect major metropolitan areas in the PAM, such as Birmingham, Alabama; Atlanta, Georgia; and Raleigh, North Carolina were not included in the congressional high-priority corridors, although these areas have experienced severe congestion in both freight and passenger travel.

Figure 8.4 presents future interstates on the National Highway System. Within megaregions, the California Farm-to-Market Corridor, US 59 (Texas), US 90 (Louisiana), US 69 (Michigan and Indiana), and US 41 (Wisconsin) have been designated by Section 1105 of the Intermodal Surface Transportation Efficiency Act (ISTEA) as future interstate highways. To incorporate the notion of economic competitiveness, the transport planning and programming process must evaluate the extent to which future designations consider global markets in addition to domestic markets.

High-Speed Rail

The Federal Railroad Administration (1997) conducted benefit and cost analysis of high-speed rail (HSR) for eight corridors in the United States. They include

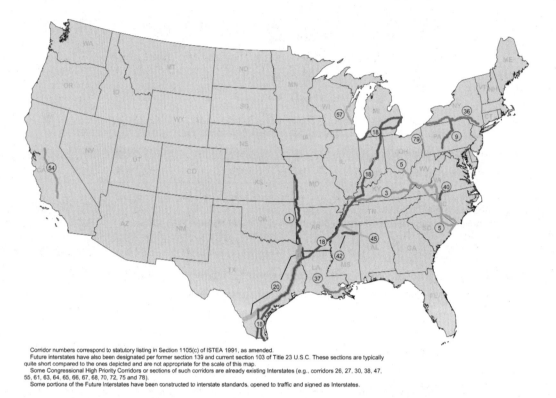

Corridor numbers correspond to statutory listing in Section 1105(c) of ISTEA 1991, as amended.
Future interstates have also been designated per former section 139 and current section 103 of Title 23 U.S.C. These sections are typically quite short compared to the ones depicted and are not appropriate for the scale of this map.
Some Congressional High Priority Corridors or sections of such corridors are already existing Interstates (e.g., corridors 26, 27, 30, 38, 47, 55, 61, 63, 64, 65, 66, 67, 68, 70, 72, 75 and 78).
Some portions of the Future Interstates have been constructed to interstate standards, opened to traffic and signed as Interstates.

Figure 8.4 Future Interstates on the National Highway System. Source: Federal Highway Administration, 2006.

existing corridors where intercity trains currently operate at speeds of more than 110 miles per hour (Northeast Corridor [Boston–New York City–Washington] and Empire Corridor [New York City–Albany–Buffalo]), five potential HSR corridors (Pacific Northwest Corridor [Eugene–Portland–Seattle–Vancouver, B.C.], California Corridor [San Diego–Los Angeles–San Francisco], Chicago Hub [Chicago–Detroit–St. Louis–Milwaukee], Florida Corridor [Tampa–Orlando–Miami], and Southeast Corridor [Washington–Richmond–Charlotte]), and the Texas Triangle (Fort Worth–Dallas–Houston–San Antonio) as a unique "nonlinear" shape. The above five potential corridors were designated under Section 1010 of the ISTEA using operational, financial, and institutional criteria and conditions that existing railroads have the capacity to run at 90 miles per hour.

In addition to the five HSR corridors under ISTEA of 1991, six more corridors were authorized as HSR corridors under TEA-21 in 1998. Since then, the Department of Transportation has designated ten corridors and their extensions (Figure 8.5).

Recently, the Passenger Rail Working Group (2007), established by Commissioner Frank Busalacchi of the National Surface Transportation Policy and

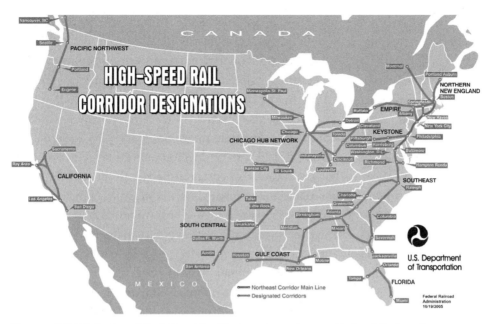

Figure 8.5 High-Speed Rail Corridor Designations. Source: Federal Railroad Administration, 1997.

Revenue Study Commission, which was created by Congress, identified the 2050 intercity passenger rail network.

Schwieterman and Scheidt (2007) indicate that about 63 percent of the proposed mileage for HSR service is included in HSR corridors that cross state lines. All but one of the forty-three states proposing routes on the HSR system have at least one interstate corridor slated for consideration. The location of the proposed HSR coincides with the economic core of most megaregions and would provide greater mobility in a more sustainable way. In fact, some corridors, such as the Chicago–Detroit–Pontiac corridor, are divided into several segments, reflecting differences in operations and in management and ownership. These segmentations may negatively affect both the development process and future operations in the long run.

Transport Planning in the Megaregion

As regions continue to expand in economic scale and functionality, complex relationships that reach beyond and across current jurisdictional and decision-making boundaries are expanding spatially. This expanding scope is seen in the sprawling growth patterns throughout the United States in the past few decades. Such growth is changing the nature and expansion of urban function into traditionally nonurban forms such as suburbs and exurbs (Lang et al. 2005). This concept may even be applied across national boundaries. Recently, the concept of regions has begun to expand beyond nations as the mutual benefits of transnational megaregions come to light. For example, the idea of the aerotropolis captures residential areas as part of functional airport-cities in one country (e.g., Dallas in the United States) that are conveniently linked to commercial areas in another country (e.g., Toronto in Canada) where a growing workforce that lives in one country works in another. This expands the live–work–play space geographically in unprecedented ways. Written about extensively by Kasarda, the aerotropolis may be a creative model for the development of large-scale infrastructure investments that enhance global competitiveness (Byrnes 2007).

As these urban functions continue to spread into traditionally nonurban areas, so do the spatial ramifications of interregional and intraregional transportation, land availability, economic competition, housing availability and affordability, natural resource management, and quality of life. They all lead to expanded spatial complexity throughout the region. Regional planning, as a measure of regional coordination, is a factor that improves the economic welfare of the region (Levine 2001). A region's success at competing on a global scale must be linked to its ability to coordinate and plan for economic functionality on a much larger scale than the city or metropolitan area. This increasing complexity and fragmentation are leading to an ever-widening spatial mismatch between a region's planning authority, its decision-making and economic functionality, and the related effects. Transportation and mobility hubs have historically proved to be advantageous to our cities and, by extension, regions (Fujita et al. 1999). Large-scale federal infrastructure planning can and does dictate how and where growth and connections may occur and therefore could support the megaregion's economy.

Transportation planning adapts to change and social needs. Table 8.5 describes the evolution of transportation planning. The next stage in the evolution is the megaregion. It responds to specific needs created by current demographic trends, global trends, and sustainable development needs. Among these are the needs to address global warming, energy security, global economic competitiveness, and social equity to strengthen established, emerging, and poorly performing regions.

Two documents from the European Union (European Spatial Planning Observation Network 2006; Harding et al. 2006) show that spatial planning plays a key role in coordinating policy and practice at multiple scales and points to challenges that must be overcome in the creation of a spatial planning framework. These challenges are highly interconnected and cannot be overcome singularly; rather, the spatial planning process must address three things to succeed. First, there must be a change in the understanding of megaregions and the functional and infrastructure connections between them. Second, it is necessary to develop effective, widely supported governance arrangements that can mobilize, sensitize, and align national, megaregion, regional, and local strategies. Third, there is

Table 8.5

Evolution of transportation planning.

Era	Type of Planning	Nature and Functions of Planning	References
1950s–1960s	Classical transportation planning	Focus was on the development of highway studies for metropolitan areas, largely to determine the best highway alignments to serve metropolitan areas.	Menendez and Cook
1970s	Neoclassical or open transportation planning	Emerged in response to changes in the planning environment. Certain groups that thought their interests were not being protected by planning officials generally mistrusted government planning. The emphasis on the land use element of transportation planning declined during this period.	Menendez and Cook
1975–1980s	Fragmented transportation planning	Planning focused on small area improvements, primarily within existing transportation rights-of-way. The Federal Highway Administration sponsored studies to enhance performance of existing transportation infrastructure in terms of efficiency, capacity, and safety. This focus was the beginning of transportation demand management.	Menendez and Cook
Mid-1980s onward	Consolidated transportation planning	Movement toward consolidated transportation planning (multimodal focus) concurrent with rising concern about increasing congestion on metropolitan and intercity transportation networks.	Menendez and Cook
1990s	Integrated transportation planning Context-sensitive solutions Environmentally conscious transportation planning	Increasing focus on improving the environment through planning (e.g., strategic environmental assessments), reducing congestion and improving the quality of life for metropolitan communities, integrating transportation and land use planning, infrastructure renewal, and asset management.	NCHRP 541, Meyer and Miller
2000s	Sustainable transportation planning; planning for megacities and megaregions	Addressing public health and advancing economic competitiveness, environmental integrity, and social equity through coordinated transportation, land use, and economic planning.	*Integrating Sustainability into the Transportation Planning Process*

the need for more effective coordination of public sector investment and expenditure over the long term. This investment provides benefits and incentives for interjurisdictional cooperation in the spatial planning process. Spatial planning success requires a governance framework that links national, regional, and local levels and is explicitly designed to build the capacity of the megaregion. This requires participatory dialogue on many levels. These frameworks are ultimately derived when there is public sector focus and investment combined with a greater understanding of functional relationships derived from empirical study and widespread participation.

Transportation Planning: A Functional Approach

In some respects we are already planning across borders. There is a tradition of planning across state lines in the United States. As required by the federal government, all urban areas with populations greater than 50,000 are subject to planning, programming, and coordinating of federal highway and transit investments under the auspices of Metropolitan Planning Organizations (MPOs). MPOs coordinate the continuing, comprehensive, and cooperative ("3-C") planning process. This responsibility is shared with local governments, state departments of transportation, and other transportation agencies. Each governor designates all MPOs within the state.

Multistate MPOs

There are approximately 384 MPOs in the United States (Turnbull 2007), and approximately 11 percent of them cross state boundaries. MPOs sign agreements that are quite varied and subject to the financial, political, and organizational preference of the local areas and state governments. Multistate MPOs face challenges that do not confront single-state MPOs. Among these are differences in public involvement procedures, planning approach, development of the short- and long-range transportation plan, funding priorities, and data collection, analysis, and manipulation. Nonetheless, multistate MPOs provide insight into some of the challenges and opportunities that confront multistate efforts of any sort. Three is the largest number of states linked in any agreement (Turnbull 2007). In the case of megaregions, we are talking about multiple states and even more differences, creating the need for a different governance structure.

North America's SuperCorridor Coalition, Inc. (NASCO) is a trinational, nonprofit trade and transportation coalition. NASCO works to make international and domestic trade more efficient and secure along existing networks of transportation systems (including highways, rail, inland ports, and deep-water ports) running north to south through the central United States, Canada, and Mexico. The nonprofit group consists of members from both the public and private sector. It was initially founded in 1994 as the I-35 Corridor Coalition. Since the entry of the United States in 1994 into the North American Free Trade Agreement, NASCO has supported corridor-related initiatives to enhance border security, cargo safety, and efficient operation of the existing transportation infrastructure.

Megaregions must capture traditional regional planning intellectual platforms but must also be responsive to the global economy. NASCO's focus on enhancing economic development through more efficient transportation is an example of one approach useful in identifying necessary improvements in the megaregion infrastructure. For example, the emerging trade corridors and the regions they traverse are an increasing part of regional planning in South America and here at home. The singular focus on moving commodities and providing trade corridors is an approach being followed in Latin America. Trade corridors have at least three distinguishing characteristics, as identified in Table 8.6. Corridors provide goods and services, they transform and enhance the value of those goods and services, and they provide access to domestic and global markets. Operating under a megaregion framework, these corridors provide more explicit linkages to domestic and global markets, coupled with the ability to influence productivity and economic performance.

Trade corridors are designed specifically to provide support for economic activity along a particular route connecting specific regions. They typically serve areas with strong economic activity and work to extend their sphere of influence by increasing economic growth and expanding to connect to other areas (Edgington et al. 2001). These corridors traverse expansive distances, connecting places that often are characterized by dissimilar social, cultural, political, environmental, and economic status. They serve as important economic linkages tied to the creation of new industries, employment opportunities, and economic expansion. In this way, trade corridors become the means by which economic integration and growth are achieved (Edgington et al. 2001).

Table 8.6
Characteristics of trade corridors.

Production, which makes available basic goods and services

Transformation, which adds value to the basic goods and services

Access to markets, both nationally and internationally

Source: Edgington et al. (2001).

Trade corridors affect impoverished areas, depressed areas, and affluent areas with clean infrastructure and high-priced urban real estate. The creation of trade corridors is often accompanied by free trade agreements. The mobility by which commodities and people are moved provides access to markets all along the corridor. Because these are expensive infrastructure investments, they must be assured of continued operation and sustainability. Therefore, minimizing the negative consequences on the environment is a responsibility they must embrace. The trade corridors and the accompanying trade agreements provide the opportunity to observe the actual role of infrastructure in supporting and creating large agglomerations and economic activity. The creation of mobility and access within and beyond the megaregion also requires a commitment of vast amounts of financial resources in infrastructure. Regional constructs and corridors that cross traditional boundaries and are linked to population and economic centers are appropriate strategies for the global economy.

The Piedmont Atlantic Megaregion

The PAM was first identified by a team within the Program of City and Regional Planning enrolled in an urban sustainability course at the Georgia Institute of Technology in the spring of 2005 (Contant et al. 2005). Using population projections, watershed boundaries, highway linkages, freight movements, commodity flows, and understandings of cultural similarities and differences, the team identified a region consisting of six states: Georgia, Alabama, North and South Carolina, Tennessee, and northern Florida (Figure 8.6). As of 2000, the PAM was home to more than 25 million people, had more than 15 million jobs, and was composed of just over 190,000 square miles.

The PAM is a rapidly growing region in terms of demographics, economic activity, and national resources consumed. Yet it faces a series of problems that transcend current political boundaries: disparities between urban and rural, a widening gap between rich and poor, overconsumption of natural resources due to sprawl, a need to diversify economically, and the desire to compete in the global marketplace. These problems are exacerbated by a lack of coordinated governance and regional planning. The PAM encompasses six states, 534 counties, and approximately 4,453 cities. This fragmentation poses a challenge within the PAM and also in other megaregions.

Environment

Consideration of environmental features is integral to the process of defining a sustainable region. The PAM's watershed boundaries, geography, and ecologi-

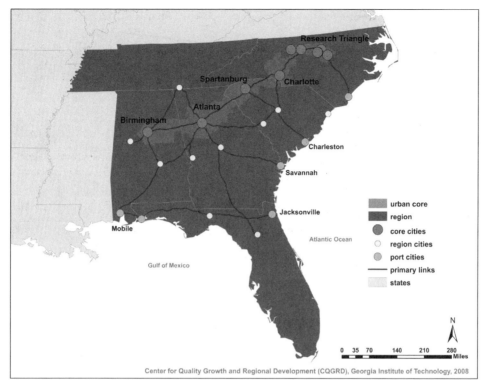

Figure 8.6 The Piedmont Atlantic Megaregion.

cally sensitive areas were evaluated. Determinations for the boundaries of our region within the United States, and for the specific delineation of what would become the urban core, were made based in part on these factors.

Watershed boundaries were the preliminary environmental tool used to make delineations. This tool is valid because it relies on natural, physical boundaries, as opposed to Metropolitan Statistical Areas (MSAs) or counties, which are human-defined boundaries. Watershed boundaries usually are ridges that separate drainage basins. These features were important because they affect water supply and allocation. Watershed boundaries dictate flows of waterways and determine where rainfall is collected.

The Southeast region consists of the following diverse physiographic features: mountains, piedmont, fall line, coastal plains, and coast (Figure 8.7). Because of our focus on long-term sustainability, defining the region using environmental criteria was an important segment of the analysis of the Southeast megaregion. An analysis was conducted to evaluate watersheds, physiographic features, and ecologically sensitive and protected areas. This information was then incorporated into the boundary definition process.

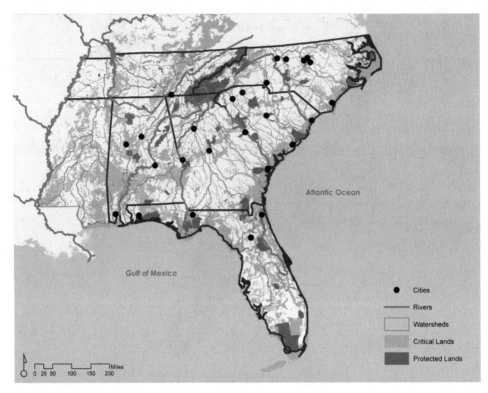

Figure 8.7 Environmental Features of the Piedmont Atlantic Megaregion.

The Southeast Corridor has experienced tremendous population growth since 1990, and projections indicate that this trend will continue through 2030 and beyond. In 1970, approximately 8 million people and 8 million jobs were in the study area. As of 2000, approximately 15,000,000 people lived within a 50-mile buffer of the study area. Projections show a 2000 to 2050 population change of 68 percent, approximately 58 million people. Figure 8.8 contours population projections for the PAM.

The PAM is a highly car-dependent region and was developed rapidly after World War II. Land uses were rigidly separated, and freeway construction was the primary transportation construction activity. Work trip data from major metropolitan areas in the region show that 92 percent of work trips are made by car (79 percent in single-occupant vehicles and 13 percent in carpools) (U.S. Census Bureau 2000).

The automobile similarly dominates noncommuting passenger travel in the region. The PAM has limited passenger rail service. Throughout the populous core, the federally supported Amtrak system runs only one train, the Crescent. Atlanta and Birmingham, both built on rail access, now have just two passenger trains a day: the northbound Crescent and the southbound Crescent. In the PAM,

2000 Population

2050 Population

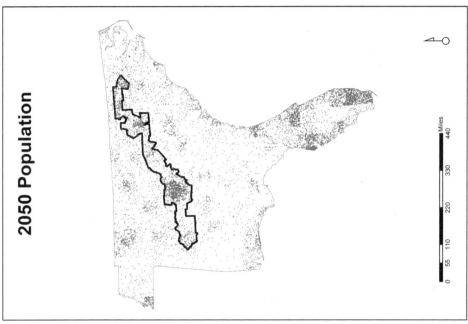

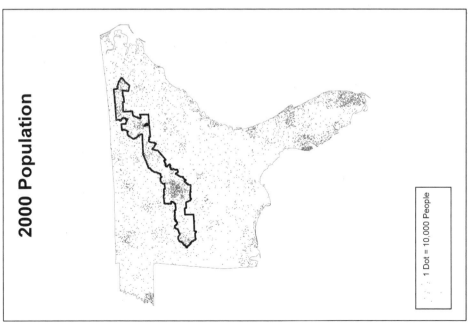

1 Dot = 10,000 People

0   55   110   220   330   440
Miles

Figure 8.8 2050 Population Projections.

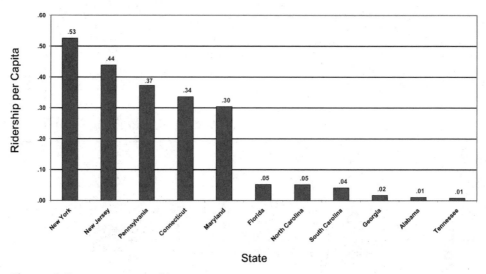

Figure 8.9 Passenger Travel by Train.

passenger train travel per capita is a small fraction of that of the Northeast (Figure 8.9). The dominance of motor vehicle travel in the PAM puts the region's economic connections at risk through rising energy prices, increased environmental regulation, roadway congestion, and other developments.

At the national and global level, the PAM is somewhat better positioned with respect to transportation; the world's busiest airports, in terms of passenger numbers and in terms of freight, are in Atlanta and Memphis, respectively. The Charlotte airport is ranked seventeenth in the world in airplane movements (Airports Council International n.d.). The region boasts major ports at Wilmington, Charleston, Savannah, Jacksonville, and Mobile. Together, the five ports accounted for $78.1 billion in foreign trade in 2003 (American Association of Port Authorities n.d.-b). Charleston's port ranked forty-second among the top fifty global ports for container traffic (American Association of Port Authorities n.d.-a).

Although this long-distance transportation infrastructure has been an economic driver in the region, it is not without cost in terms of environment degradation and social equity. For example, airports generate noise and air pollution, with the bulk of the burden borne by nearby residents. Waterborne shipping affects the ocean and coastal ecosystems as global trade rapidly accelerates to provide consumers foreign goods that were previously produced locally or regionally.

The megaregion's dependence on the car becomes all the more potentially damaging when one considers future growth in commuting patterns. In 1990, 36 percent of commuters in the four main MSAs in the corridor (Birmingham, Atlanta, Charlotte, and Raleigh–Durham) spent 30 minutes or more traveling one way to work; by 2000 it was almost 42 percent. Although the percentage increase is important, examining its impact in the context of population growth is more significant. In 1990, 648,000 people had a commute time of more than 30 minutes. In 2000, that number rose to more than 1.2 million commuters traveling more than 30 minutes to work. In 1998, average annual daily traffic was concentrated inside the eight MSAs. By 2020, the latest date for which projections are available, traffic volumes will increase slightly between the MSAs, especially in the Charlotte to Raleigh–Durham segment.

The corridor will also experience an increasing number of truck trips. This increase is more significant than that of overall traffic volumes. As in much of the country, freight movement has gravitated to truck modes rather than rail. For individual shipments, approximately 91 percent of all freight is moved by truck in the PAM. The negative consequences of such growth are not limited to lost productivity due to congestion. Air quality is a concern throughout the PAM. If current transportation trends continue, air quality will continue to deteriorate because some of the primary sources for air pollution in the PAM are industrial and vehicular (American Lung Association 2004). The corridor's history of failing to meet national air quality standards, particularly for the Atlanta MSA, will be difficult to overcome given the increasing population projected for the Southeast Corridor, and the majority of major metropolitan areas will continue to experience air quality problems. The smaller metropolitan areas are also experiencing increasing problems with nonattainment. A number of projects have been discussed for the PAM. Many of these cannot proceed under existing planning and financial requirements. However, a number of them could move forward under the megaregion planning approach. They include the following:

- Develop a climate change initiative to be implemented throughout the PAM.
- Design an intermodal system of hubs to facilitate passenger and freight movement throughout the PAM.
- Identify and improve major choke points for passengers and freight throughout the PAM.
- Evaluate the costs and benefits of implementing a truck-only toll system throughout the PAM.
- Consider a high-speed passenger and freight rail from Savannah to Knoxville, Tennessee.
- Construct new ports with input from other states, such as North Carolina, South Carolina, and Georgia.
- Identify priority connections from the PAM to the gateways from which significant exports and imports originate in order to ensure efficient and effective movement.

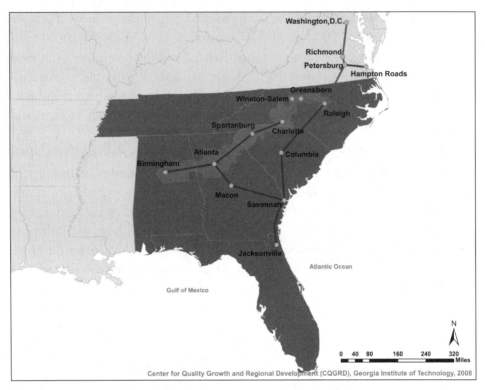

Figure 8.10 High-Speed Rail in the Southeast.

- Evaluate high-speed rail from Charlotte, North Carolina to Atlanta, Georgia and from Atlanta to New Orleans, Louisiana. An additional route from Savannah, Georgia to New Orleans could also be evaluated. It is critically important that PAM develop an extensive transit network between cities along significant corridors that includes both high-speed and commuter rail.

Further study is necessary to develop feasible transit corridors for such a low-density region, but a directive to create more sustainable transportation systems is part of the solution for transportation challenges in the PAM. One example is the currently proposed construction of a high-speed rail system that would connect the Southeast megacity corridor and also include Washington, D.C. to Savannah, Georgia and Jacksonville, Florida (Figure 8.10).

The system would increase transportation options, ease traffic congestion, improve air quality, and facilitate economic redevelopment. It could become the backbone linking the core cities along strategic corridors, thereby creating a transit network to meet the needs and future growth in the Southeast megacity corridor. The implementation of this transit network will require leaders in the core cities along the corridors to engage in infrastructure planning that transcends the boundaries of the geographic areas they represent.

Conclusions

The challenges to the implementation of a megaregion approach are extensive, beginning with the need to compete in the global marketplace while preserving our national and regional identities. A pervasive challenge is the need to plan more effectively for megaregions, given their increasing significance as America's platform to operate more globally. The most significant challenge is to craft a new vision that creates greater opportunity for our communities, cities, and regions and resonates in the context of the new economy. The nation's surface transportation program is confronting a number of long-term challenges as we consider the next reauthorization cycle. The carrying capacity of our freight network is severely constrained, and congestion has a stranglehold on urban and regional mobility. The purchasing power of the highway trust fund is being eroded, and there is much to indicate that we are poorly prepared to provide mobility linked to economic opportunity for the increasing population of the country.

At the same time, the threats to maintaining a high quality of life occur at a time when our citizens are demanding safe travel environments that promote mobility, facilitate social interaction, and increase the opportunity for physical activity. Perhaps the biggest incentive for creating a new vision with more sustainable travel practices is the need to reduce our dependence on fossil fuels and engage in more sustainable ways to provide mobility.

Increasing global competition, climate change, national security, escalating energy costs, and congestion are the priorities to be addressed as we develop transportation plans for the foreseeable future. In addition, large amounts of resources must be committed to maintaining our existing infrastructure and integrating new technologies to improve system performance.

Increasing intermodal connections inside and outside the United States must be an increasing component of any transportation initiative. These investments and improvements must be structured to support and enhance new and old markets that are critical to increasing our economic competitiveness. It is this link between infrastructure investment that must be addressed in a more fundamental and explicit way. The megaregion presents an opportunity to accomplish multiple objectives, recognizing the constantly changing global environment in which we currently live.

Note

1. "Air and truck" includes shipments by air or a combination of truck and air. "Other intermodal" includes shipments typically weighing less than 100 pounds by parcel, U.S. Postal Service, or courier and shipments of all sizes by truck–water, water–rail, and other intermodal combinations. "Pipeline" is included with "unknown" because region-to-region flows by pipeline are subject to uncertainty. "Rail" includes any common carrier or private railroad.

"Truck" includes private and for-hire trucks. "Truck and rail" includes shipments by a combination of truck and rail. "Water" includes shallow draft, deep draft, and Great Lakes shipments. "Shallow draft" includes barges, ships, or ferries operating primarily on rivers and canals; in harbors; and on the Saint Lawrence Seaway, the Intra-coastal Waterway, the Inside Passage to Alaska, major bays and inlets, or the ocean close to the shoreline. Deep draft includes barges, ships, or ferries operating primarily in the open ocean (FHA 2006).

References

Airports Council International. n.d. *Traffic Movements 2004 Preliminary 2005*. Retrieved September 4, 2005 from www.airports.org/cda/aci/display/main/aci_content.jsp?zn=aci&cp=1-5-54-57_9_25.

American Association of Port Authorities. n.d.-a. *United States Waterborne Foreign Commerce 2003–2005*. Retrieved April 9, 2005 from www.aapa-ports.org/pdf/2003_US_PORT _RANK INGS_BY_CARGO_VALUE.xls. http://www.aapa-ports.org/pdf/2003_US_PORT _RANK INGS_BY_CARGO_VALUE.xls).

————. n.d.-b. *World Port Rankings: 2003–2005*. Retrieved September 4, 2005 from www.aapa-ports.org/pdf/WORLD_PORT_RANKINGS_2003.xls.

American Lung Association. 2004. *State of the Air: 2004*. American Lung Association, New York.

American Society of Civil Engineers. 2005. *2005 Report Card for America's Infrastructure*. Retrieved 2005 from www.asce.org/reportcard/2005/index.cfm.

Byrnes, N. 2007. Home is where the airport is. *BusinessWeek*, August 20 and 27.

Cohen, J. E. 2005. Human population grows up. *Scientific American* Special Issue: Crossroads for Planet Earth, September.

Contant, C., C. L. Ross, J. Barringer, C. Blengini, K. Leone de Nie, L. Lyman, et al. 2005. *The Piedmont Atlantic Megalopolis (PAM)*. College of Architecture, Georgia Institute of Technology, Atlanta.

Dreier, P., J. Mollenkopf, and T. Swanstrom. 2001. *Place Matters, Metropolitics for the Twenty-first Century*. University of Kansas Press, Kansas City.

Edgington, D., A. Fernandez, and C. Hoshino. 2001. *New Regional Development Paradigms, Volume 2. New Regions: Concepts, Issues, and Practices*. Greenwood, Westport, CT.

European Spatial Planning Observation Network. 2006. *Governance of Territorial and Urban Policies from EU to Local Level. Final Report*. Draft version May 31, 2006, project 2.3.2. Retrieved October 16, 2006 from www.espon.eu/mmp/online/website/content/projects/243/374/file _2186/draft_fr-2.3.2-full.pdf.http://www.espon.eu/mmp/online/website/functions/home/homepage/index_EN.html.

Federal Highway Administration (FHA). 2001. *Highway Statistics 2001*. U.S. Department of Transportation. Washingon, D.C.

————. 2006. *Freight Analysis Framework (FAF) Version 2.2, User Guide: Commodity Origin–Destination Database: 2002–2035*. U.S. Department of Transportation. Washington, D.C. Retrieved 2008 from ops.fhwa.dot.gov/freight/freight_analysis/faf/faf2userguide/index .htm.

Federal Railroad Administration. 1997. *High-Speed Ground Transportation for America*. U.S. Department of Transportation. Washington, D.C. Retrieved 2008 from ntl.bts.gov/data/hsgt.pdf.

Fujita, M., P. Krugman, and A. Venables. 1999. *The Spatial Economy: Cities, Regions, and International Trade*. MIT Press, Cambridge, MA.

Harding, A., S. Marvin, and B. Robson. 2006. *A Framework for City-Regions*. ODPM, London. Retrieved October 16, 2006 from www.communities.gov.uk/index.asp?id=1163565.

Isard, W., I. Azis, R. Drennan, R. E. Miller, S. Saltzman, and E. Thorbecke. 1998. *Methods of Interregional and Regional Analysis*. Ashgate, Burlington, VT.

Jones, C. 2007. *Economic and Equity Frameworks for Megaregions*. Regional Plan Association, New York.

Lang, R. E., E. J. Blakely, and M. Z. Gough. 2005. Keys to the new metropolis: America's big, fast-growing suburban counties. *Journal of the American Planning Association* 71(4):381–391.

Levine, J. N. 2001. The role of economic theory in regional advocacy. *Journal of Planning Literature* 16(2):183–201.

Meyer, M., and Eric Miller. (2001) Urban Transportation Planning. McGraw Hill, New York.

National Cooperative Highway Research Program (2005). Consideration of Environmental Factors in Transportation Systems Planning. Transportation Research Board. Washington D.C.

Passenger Rail Working Group. 2007. *Vision for the Future: U.S. Intercity Passenger Rail Network through 2050.* Washington D.C. Retrieved 2008 from http://www.railtrends.com/www.dot.state.wi.us/projects/state/rail-vision-2050.htm.

Puentes, R. 2008. *A Bridge to Somewhere: Rethinking American Transportation for the 21st Century.* The Brookings Institution (Metropolitan Policy Program), Washington, D.C.

Ross, C. L., M. Woo, J. Barringer, K. Leone de Nie, H. West, and J. L. H. Doyle. 2008. *Identifying Megaregions in the US: Implications for Infrastructure Investment.* ACSP-AESOP 4th Joint Congress, Chicago.

Schwieterman, J. P., and J. Scheidt. 2007. Survey of current high-speed rail planning efforts in the United States. *Transportation Research Record* 1995(1):27.

Turnbull, K. F. 2007. *The Metropolitan Planning Organization, Present and Future: Summary of a Conference.* Transportation Research Board, Washington, D.C.

U.S. Census Bureau. 2000. *U.S. Census 2000.* Retrieved from www.census.gov.

Yoder, S. 2006. Presentation material for Detroit River International Crossing Study. Federal Highway Administration (FHWA) Resource Center.

Zhang, M., F. Steiner, and K. Butler. 2007. Connecting the Texas Triangle: Economic integration and transportation coordination. In *Healdsburg Research Seminar on Megaregions.* Lincoln Institute of Land Policy, Healdsburg, CA.

9

Investing in Megaregion Transportation Systems

Institutional Challenges and Opportunities

William D. Ankner and Michael D. Meyer

The population, economic wealth, and cultural resources that define modern societies will probably continue to concentrate in increasingly well-defined megaregions of the United States and of other countries. However, whereas economic markets become more integrated and interdependent within a megaregion construct, government remains highly fragmented. Accordingly, strategies for investing in megaregion transportation systems are seldom tied to an overarching vision of what such investment means to the broader economic prosperity of megaregion communities.

In the United States myriad organizations and agencies are involved in developing and managing the transportation network. Such organizations include federal, state, and local transportation agencies, metropolitan planning organizations, airport authorities, seaport and cargo authorities, mass transit agencies, and expressway and tollway authorities. In addition to government organizations, the transportation investment decision-making process usually involves numerous advocacy groups, trade organizations, business associations, and public interest groups. And ultimately, state and local elected officials adopt the policies and approve the funding that supports the transportation system, usually with very parochial perspectives on what this funding should do for their constituents.

Within this complex dance of players, how do megaregions ensure the efficient mobility of people, goods, and services while remaining competitive? Megaregions would intuitively benefit from a well-connected and linked transportation infrastructure (air, rail, water, transit, highways) in a way that is cost effective and increases the competitiveness of the regional economy (Reconnecting America 2002). But how exactly can this be accomplished? In particular, how does one put in place a financing strategy that cuts across jurisdictional boundaries and targets the facilities and services most important for regional competitiveness and a high quality of life for the region's citizens?

The purpose of this chapter is to describe the characteristics of megaregion transportation systems and the institutional framework for investment decision making. The dimensions of this framework that are particularly challenging for megaregion-level investment are identified, and potential investment strategies for promoting such investment are proposed. The final section recommends actions that government agencies can take to promote investment in megaregions that will support and guide expected economic growth.

Investment in Megaregion Transportation Systems: Needs and Institutional Challenges

Many studies have been undertaken over the past few years on megaregion development and the challenges it presents to national economic growth. Each of these studies has identified investment in transportation systems and services as a key to the future success of a particular megaregion, in some cases identifying very specific services that should be supported (such as Amtrak in the U.S. Northeast megaregion). The types of transportation recommendations found in these studies include the following:

> The goal for Northern California is then to concentrate new jobs and housing in core areas at the coast and inland, including existing downtowns such as Sacramento, Oakland, Stockton, and Modesto. We should then create direct transit linkages between these nodes to enable workers from throughout the megaregion access to the greatest range of job opportunities. Further, we should look to build economic districts around other key transportation nodes such as high-speed rail stops and airports, so long as there are plans for transit linkages to the airports. (Metcalf and Terplan 2007)

> To strengthen the economies of the region's metropolitan areas, the Great Lakes states and the federal government should design and embrace a new competitive vision for transportation policy that includes high-speed rail, greater access to ports and freight hubs, and better maintenance and preservation of existing highway and transit systems. (Austin and Affolter-Caine 2006)

In a discussion on the Texas Triangle megaregion, "a megaregion approach also calls for new ideas, methods, and tools for planning beyond the current toolbox of metropolitan planning organizations (MPOs). For instance, given the geographical scale of the megaregion, travel options to be considered should include air, high-speed rail (HSR) and telecommunications, along with the conventional list of non-motorized modes such as cars, buses, metro, and light rail transit" (Zhang et al. 2007).

> Enhance northeast corridor mobility, including intercity and high-speed rail, highways, airports, seaports, and goods movement, with an aggressive investment strategy that moves from the municipal to the megaregional scale. . . . Collective action is needed to decongest these systems, create new capacity for improved passenger and goods movement, and provide a framework for economic development for the next half century. . . . The Northeast states should collaborate on measures to reduce air and seaport congestion to move goods more efficiently and effectively. Solutions should focus on improving connections between modes, removing bottlenecks, and enhancing the landside connections to maritime ports to move logistics functions inland. (Regional Plan Association 2007)

One of the characteristics common to almost all these studies is that although many transportation investment needs are identified, very seldom is there a recommendation on where the funds will come from to pay for these improvements. Given the investment associated with the recommended strategies and the institutional challenges associated with creating a megaregion-level investment strategy, perhaps it is not surprising that finance is left to future discussions. Recent research on cross-boundary transport investment in Europe also found that project financing in a cross-boundary environment was the most important challenge facing project implementation (Crocker 2007).

Financing new megaregion-level investments becomes even more of a challenge when one considers the following:

- In most of the developed world, but particularly in the United States and Europe, the transportation system is facing significant needs in keeping current infrastructure and services in working condition. In the United States alone, the past 50 years of investment in the nation's transportation infrastructure can be measured in the trillions of dollars. Much of this infrastructure is now in need of repair and reconstruction, commanding much of the attention of state and metropolitan transportation officials and leaving a diminishing amount of resources for adding new system capacity.
- Transportation finance in the United States is in a period of transition, if not turmoil. The federal aid program that has been the major player for the past 50 years of major highway investment is being pressured from many

fronts. The purchasing power of the motor fuel gas tax receipts that have been the foundation of the federal and state aid programs for many years has been eroding significantly over the past 10 years (Transportation Research Board 2006). With very few political leaders willing to raise the gas tax for fear of voter backlash, the amount of revenue available for transportation investment continues to decline. As of this writing, the federal Highway Trust Fund, the repository of federal motor fuel gas tax receipts in the United States, is expected to become insolvent sometime in 2009.

- Although public–private partnerships have been used in many parts of the world to finance transportation facility investment, the record in the United States is still evolving. Many are counting on private investment for the capital needed to provide new facilities and services, and it is likely that such investment will find itself in the financing mix for transportation capital programs. However, it is not clear whether this investment will result in sufficient levels of funding to provide the mobility and accessibility necessary to support the economic growth that is expected in megaregions.

- The institutional and government structure in megaregions will itself pose significant challenges. The government structure for public sector transportation investment in the United States is a legacy of a federally aided transportation program (in the case of state departments of transportation) and of an acknowledgment in the 1970s that metropolitan areas are the best focus for a comprehensive and coordinated transportation planning process (and thus the creation in 1974 of the metropolitan planning organization). Organizational mission statements, study boundaries, problem definitions, and funding allocations often stop at the border with neighboring jurisdictions. Trying to expand the scope of a transportation problem beyond the current mandate of a government agency (e.g., looking at a megaregion's transportation needs) would probably face significant obstacles.

- The U.S. government has slowly been reducing its participation in transportation investment programs. Beginning in earnest during the administration of President Reagan with a strong push to devolve as much responsibility as possible to the states, the federal government has slowly become a smaller contributor to state and metropolitan transportation programs. This has resulted in many states and metropolitan areas raising their own funds through sales tax and gas tax increases. Given the increasing use of locally raised transportation funds to support capital investment and the local politics of distributing these funds around the jurisdiction, it once again becomes difficult to rely on this funding source as a means of improving megaregion-specific transportation infrastructure, except to the extent that the megaregion and jurisdictional needs overlap.

- To the extent that existing government funding can be used to support megaregion-level transportation investments, many of these funding programs are category specific. Highway Trust Fund dollars for transit investment are still limited, unless "flexed" by a state for such an investment. And even though Highway Trust Fund dollars are available for investments other than roads, they cannot be used to finance intercity rail passenger service. Other funds must still be used to augment transit funding. In addition, except for some special cases, Highway Trust Fund dollars cannot finance facilities for private freight intermodal connections or freight rail infrastructure. Even if federal dollars were more flexible, the state dollars used to match federal grants often are restricted in a state's constitution to only road-related uses, thus limiting the amount of investment dollars available for other modes of transportation. Airport and Airway Trust Fund expenditures, a national financing mechanism similar to the Highway Trust Fund but only for airports, are also restricted. They can be used only on airport property and only for direct aviation projects.
- Finally, even if current funding programs are to be the source of funding for megaregion-level investments, much of the current funding (for highways, in particular) comes from sources that are uncertain in the long run. For example, both federal and state highway funding comes predominantly from petroleum-based gas taxes. With conversion to alternative-fueled vehicles, greater fuel efficiency, and perhaps even changing travel behavior patterns, it is not likely that such taxes will provide a stable platform for transportation funding in the future. Changing to a distance-based fee or charge for network use seems to be the best solution, but the steps necessary to do so are likely to be challenging.

In sum, much of the research that has examined the evolving characteristics of megaregions has concluded that the transportation sector is a critical focus for investment in support of future megaregion economic success. However, the challenges of creating a megaregion-focused transportation financial strategy are formidable, and without identifying strategic approaches to overcoming some of these challenges, it is difficult to see how the most cost effective transportation investment at this scale would occur.

Multijurisdictional Structures and Financing Models: Some Examples

The few reports and studies on megaregions that have discussed financing strategies have identified a range of options, often in very general terms. In a prospectus on the concept of megaregion development, Carbonell and Yaro (2005) note that much of the transportation investment needed to support the evolving megaregion development pattern would be financed "through user fees and public–private partnerships." They also suggest that it "should be possible to employ modest payroll or other taxes to finance some of these investments." Others suggest a more traditional approach. Todorovich (2007) recommends "raising the gas tax at least to the inflation-adjusted level of the past and probably greater, combined with an assortment of revenue raising measures at the state and local levels, including the greater use of tolling, public–private partnerships . . . dedicated sales taxes, and general revenue sources." And the Regional Plan Association (2006) notes that

> public authorities can use their tax-free status to attract private dollars through bond issuances, sales, and lease-back arrangements. New user fees, such as congestion pricing or high occupancy toll (HOT) and truck only toll (TOT) lanes, link charges to those who benefit the most from new investments, creating new revenue streams. And value recapture models, such as tax increment financing, allow future increases in land values to finance today's infrastructure investments.

The challenges facing multijurisdictional financing of transportation infrastructure notwithstanding, experience shows that such investments have occurred. The U.S. interstate highway system is a classic example of such cross-jurisdictional implementation and financing. In this case, the federal government played a central role in establishing the vision and the financing mechanism for supporting system development. As the interstate highway system reached completion in the 1990s, it was not clear what role the federal government was going to play in future transportation investments. As a result, several alternative forms of multistate planning have evolved over the past 15 years in the United States that provide interesting models for a megaregion-specific transportation investment policy. In addition, the European experience with investing in cross-border transportation projects illustrates another set of approaches for overcoming cross-jurisdictional challenges.

Clearly, many of the improvements that will be undertaken by single jurisdictions or by metropolitan areas within a megaregion will also enhance transportation system performance. However, the significant institutional challenge is promoting multijurisdictional transportation accessibility that serves internal megaregion transportation needs, providing mobility that connects megaregions to each other and to the rest of the country, and ensuring the viability of transportation facilities and services that connect a megaregion to the rest of the world market (e.g., ports, airports, and the transportation infrastructure that serves these intermodal centers). Thus, although there are often substantial challenges in raising the funds necessary to support a community's transportation system, the following examples focus on multijurisdictional finance, most at the state or national levels.

Corridors of National Significance

Beginning in the early 1990s with concern about the impacts of free trade agreements (most notably the North American Free Trade Agreement) on the U.S. transportation system, the U.S. government has become increasingly interested in major transportation corridors and in the strategies that could be adopted to improve traffic flow. Over the past 15 years of federal transportation legislation, the U.S. Congress has identified forty-four transportation corridors considered to be nationally significant. The criteria for selecting highway projects in these corridors included the extent to which

- The corridor linked two existing segments of the interstate highway system.
- The project facilitated major multistate or regional mobility, economic growth, and development in areas underserved by highway infrastructure.
- Commercial traffic in the corridor had increased since enactment of the North American Free Trade Agreement and traffic was projected to increase in the future.
- International truck-borne commodities moved through the corridor.
- The project will reduce congestion on an existing segment of the interstate highway system.
- The project will reduce commercial and other travel time through a major freight corridor.
- Federal funds will be leveraged (Federal Highway Administration 2006).

The federal share of project cost was generally 80 percent, subject to a sliding-scale adjustment for special circumstances, such as a 90 percent federal share when high occupancy vehicle lanes were to be added to an interstate highway corridor.

Figure 9.1 shows an example from a national study funded under this initiative. The I-10 National Freight Corridor Study included eight states and fifteen major urban areas (Wilbur Smith and Associates 2003). The objectives of the corridor study were to assess the importance to the United States and to adjacent states of the freight moving on I-10, identify current and future traffic operations and safety problems along the corridor that could impede the flow of freight, and identify and evaluate strategies, including multimodal strategies, to facilitate freight movement. Of the many recommendations resulting from this study, the ones of most relevance to this chapter include making the case for in-

Figure 9.1 I-10 National Freight Corridor Study.

creased national investment across all transportation modes, developing and implementing a corridor-level intelligent transportation system (ITS) architecture, and coordinating investments in the corridor, focusing on those communities that bridge the corridor. The study noted that the anticipated capital needs in the corridor were estimated to cost $21.3 billion (2000 dollars), with a shortfall of $12.6 billion. Most of these capital needs were in urban areas.

The Corridors of National Significance program is illustrative of other targeted funding programs that have surfaced from recent federal legislation. In addition to this program, other initiatives have been established for coordinated border infrastructure and freight intermodal distribution centers. The targeting of such programs and project types provides an example of the types of focused investment that might address megaregion transportation investment needs. In addition, these initiatives have begun the process in the United States of examining how public dollars can be used to improve facilities and systems that would greatly benefit private freight operators.

Corridors of the Future

Another corridor-oriented initiative from the U.S. Department of Transportation (DOT) was the Corridors of the Future Program, a program created in 2007 under a broader national congestion reduction strategy. The primary goal of the program was to "encourage states to explore innovative financing as a tool to reduce congestion on some of our most critical trade corridors, improve the flow of goods across the United States, and enhance the quality of life for U.S. citizens" (U.S. DOT 2007). Interestingly, the DOT identified its role in this program as facilitating and accelerating the development of the corridors by helping project sponsors break through the institutional and regulatory obstacles associated with multistate and multimodal corridor investments. The corridors that were selected as part of this national program represented 22.7 percent of the U.S. daily interstate travel.

The Interstate 5 (I-5) corridor in the Western United States exemplifies the types of corridors selected under this program. The I-5 corridor extends from the U.S. border with Canada, through the states of Washington, Oregon, and California, to the U.S. border with Mexico. The I-5 corridor is more than 1,350 miles long, with approximately 550 miles in urban areas. More than 65 percent of these urban miles are considered to be heavily congested during peak periods. The proposed corridor improvements included highway projects in individual states, improved regional traffic management systems in two major urban areas, inclusion of regional freight and passenger rail improvements in a portion of the corridor, ITS improvements and an alternative fuel demonstration program.

Of relevance to this chapter, the types of financing strategies proposed for corridor improvements ranged widely, from use of variable pricing tolls (with 100 percent electronic toll collection) to use of traditional federal and state grant programs. This application illustrates the combination of financing strategies that probably will characterize the investment strategy at the megaregion level.

I-95 Corridor Coalition

The I-10 and I-5 corridor initiatives are examples of how states will respond to federal programs in which some form of financial incentive motivates participation, in both cases federal dollars. In contrast, the I-95 Corridor Coalition is a voluntary group of transportation professionals working toward better managing the I-95 corridor in the Eastern United States. The I-95 corridor extends from the Canadian Atlantic provinces and Maine to Florida. According to the coalition,

> In 2006, 110 million people lived in corridor region. The corridor region occupies 10 percent of the nation's land area but contains 37 percent of its population. At 272 people per square mile, it is over three times more densely

populated than the United States. The states in the coalition region contributed $4.7 trillion to the national gross domestic product (GDP) in 2006, constituting 37 percent of the nation's GDP. (I-95 Corridor Coalition 2007)

The coalition notes that it has also "served successfully as a model for multi-state/jurisdictional interagency cooperation and coordination since 1993." Initially focused on studies and tests of incident management and traveler information technologies, the coalition now includes a variety of important efforts, including corridor-wide information systems, policy and vision studies, multimodal and intermodal issues, and financing of solutions to major highway and rail bottlenecks and choke points.

Interestingly, the I-95 Corridor Coalition was selected as one of the U.S. DOT's Corridors of the Future. In its application, the coalition explicitly linked its transportation needs to serving the megaregions through which the corridor runs. As noted, these transportation networks were to serve transportation needs at four scales within and between these megaregions (I-95 Corridor Coalition 2007):

- *Within metropolitan areas in the coalition's megaregions,* where the focus is on managing congestion and improving metropolitan transit and commuter rail services.
- *Within megaregions,* where the focus is on intercity highways serving automobile, bus, and truck traffic and on intercity air and rail services for passengers.
- *Between megaregions in the coalition region,* where the focus is on serving industries and distribution centers dependent on the region's interstate highway system and the north–south freight rail network and serving longer-distance business and recreation travel by rail and air.
- *Between megaregions in the corridor and other national and global trade blocs,* where the focus is on providing reliable connections to ports, airports, transcontinental highways, and rail lines.

As part of its application, the coalition agreed to develop innovative financing approaches, including model legislation for multistate transportation infrastructure banks and public–private partnerships, which states can use to implement projects that address major highway and rail bottlenecks. The coalition's goal is to "reduce long-term congestion by providing a framework for public–public and public–private investment to eliminate or reduce the delays caused by nationally and regionally significant highway bottlenecks and rail choke points that are too expensive for a single state to fix" (I-95 Corridor Coalition 2007).

The European Union

The Treaty of Rome (1957) established the political basis for the European Union's (EU) responsibility (at the time the European Economic Community) for establishing a common transport policy. This treaty defined the goal of "promot[ing] the free flow of goods and people throughout the Union" (Farrel 1995). The EU has embarked on an ambitious plan to create a Trans-European Transport Network (TEN-T) covering the entire twenty-seven EU countries by 2020, representing an investment of more than $896 billion in 2000 dollars (600 billion euros). A network of thirty corridors throughout the EU have been identified, and of the 120 identified project segments in these corridors, 43 (more than one third) involve a cross-boundary segment between EU member states (European Commission 2005).

In 2001, the Directorate General for Energy and Transport of the European Commission issued a white paper on transport called "European Transport Policy for 2010: Time to Decide." The white paper stressed the importance of using transport links in integrating the enlarged EU. However, as the white paper noted, one of the main obstacles to the completion of the TEN-T was the lack of progress on the cross-border segments between member states of the EU (European Commission 2001). Indeed, the EU has identified the provision of cross-boundary transportation infrastructure and services as one of the largest challenges facing transportation in Europe.

The cross-boundary challenge in developing the TEN-T has been noted by others as well. Turró (1999) presents one of the more comprehensive examinations of the technological, political, and financial challenges facing the construction of the TEN-T. Political action across traditional national boundaries for funding, planning, and construction was highlighted as the most important challenge to completing the TEN-T. Roll and Verbeke (1998) examined the financing of the European high-speed train network and discovered that direct government financing of the networks covered about 40 percent of the project costs, except in France and Italy, where the national rail infrastructure was self-financed. Ross (1994) notes that historically in Europe most rail and other infrastructure investment has been by state-owned companies more interested in unifying the country and therefore more focused on national investment goals rather than operating from a European perspective.

With respect to the TEN-T priority projects, "the public financing capacities of the European Union member states remain constrained; the level of investment in transport infrastructure has fallen in all member states and now amounts to less than 1 percent of gross domestic product. Similarly, the new financial perspectives of the EU for the period 2007–13 provide only a limited increase in the budget available for TENs" (European Commission 2005). Accordingly, transportation system investment in Europe relies on a wide range of financing strategies. For example, the EU is attempting to leverage public investment in transportation facilities to entice private investment (Rienstra and Nijkamp 1997). Such a strategy has been successful in several cross-border projects, such as the Oresund Bridge, the new Brenner Tunnel through the Alps, and the international portion of the Lyon–Turin high-speed rail line (Crocker 2007). In particular, the EU is using the European Investment Bank to increase the completion rate of the TEN-T, leading to the development of specialized financial instruments such as the "TEN Investment Facility," specifically designed to strengthen development of the TEN and increase private sector participation (Barrett 2005).

The European financing context is very different from that of the United States, which has relied on public funding for most of its road infrastructure. The EU strategy of using public money to leverage private investment is an explicit recognition that there are insufficient public resources available to build all the proposed continental projects. In the absence of alternative sources of funding, either additional public funding must be provided (taking funding away from other projects), or the overall capital investment program must be stretched over a longer time period. As chronicled by Dunn (1995), France attempted to finance motorways through dedicated motor fuel taxes but met resistance from the finance ministry and instead ended up with a series of national motorways. More than 70 percent are controlled by toll companies, of which seven are designated as "mixed economy" companies, similar to authorities in the United States, and one is a private concessionaire.

Cross-Jurisdictional Overview

Crocker (2007) identifies several organizational arrangements that were used in Europe and the United States to implement cross-jurisdictional projects (Table 9.1). Crocker also notes that in some cases geographic equity played a critical role in garnering the financial support necessary to implement a project. As Crocker notes,

> While this factor is most prevalent in the voting control of the organization, either through political appointment or shareholding, it is worth noting that in two cases, establishment of Sound Transit in Seattle and the construction agreement of the Belgian portion of the Paris Brussels Cologne/Frankfurt Amsterdam London (PBKAL) high-speed rail axis, one of the important factors was that construction physically takes place in each of the involved entities within a specified time period. The investment that was to take place was explicitly spelled out with a timeline for completion. This suggests that the method garnering

Table 9.1

Institutional and financial arrangements: Selected TEN-T projects and operations.

Arrangement	Location
Third-party agency with oversight board representing geographic area	Oresund Bridge (Oresund Konsorteit) Channel Tunnel (Eurotunnel)
Each country responsible for construction on its own territory	Paris–Brussels high-speed train (SNCF and Infrabel) Brussels–Amsterdam (Infrabel and High Speed Alliance) Brussels–Cologne (Infrabel and Deutsche Bahn)
Operating with funding contributions from participating jurisdictions	PBKA Operations (Thalys) PBL Operations (Eurostar) offering seamless European service
Independent operator with fees paid to use infrastructure	France–Brussels rail service (Train à Grand Vitesse by SNCF to Brussels) Germany–Brussels rail service (ICE: France's high speed rail service service by Deutsche Bahn to Brussels) Netherlands–Brussels rail service (High Speed Alliance to Antwerp and Brussels) Channel Tunnel (freight service) Oresund Bridge (sale of rail operating rights)

Source: Crocker (2007).

support for places that might be reluctant to construct or operate cross-boundary services is to develop a detailed work plan that specifically spells out the investments to be made and that shares those investments proportionally across the involved governments.

A Range of Financing Strategies and Mechanisms for Transportation Investment

Two questions must be considered when developing a financing strategy for megaregion transportation investment: What types of revenue sources can be considered? And institutionally, how can these funds be managed and administered?

Public Finance Strategy

For megaregions, the least controversial financing strategy from the state, regional, and local government perspective is to seek funds from a national government or a supranational organization. These funds could be part of a national corridor program or some other targeted federal program or could simply be the funds that are normally allocated to states as part of the federal aid program. In the latter case, special consideration would have to be given to funding the projects that most benefit megaregion transportation needs, similar in concept to the program criteria noted earlier for the corridors of national significance. Institutionally, a national program would probably place the least pressure on existing institutional structures and relationships. The success of such a program would depend on the availability of funding. It would also be desirable to have all types of megaregion transportation projects be eligible for such funding (e.g., highways, intercity transit, high-speed rail, freight infrastructure).

Absent a national program and thus national dollars, a variety of funding sources can be considered for providing needed transportation revenues. Table 9.2 shows an assessment of the different revenue sources that might be part of a multijurisdictional metropolitan area where, in this case, *multijurisdictional* is defined as spanning more than one state (Institute of Transportation Studies and ICF 2005). This table subjectively assesses the effect and feasibility of each type of revenue source based on several criteria. For example, financial effectiveness is defined as the degree to which a funding source provides a stable foundation for transportation investment over time and whether the level of funding will increase. The efficiency criteria relate to the degree to which the funds can be collected and the resulting impact on travel behavior. Equity reflects the geographic and political issues associated with making sure those who pay receive benefits for their contribution. And political acceptability is the degree to which multiple jurisdictions can reach agreement on a particular financing strategy. As can be seen in the table, the assessment portrays political acceptability as being very poor for almost all of the strategies.

Table 9.2 identifies the types of revenue sources that could be used to fund transportation investments. It is important to note that that many jurisdictions are incurring debt by using the municipal bond market to borrow investment funds. These bonds have to be paid off over the life of the bond issue, which means that some revenue source must be available to pay the debt service. The revenue sources in Table 9.2 illustrate the types of strategies that could be used when considering debt financing as well. This so-called debt financing is becoming more common than it once was.

Institutionally, an important consideration for using any of these funding strategies at a multijurisdictional level is the organizational structure for generating and allocating the revenues beyond one jurisdiction. Historically, such structures have included the following:

Table 9.2

New regional revenue sources in a multijurisdictional metropolitan planning organization.

	Revenue Criterion					
	Financial Effectiveness		Transportation Efficiency	Fiscal Efficiency	Equity	Political Acceptability
Revenue Source	Stability	Growth Potential				
Direct User Fees						
Fuel tax on motor and diesel fuels	+	–	+	++	–	–
Sales tax on motor and diesel fuels	+	+	+	++	–	–
Aviation fuel tax	+	+/–	–	++	++	+
Flat tolls (facility based)	+	+	+	+	+	+/–
Variable Tolls						
Area-based tolls	+	+	++	+/–	+/–	+/–
Time-based tolls	+	+	++	+/–	+/–	+/–
Congestion-based tolls	+	+	++	+/–	+/–	+/–
Emission fees	+/–	+/–	–	–	–	–
Annual VMT fees	+	+	–	–	–	–
Nonuser Fees						
Vehicle sales tax	+	++	–	+	–	–
Vehicle license and registration fees	+	++	–	+	–	+/–
Sales tax	+	++	–	++	–	+/–
Property tax	+	++	–	+	+	–
Commercial development tax	+	++	+	+	+	–
Residential development tax	+	++	+	+	+/–	–
Per capita tax from jurisdictions	+	+	–	+	+/–	–

++ Very good
+ Good
+/– Neutral, depending on circumstances
– Poor
— Very poor

Source: Institute for Transportation Studies and ICF (2005).

- *Regional government and regional service providers*: There are only a handful of examples of regional entities providing services at a level comparable to multiple metropolitan areas; however, state support could contribute to the development of more such models, especially for regional service providers.
- *Area-wide special districts or authorities*: State legislation could incorporate MPOs, counties, and other jurisdictions in a targeted area as a special district for transportation planning and finance.
- *Interstate compacts and compact agencies*: A number of such compacts exist for a variety of reasons, not all related to transportation. Such compacts often have to obtain approval from the federal government.
- *Federally designated regional commissions and semi-independent federal corporations*: Although the federal government can create regional authorities, the trend in recent years is to reduce the level of federal government involvement in state and regional decision making (Institute of Transportation Studies and ICF 2005).

As was described earlier, multiple jurisdictions can also sign memoranda of understanding that outline how investment decisions will be made in targeted corridors (similar in concept to the I-95 Corridor Coalition). In this situation, no formal government organization has to be created, simply the adoption of an agreement to cooperate and coordinate investments for the benefit of the corridor.

Public–Private Finance Strategy

Although transportation investment in most countries is the responsibility of the public sector, a great deal of interest has been generated over the past two decades in public–private partnerships (P3), which are viewed as a way of augmenting public investment in transportation facilities and in promoting more cost-efficient operations. A range of P3 models exist, from complete private operation of a facility to concession arrangements that permit a private firm or consortium to build and operate a facility in exchange for a revenue stream over a specified time period. A P3 equity partnership approach is an opportunity to change the way transportation investment has occurred in the past. Because so many governments are expecting P3s to be an important part of their future investment strategy, the following paragraphs will further discuss the important characteristics of such arrangements.

Investment equity views the public and private sectors as real partners in a transportation investment project. Both share in the risks and profits of the project over the long haul. Each brings to the project its relative strengths. For example, public agencies have the best resources to do the up-front, high-risk work of project development, environmental assessment, community outreach, and condemnation. The private investor's contribution is construction efficiency, quality, and the ability to generate revenues.

Two major decision factors important to P3 projects are risk and return on investment. The level of certainty with project costs, revenues, rate of return, and timing dominate private sector concerns with public sector infrastructure investments. Great uncertainty in any of these will result in either no P3 project occurring or the need for a large financial offset to the investors to mitigate the risks created by the uncertainty. Private investors use valuation factors to determine the price and level of revenues they are willing to accept. Relevant factors that drive valuations include the following:

- *Investment fund push*: The entry of foreign financial investors into the transportation sector has changed the United States' private investment marketplace, which was dominated in the past primarily by strategic investors, such as construction firms, engineering firms, and equipment suppliers. The international players not only bring in new money but also change the way business is done and increase the competitiveness of potential deals. However, many international investors are not used to U.S. laws concerning transportation decision making. The issue of transparency of investment deals becomes a critical issue.

- *Market creation*: The U.S. toll road P3 market is still fairly small, but it is increasing as new entries seek to establish a U.S. presence. Aggressive bids may be made not only based on the project but also with an eye toward increasing the size of the toll market. Indeed, recent high bids for some transportation facilities have probably increased government interest in additional concession opportunities.

- *Market share*: Given that the market is likely to expand, investors may be more concerned with maximizing market share and developing a strong reputation in order to increase their chances for other projects.

- *Integrated bidders*: Large, consolidated firms are able to profit from every service in a design, build, operate, and maintain concession, thereby increasing the profitability of the whole. This is a new experience for U.S. transportation projects, which have historically relied on the fragmented design bid and construction bid process, in which the parties were forced to be separate and the public sector absorbed much of the design and construction risk.

- *Discount rate*: Long concession timeframes (some more than 50 years) enable bidders to set a base discount rate that ensures that they cover debt service while forecasting larger but speculative equity returns.

- *Risk profile*: The risk profile, and hence return rate, of a long-term concession may change over time. For example, in the startup period, construction cost and traffic uncertainties are likely to be heavily discounted. However, once a road has a traffic history, the risk is greatly diminished, and the investor will have the opportunity to refinance or sell the transaction. Once major rebuilding is needed in 30 years or more, a different risk profile may come into play.
- *Tax and depreciation laws*: The financial profile of investors, and the accounting rules under which they operate (which may differ by country), can affect the value of tax benefits from operating losses and depreciation. This can become a significant factor in the value of the project to the investor.
- *Exchange rates*: The U.S. dollar–euro exchange rate currently favors foreign participation in the U.S. P3 market. Although the theory of purchasing power parity dictates that the long-term equilibrium exchange rate between two currencies converges to one, significant short- to medium-term swings exist in which market exchange rates can diverge significantly from the long-term equilibrium rate. This could provide foreign-based firms with an opportunity to increase their return for infrastructure over U.S. currency-based firms or consortia.
- *Use of special purpose entity (SPE) structures*: The use of an SPE ("holding company") in the corporate finance setting is well known. The strategic use of this organizational structure allows investors to act aggressively in acquiring infrastructure assets. A parent firm can quickly create a holding company comprising several hundred controlled entities. Although holding companies fulfill a wide array of functions, in toll road acquisitions they critically hide the acquirers' true debt profile.

Each of these valuation factors is an important consideration in a private decision to invest in a public facility. Perhaps most important is the need to have a sufficient revenue stream to guarantee a high level of return to the investors. This naturally focuses attention on the high-volume roads (where tolls would generate such a return) or where the government provides some level of subsidy to entice private investment. From a megaregion perspective, this might not be a serious limitation in that many of the infrastructure facilities that would be in critical need of investment are likely to be high-volume facilities. However, in most cases in the United States, this investment has been targeted on high-volume highways, with very little attention given to transit.

One final financing tool that merits discussion is the concept of a state infrastructure bank. This concept provides public agencies greater flexibility in leveraging transportation dollars. Under this concept, states can lend with favorable conditions their allocated federal funds to revenue-generating projects with public or private sponsorship or to a project as subordinated debt with extended repayment periods. In essence, the infrastructure bank is a revolving fund, providing easier terms for investment but not generating new dollars. A similar infrastructure "bank" could be developed for a megaregion investment program, in this case where multiple states would have to participate. Low- or no-cost loans from the bank could be targeted specifically to projects whose purpose is to enhance megaregion transportation system productivity.

A Megaregion Transportation Investment Strategy

Identifying and arriving at a consensus on the mechanisms and strategies for megaregion transportation investment will be challenging. With numerous jurisdictions and government agencies responsible for different components of the transportation system, developing a plan and investment program that reflect megaregion priorities would probably run into political, legal, and administrative obstacles. However, investing in transportation is a likely prerequisite for the future economic success of megaregion communities. Thus, providing some means of financially supporting needed megaregion transportation investments will probably be an important metric by which national transportation policies can be measured. What should such a strategy consist of?

Role of the National Government

Given the multistate nature of most megaregions, there is a strong national government role (in the United States, this would be the federal government) in fostering needed investment (in the European case, this would be a supranational government role). As seen in the examples provided earlier, this role should include national funds that can be used to leverage funds from other government agencies and private investors. With the level of needed investment in most megaregions probably reaching hundreds of billions of dollars, only the federal government could develop a nationally applied strategy to invest in megaregion transportation systems. Recommended actions include the following:

- Develop a *national multimodal transportation strategy* that recognizes the importance of megaregions for the future of the nation and that quantifies the economic benefits of having high-performance transportation systems that serve internal travel, travel between megaregions, and access to global markets.

- Develop a *megaregion investment program* as part of the national federal aid program, similar in concept to the corridors of national significance. This program would provide a portion of the investment needed for megaregion-level investments, where criteria for a megaregion-level facility or service would be specified. The intent of this program would be to act as a catalyst for other investors.

- Explicitly recognize *freight movement as a national economic issue* and promote federal programs that foster both public and private investment in freight infrastructure.

- Enable multiple states to form *megaregion-level planning and investment organizations*, where appropriate, that would promote transportation investments across jurisdictional boundaries.

- Enable *multistate infrastructure banks* that can act as a vehicle for providing low-cost loans to project developers.

- Establish as part of the formal, federally certified state and metropolitan transportation planning process *an examination of megaregion transportation issues* as they affect a state or metropolitan area. Although in many cases this examination might result in very little concern at this time, such a requirement would begin the process of educating decision makers on the broader economic market in which they live.

Role of State Governments

Even with a national transportation policy that recognizes the importance of megaregions, much of the impetus for transportation investment will probably come from the states. It seems likely that strategic partnerships across regional and state boundaries will have to be created to deal with the challenges associated with megaregion-scale investment. This already happens for bordering jurisdictions and especially for large-scale projects, such as bridges over rivers that serve as state boundaries. Such collaboration was key to the connected interstate highway system in the United States and the high-speed rail network in Europe. However, the new element of this approach is the need to have more than one state or major metropolitan area as part of a megaregion planning and investment strategy. This greatly increases the level of complexity and uncertainty associated with roles and responsibilities. Recommended actions include the following:

- Work with other states to advocate and develop *multistate national programs* aimed at megaregion transportation investment. In most Western countries, much of what happens nationally is generated from state and local innovations. As noted earlier, the national corridor programs in the

United States were defined by Congress—that is, the idea for such an effort came from legislative delegations representing the states. The states most affected by megaregion development can play a critical role in forming a national transportation agenda that acknowledges the important role of megaregions.

- Incorporate *megaregion needs and respective roles* of state agencies into the statewide transportation planning process. The planning process can be an important platform for identifying the transportation needs of the state and educating decision makers about the broad outlines of the future challenges facing a state's transportation system.

- Develop *strategic partnerships* with other states that make up the megaregion. In some ways, this is similar to the I-95 Corridor Coalition, in which states along I-95 have recognized the importance of travel along this corridor. These partnerships might take the form of compacts in which formal responsibilities and roles are outlined, or simply informal agreements to work together. In addition, the concept of a multistate infrastructure bank that targets megaregion-level investment opportunities should be examined.

- Identify with their partners the transportation facilities and services that are significant from a megaregion perspective. The identification of such a *strategic system* is a critical foundation for a megaregion investment program in that it targets investment in the facilities and services that provide the best megaregion connectivity.

- Create *megaregion-wide investment strategies and programs* aimed at improving the economic integration and position of the megaregion. These strategies and programs should be multimodal and focus not only on travel internal to the megaregion but also on transportation opportunities that connect the megaregion to the rest of the nation and to the world market.

- Incorporate *freight infrastructure needs and freight flows* more strategically in statewide planning and investment. Many of the major ports of entry into the United States are state facilities or are served by highways under state control. Given that much of the economic success of megaregions will be linked to global trade, expediting flows to and from these ports of entry is an important planning goal.

Role of Metropolitan Areas

Metropolitan areas are the most important economic units within a megaregion. Not only do they serve as major population and employment centers, but they are also the most important locations for generating economic wealth. However, they are also often the location of the most parochial perspective on transportation investment, that is, targeting investment to benefit local constituencies at the expense of regional or state needs. But given that most of the major transportation facilities and services in a megaregion are in place primarily to serve metropolitan areas, the success of a megaregion-level investment program will depend to a large extent on the willingness of metropolitan areas to acknowledge their position in this broader economic construct and to establish an investment program that emphasizes the importance of megaregion-level travel. Recommended actions include the following:

- The *metropolitan transportation planning process*, which is used to update the metropolitan transportation plan every 3 to 5 years, should examine the role of metropolitan areas in a megaregion economy. This effort not only would provide important information on the transportation system needs for the region to be successful in such an economy but also would raise awareness of each metropolitan area's respective role.
- Identify a *strategic transportation system* in the metropolitan area that serves primarily intercity or megaregion travel. This system can then become the focus of investment priorities.
- Develop a *metropolitan transportation investment program* that consists of many different funding sources, both public and private, so as to provide the broadest possible foundation for investing in the region's transportation system.
- Conduct *planning studies* in the corridors where intercity passenger and freight movements are major components of travel flow. These corridor studies could be conducted in conjunction with other metropolitan areas served by the same corridors so as to broaden the planning perspective on the travel market being served.
- Work with national and state legislative leaders in establishing *multistate investment programs* that target megaregion transportation investment. This is similar to the bottom-up approach to creating national transportation programs. Because of the large numbers of people who reside in metropolitan areas, they have a very large representation in national and state legislative bodies. This political influence can be used to develop programs that will benefit megaregion transportation systems.

Role of Private Investors

As indicated earlier, many countries are emphasizing public–private investment strategies as a major means of meeting future investment needs. For multijurisdictional corridors, and especially for those in megaregions that are often quite large, a public–private investment strategy might be the best approach to overcoming jurisdictional barriers to joint investment. Not only do private investors have the ability to invest in multiple state jurisdictions (which most state governments do not), but they can often respond much faster than most governments in providing needed system capacity improvements. This is not to say that planning process requirements and environmental conditions can be ignored but simply that private investors have more flexibility working in multiple jurisdictions at one time. Given the expected increase in volume on megaregions' major transportation facilities, a prerequisite for private investor interest, it seems likely that public–private partnerships will play a critical role in providing megaregion system capacity in future decades.

Conclusions

One of the challenges in providing coordinated and integrated transportation systems for megaregions is overcoming the traditional, jurisdiction-specific institutional structures for funding such systems. Historically, states and municipalities have used their transport funding to the benefit of their specific jurisdiction and have not looked beyond their own boundaries to consider the much broader benefits of investment from a multijurisdictional perspective. This chapter has examined the institutional challenges that relate to funding transportation infrastructure and service provision from a megaregion perspective.

Examples do exist of multijurisdiction funding programs created by national and state governments to invest in transportation facilities and services that extend through many states and metropolitan areas. Although very few of these programs have been portrayed as megaregion-serving investment programs, in reality this is what they are. The European TEN-T and the corridors of national significance described in this chapter serve such a function. The interesting characteristic of such programs is that each has identified obtaining multijurisdictional cooperation and collaboration on joint action as one of the most important obstacles to successful program implementation.

Megaregions will continue to evolve into the economic engines that drive national economies. The ability of megaregion passenger and freight transportation systems to serve these growing economies will largely define the level of economic success that will be achieved. There is a strong national government role in providing resources and an institutional structure for addressing these transportation needs. Funding should be targeted to these needs, with both public and private investment being part of the financing strategy. States and metropolitan areas also have important roles to play in broadening their perspective on how critical transportation facilities and services that cross jurisdictional lines should be funded.

Although the selection of specific investment strategies will often reflect the political and institutional circumstances of a given situation, it seems likely that the financing structures that would be of most interest to the United States for megaregion transportation infrastructure will include both public and private investment. Multistate compacts in which megaregion-level investment strategies will be targeted on the most important bottlenecks will probably be a common institutional arrangement in the future. Such compacts will provide a megaregion-level perspective on transportation priorities but will also permit state investment that respects state boundaries. Public–private partnerships also represent an approach that will be of great benefit to the United States. The major benefit of private sector involvement, which has usually been portrayed as bringing additional investment dollars into the transportation system, is considered in this chapter as one of breaking down the barriers that pervade multijurisdictional investment situations. Finally, a megaregion-level investment strategy would be much easier to achieve if the national government played a role in supporting the strategy, most importantly with national transportation funds. If funding is not an option, then the national government can play an important convening role in getting all the actors to focus on the transportation problems facing the megaregion.

For many years, transportation planners and policymakers have acknowledged that dealing with the institutional issues is the most challenging aspect of transportation investment decision making. A megaregion perspective on such decision making is even more complicated. And yet, given the importance of such a perspective to the future economic success of the nation, these challenges must be dealt with successfully.

References

Austin, J., and B. Affolter-Caine. 2006. *The Vital Center: A Federal–State Compact to Renew the Great Lakes Region.* The Brookings Institution, Washington, D.C.

Barrett, T. C. 2005. *EIB Experience in Financing Trans-European Networks and Public–Private Partnerships* [Presentation]. European Investment Bank, Moscow.

Carbonell, A., and R. D. Yaro. 2005. Megaregions. *Land Lines.* July, 2008.

Commission of the European Communities. 2006. *Keep Europe Moving—Sustainable Mobility for Our Continent: Mid-Term Review of the European Commission's 2001 White Paper.* European Commission, Brussels.

Crocker, J. 2007. *Organizational Arrangements for the Provision of Cross-Boundary Transport Infrastructure and Services.* Unpublished Ph.D. dissertation, Georgia Institute of Technology, Atlanta, GA.

Dunn, J. A. Jr. 1995. The French highway lobby: A case study in state–society relations and policymaking. *Comparative Politics* 3.

European Commission. 2001. *White Paper—European Transport Policy for 2010: Time to Decide.* Office for Official Publications of the European Communities, Luxembourg.

————. 2005. *Trans-European Transport Network: TEN-T Priority Axes and Projects 2005*. Office for Official Publications of the European Commission, Luxembourg.

Farrel, S. 1995. *Financing European Transport Infrastructure: Policies and Practice in Western Europe*. Macmillan, Hampshire, UK.

Federal Highway Administration. 2006 *National Corridor Infrastructure Improvement Program*. Retrieved November 12, 2007 from www.fhwa.dot.gov/safetealu/factsheets/corridors.htm.

I-95 Corridor Coalition. 2007. *Corridors of the Future: Application*. Retrieved November 1, 2007 from www.i95coalition.org/travinfo_corridors-of-the-future.html.

Institute of Transportation Studies and ICF. 2005. *Metropolitan-Level Transportation Funding Sources*. Transportation Research Board, Washington, D.C.

Metcalf, G., and E. Terplan. 2007, November/December. The Northern California megaregion. *Urbanist* 4–25.

Reconnecting America. 2002. *Missed Connections: Finding Solutions to the Crisis in Air Travel*. Oakland, CA.

Regional Plan Association. 2006. *America 2050: A Prospectus*. Regional Plan Association, New York.

————. 2007. *Northeast Megaregion 2050: A Common Future*. Regional Plan Association, New York.

Rienstra, S. A., and P. Nijkamp. 1997. Lessons from private financing of transport infrastructure: Dutch infrastructure in the 19th century and European projects in the 20th century. *Revue Economique* 48(2).

Roll, M., and A. Verbeke. 1998. Financing of the trans-European high-speed rail networks: New forms of public–private partnerships. *European Management Journal* 16(6):706–713.

Ross, J. F. L. 1994. High-speed rail: Catalyst for European integration? *Journal of Common Market Studies* 32(2):191.

Todorovich, P. 2007. *A Transportation Strategy for 21st Century America*. Regional Plan Association, New York.

Transportation Research Board. 2006. *The Fuel Tax and Alternatives for Transportation Funding*. National Academy Press, Washington, D.C.

Turró, M. 1999. *Going Trans-European: Planning and Financing Transport Networks for Europe*. Pergamon, Amsterdam.

U.S. Department of Transportation. 2007. *Corridors of the Future*. Retrieved October 30, 2007 from www.dot.gov/affairs/dot9507.htm.

Wilbur Smith and Associates. 2003, May. *The I-10 National Freight Corridor Study*. Retrieved January 12, 2008 www.i10freightstudy.org/7_reports.html.

Zhang, M., F. Steiner, and K. Butler. 2007. *Connecting the Texas Triangle: Economic Integration and Transportation Coordination*. Paper presented at the Healdsburg Research Seminar on Megaregions, Healdsburg, CA.

10

Social Equity and the Challenge of Distressed Places

Norman Fainstein and Susan S. Fainstein

For nearly two centuries social analysts have been blaming place as a contributor to economic hardship and even as its main cause. Victorian and Progressive social reformers identified slums as the sources of poverty and disease (Ward 1989). Twentieth-century American sociologists added ethnicity (Wirth 1928) and then race in establishing the concept of the ghetto (Cayton and Drake 1945) and the "dark ghetto" (Clark 1965). Proponents of urban renewal spoke of eliminating slums and blight (Gelfand 1975). The architects of the "War on Poverty" described neighborhoods of "tangled pathology" (O'Connor 2001). For a very long time, social scientists and policymakers have identified distressed places as a principal cause of social inequality rather than merely as a spatial expression of its symptoms. In recent years the terminology has changed a bit—from "slums" to "neighborhoods of concentrated poverty," from the "undeserving poor" to the "underclass," from "ghettos" to "racially isolated places"—and the list of similar concepts is long (Fainstein 1993; Katz 1993). Major works that emphasize place-based factors in the explanation of poverty are well known (Wilson 1987; Jencks and Peterson 1991; Jencks 1992; Massey and Denton 1993; Jargowsky 1997; Goetz 2003; Dreier et al. 2004).

However, their authors often disagree sharply on the explanatory importance of race, segregation, culture, social structure, and political institutions. When the subject matter becomes immigrants, the whole causal structure may be turned on its head. Specialists on immigration—on a parallel and noncommunicating track with those concerned about poverty and race—often find positive aspects to concentrations of poor ethnic minorities. Instead of pathology, they see "immigrant enclaves," "employment networks," and "facilitative linguistic and cultural communities" (Muller 1993; Borjas 1999), and students of politics find that racial segregation and common economic interests provide a base for political empowerment, one that would probably be lost in a fully integrated world (Piven and Cloward 1967). Not surprisingly, the theoretical and political orientations of the analyst and the group or place in question determine the preferred form of intervention. In starkest terms, whether to direct resources to the distressed place or to "deconcentrate" the affected population (either forcibly or by providing incentives and breaking down barriers to spatial mobility) are the only options given.

The significance of place—whether place is defined at the neighborhood, municipal, or metropolitan level—is still very much a question in play. In fact, there are many reasons to believe that class power, racial subordination, and public policy tell us far more about poverty and income inequality than does spatial organization. From this perspective, spatial arrangements are largely an important expression of social inequality and only secondarily its cause. Recent evidence about spatial inequality at all levels of aggregation provides further credence to this point of view.

A discussion of social equity and the challenge of distressed places focuses on metropolitan areas because they are where most Americans live.[1] Our concern in this chapter is with metropolitan areas in two senses. They are the places where the national political economy finds its spatial expression. Beyond that, everyone lives in real space and in the built environment. Whatever the importance of neighborhood or spatial effects as causal determinants of social mobility, economic inequality, and poverty, the character of place absolutely matters to everyone, for it is a critical dimension of the quality of life.

In the following sections, we will first describe the shape of metropolitan inequalities. Then we argue that redeploying people in space will not dramatically alter their life chances. Next, we turn to the most commonly prescribed reform measure for remedying spatial inequity—metropolitan consolidation—and contend that it holds little promise for erasing disadvantage. Finally, we show that state governments already have the capacity to deal with spatial inequality and suggest a number of policies that would promote greater equity within metropolitan areas and across regions.

Changing National Contours

Between World War II and 1980, the American landscape was formed by economic and political forces that produced what used to be called "the urban crisis," with its well-known spatial expressions at the municipal and metropolitan levels. The continued migration from the countryside of all Americans, but especially poor black people from the South and poor Hispanic people from Puerto Rico, made central cities the homes of racial minority groups. National policy precipitated suburban housing development, and official and unofficial racist practices ensured that the new suburbs would become a segregated white world. The decline of city-centered manufacturing, decentralization of employment, efforts to integrate city schools, crime, and sometimes violent black–white conflict all facilitated the "white flight" that reached its peak in the 1970s. The resulting configuration was one of fiscally stressed central cities—their downtowns dying, their neighborhoods increasingly housing the poor and people of color—surrounded by economically thriving, white, middle- and upper-class suburbs with their good schools and single-family houses. Although the American pattern has always been more complex than that conveyed by the metaphor of the doughnut—a sweet roll with a hole in the center—the image still captured the essential features of metropolitan inequality.[2]

For the last quarter century, however, global economic forces and national politics have combined to superimpose new patterns on the American metropolitan landscape. First, immigration, arguably on a scale greater than at any time in American history, has resettled old cities and created a complex politics of race, ethnicity, and nativity that is transforming our previously dichotomized black–white society. Second, the decline in overt racism, improved educational attainment, and higher incomes in the black population have combined with affirmative government programs to facilitate the growth of a black middle class.[3] Third, economic inequality has grown steadily since the mid-1970s, with stagnating incomes for the poor and the middle class. The great bulk of economic growth is being captured by the top fifth of the population—and an increasingly disproportionate share by the top 5 percent, 1 percent, and 0.01 percent (Piketty and Saez 2003; Saez 2007).[4] The new Gilded Age in America has been expressed spatially with the renaissance of some downtowns, the building of luxurious, gated suburban and exurban communities, and the general decline of middle-income suburbs. Table 10.1 shows the income distribution in the United States.

In this chapter we will use recent data to flesh out the American pattern of spatial inequality and the changes it is undergoing. Most of this evidence is drawn from analyses of the 2000 Decennial Census and the 2005 Current Population Survey. As we will see, old patterns are still dominant, with the metropolitan terrain of inequality becoming ever more complex. Time-honored generalizations are breaking down and a contextual understanding of specific places—whether large regions, metro areas, municipalities, or neighborhoods—is becoming increasingly essential to description, explanation, and effective policy.

Table 10.1

Income distribution in the United States.

	1979	1999	2005
Income of households[a]			
Poorest quintile	17,442	20,073	19,178
Median	41,015	47,599	46,326
Richest quintile	72,259	92,813	91,705
Top 5 percent	116,670	166,340	166,000
Income share of households[b]			
Poorest quintile	4.1	3.6	3.4
Middle quintile	16.8	14.9	14.6
Richest quintile	44.2	49.4	50.4
Gini coefficient[c]	.404	.458	.469

[a]Measured in constant 2005 dollars, adjusted for prior years with CPI-U-RS. CPI Research Series Using Current Methods

For the poorest quintile the dollar figure represents the income cutoff for the upper limit; for the richest quintile and richest 5 percent the dollar figures are the cutoffs for the lower limits. For example, in 1979 a household with an income at or below $17,442 (in 2005 dollars) would be in the lowest quintile of the distribution; a household with an income at or above $116,670 would be in the highest 5 percent of all households.

[b]The figures represent the percentage of all household income received by the respective quintile. For example, the share of household income of the poorest quintile in 1979 was 4.1%, and that of the richest quintile was 44.2 percent.

[c]The Gini coefficient here measures inequality in the distribution of income between households; the higher the coefficient, the greater the inequality.

Source: U.S. Census Bureau (2006), Table A-3.

Inequality at the Regional and Metropolitan Levels

At the regional level, the prosperous 1990s produced a general improvement in aggregate economic indicators across the country. But closer examination showed new cleavages in the Sunbelt, the most notable being the bifurcation of California into a prosperous north and an increasingly troubled south. Using an index of prosperity that reflects both growth and equity, John Logan (2002) found that Los Angeles and nearby metropolitan areas suffered significant declines on his index, in large part because of Mexican immigration. In other places, most notably New York City, despite substantial population growth, gentrification at the center, and skyrocketing real estate prices, aggregate prosperity declined. These spatial effects and the muddling of the old Snowbelt–Sunbelt dichotomy were the result of highly differential immigration patterns, the restructuring of the U.S. economy, and, as previously noted, escalating inequalities in the distribution of income. Whereas average per capita income in Logan's 331 metro areas (en-

Table 10.2

Inequality between central cities and suburbs.

A. Ratio of Central City to Suburban Per Capita Income

1960	1.05
1970	0.96
1980	0.89
1990	0.84
2000	0.83

Source: Dreier et al. (2004), Figure 2.1.

B. Poverty in the United States and 100 Largest Metropolitan Areas

	Number (thousands)		Percentage (%)	
	1999	2005	1999	2005
United States	33,900	38,232	12.4	13.3
Metro	20,629	23,195	11.6	12.3
Central City	10,380	10,958	17.9	18.8
Suburb	10,250	12,236	8.5	9.4

Source: Berube and Kneebone (2006), Figures 1 and 2.

compassing 225 million people) rose by 12.8 percent between 1990 and 2000, median income, a measure of middle-class welfare, rose by barely half that amount, 6.7 percent, in constant dollars (Logan 2002).

The increasing complexity of economic inequalities caused deviations from the old pattern of suburban prosperity and central city decline. Table 10.2A shows central city versus suburban per capita income since 1960 for the eighty-five largest metropolitan areas. Central city fortunes have monotonically declined for more than 40 years, from central cities having an advantage in 1960 (105 percent of suburban income) to a significant and increasing disadvantage in the ensuing decades. The central city disadvantage did not significantly worsen in the 1990s because the central city economic collapse, on average, ended in that decade.

Moreover, there were sharp regional differences in the suburban/urban income ratio. Nearly all the inequality, measured in a gross contrast between central cities and suburban ring, was found in the Northeast and Midwest. Southern and Western metropolitan areas, with their generally much larger central cities, showed far less difference in 2000, with the central city/suburban ratio standing at 99 percent in Western and 92 percent in Southern metropolitan areas.

With titles such as "The Urban Turnaround" and "Downtown Rebound," urban scholars found real, if not overwhelming, evidence for the reanimation of older central cities. Simmons and Lang (2003) determined that of thirty-six older cities, mainly in the Northeast and Midwest, which had been steadily losing population since 1950, fifteen grew in the 1990s. In a study of twenty-four down-towns of major cities, Sohmer and Lang (2003) show that three quarters gained residential population in the decade. Even in notoriously declining cities such as Cleveland, Baltimore, Philadelphia, and Detroit, which lost population even in the 1990s, downtown residence actually expanded. Many downtowns showed sharp increases in the population of highly educated and young households (Birch 2006). Playing on the title of a 1925 article by Lewis Mumford, Fishman (2005) describes the components of a "fifth migration" back into the old center cities: "downtown reurbanism," "immigrant reurbanism," "black reurbanism," and "white middle-class reurbanism." Thus, economic development, gentrifica-tion, and repopulation are producing growth in parts of some central cities, even while many of their older, first-ring suburbs have come to look more like the inner cities of past decades (Puentes and Warren 2006).

To be sure, the suburbs were never as uniformly prosperous or as homoge-neous in social class as suggested in media images and doughnut (or noose) metaphors. Still, the 1990s marked an unprecedented increase in suburban eco-nomic diversity. Older suburbs, especially those adjacent to low-income city neighborhoods or the recipients of major immigrant inflows, became smaller ver-sions of the inner cities. In fact, by 2005 the number of poor people in suburbs exceeded that in central cities by more than a million (see Table 10.2B), with the percentage of the suburban population under the federal poverty line increas-ing from 8.5 to 9.4 in just 5 years.

As suburbs have turned black and Hispanic, some have become demonized as slums, ghettos, and high-crime districts. Yet—perhaps surprisingly to most Americans—a great deal of suburban poverty is accounted for by non-Hispanic whites, who made up 44 percent of poor people in 2005 (about 16 million of the 37 million Americans in poverty) and who lived mainly in the suburbs (U.S. Cen-sus Bureau 2006, Table B1). Largely invisible because they tend not to be con-centrated in particular neighborhoods or municipalities and because of their "colorlessness," the non-Hispanic, white poor add to the economic diversity of the new suburbia.

Other indicators reinforce findings about the suburbanization of poverty. Whereas the distribution of family income has become increasingly unequal for more than three decades, the spatial expression of that inequality at the neigh-borhood[5] level has become even more skewed. One way to see this trend is to ex-amine the distribution of metro families among income levels and then compare

Table 10.3

Economic inequality in the 100 largest metropolitan areas.

	1970	1980	1990	2000
A. Metropolitan residential distribution by family and neighborhood income				
Family income				
Poverty (50% of metro median or less)	17.2%	18.7%	20.1%	20.6%
Middle (80–120% of metro median)	28.0%	24.7%	22.9%	21.5%
High (150% of metro median or more)	23.6%	24.7%	26.3%	28.1%
Neighborhood income				
Poverty	3.5%	7.5%	9.1%	8.2%
Middle	58.2%	49.9%	44.4%	40.9%
High	4.9%	6.8%	9.7%	11.8%
B. Suburban residential distribution by per capita income of the suburb				
Low (75% of metro income or less)		8.4%	17.4%	18.1%
Middle (75–125% of metro income)		74.9%	63.4%	60.8%
High (125% of metro income or more)		16.7%	19.2%	21.1%
C. Ratio of per capita income of richest suburbs (top 5%) to poorest (bottom 5%), 50 largest metro areas		2.68	3.41	3.51

Sources: A, Booza et al. (2006), Table 2; B, Swanstrom et al. (2006), Figure 6; C, Dreier et al. (2004), Figure 2.6.

the family distribution to that of neighborhoods. Table 10.3A identifies three different income brackets, each specified by the median income of a particular metropolitan area at a given time. It defines poor families as those with incomes that are less than 50 percent of the metro median.[6] Middle-income families have incomes between 80 percent and 120 percent of the metro median, and high-income families have incomes greater than 150 percent of the median. The data indicate that between 1970 and 2000 the percentage of both low- and high-income families increased, while those in the middle declined (from 28.0 percent in 1970 to 21.5 percent in 2000).

The decline of the middle-income family is reflected in the sharper decline of the middle-income neighborhood.[7] Defining neighborhoods by their median incomes as low-, middle-, or high-income in the same way as we did family incomes, we see a similar phenomenon of the contraction of the middle and the growth of both poor and high-income categories. But in the case of neighborhoods, the changes are truly startling, with a drop of more than 17 percent in the number of middle-income neighborhoods between 1970 and 2000 and more than a doubling of the percentage of low- and high-income areas. Excluding central cities from the calculation, we see clear evidence of growing spatial inequality between suburbs (Table 10.3B), with a decline of the middle and growth at the two extremes.[8] These data reveal an especially large increase since 1980 in the number of residents living in low-income suburbs.

Another way to measure income inequality between suburbs is to array all the suburbs in a metropolitan area by their per capita income and then examine a measure of inequality in that distribution over time. Table 10.3C compares the per capita income that defines the wealthiest suburbs (the top 5 percent)[9] in each of the fifty largest metro areas to the income that defines the poorest (the bottom 5 percent). The larger that ratio is, the more inequality between suburbs. Averaged across all fifty metro areas, the income ratio increased from 2.68 in 1980 to 3.51 by 2000, a growth of 31 percent in economic inequality between the suburbs.

Thus, by several measures we find that while economic inequality between suburbs and central cities has declined modestly in recent years, economic inequality has grown substantially within metropolitan areas measured at the neighborhood level and among metropolitan suburbs measured at the municipal level. The American picture of consistently prosperous suburbs and homogeneously impoverished central cities is becoming less useful as a description of economic inequality. So too, is that of the black city surrounded by white suburbs.

Racial Diversity and Segregation

The suburbs of metropolitan areas are far more racially diverse than at any time in American history. In the 1990s alone, the suburban minority population increased from about 19 percent to 25 percent, with the most substantial growth in the Hispanic population (Table 10.4A). By 2005 racial minorities made up 27 percent of all suburban residents. Similarly, the percentage of each racial group that was suburban also increased in the 1990s. Today it simply makes no sense to speak of Hispanics, much less Asians, as inner-city populations. Even the highly centralized black population is reaching the threshold of being half suburbanized.[10]

Yet the minority population remains living in segregated neighborhoods throughout metropolitan areas. The most commonly used indicator of segregation is the dissimilarity index, which measures the percentage of a population that would have to change census tracts (or whatever unit is being considered) in order to achieve a distribution in each tract that matches its share of the metropolitan population.[11] By this indicator, black–white segregation decreased between 1980 and 2000, but it still remained very high at .640 (Table 10.4C).

Table 10.4

Metropolitan racial diversity and neighborhood segregation.

		1980	1990	2000
A. Percentage of suburban population				
Black			7.1%	8.4%
Hispanic			8.5%	12.1%
Asian			3.2%	4.4%
White			81.2%	75.1%
B. Percentage of racial group in suburbs[a]				
Black			33%	39%
Hispanic			46%	50%
Asian			51%	55%
White				
C. Neighborhood residential segregation				
Black/white[b]				
	Dissimilarity	.727	.678	.640
	Isolation	.655	.614	.591
Hispanic/white[c]				
	Dissimilarity	.502	.500	.509
	Isolation	.454	.508	.552

[a]Metropolitan areas with populations of 500,000 or more in 1990.
[b]For 270 metropolitan areas with significant black populations. National mean weighted by SMA (Simple Moving Average) black population.
[c]For 123 metropolitan areas with significant Hispanic populations. National mean weighted by SMA Hispanic population.
Sources: Section A of Table 10.4 Frey (2003), Table 9.7; Section B of Table 10.4 Katz (2005); Section C of Table 10.4 U.S. Census Bureau (2002), Tables 5-1, 6-1.

Hispanic/white segregation was somewhat lower over the period but showed no decline.[12]

Another indicator of segregation, the isolation index, measures the percentage of the minority population in the neighborhood of the average minority person. For blacks, the isolation index also declined, although it remained high. The large increase of the Hispanic population made the neighborhood composition of the typical Hispanic person more homogeneous in the final decades of the twentieth century. On average a Hispanic person was living in a neighborhood in 2000 that was about 55 percent Hispanic. Thus, whereas a few decades ago most minority members were confined to central cities that were themselves highly segregated at the neighborhood level, the new American pattern is of minority groups living in racially segregated neighborhoods in both cities and suburbs.

Immigration

The scale of immigration is transforming metropolitan America. The aggregate numbers are impressive. More than twice as many foreign-born people are living in the United States now as during the last great wave of immigration in the early twentieth century. By 2005 the immigrant population had topped 35 million, more than 12 percent of the entire country (Table 10.5A). Immigration has accounted for most of the increase in population growth of older cities. In recent years, however, immigrant population growth in the suburbs has been even more rapid. In the 1990s about 4.8 million immigrants were added to the population of the suburbs in the largest U.S. metropolitan areas, compared with 3.4 million to their central cities (Table 10.5B).

This tremendous increase in the foreign-born population, since its low point in 1970, is transforming metropolitan inequalities in profound ways and changing the meaning of race and racial categorization.[13] Black–white politics has become multidimensional. In many settings, descendants of U.S. slaves are a minority of black people with African ancestry. The largest "minority" group in America is now Hispanic. The great political and policy debates of the present moment are about neither racial nor economic equality but rather about illegal immigrants and immigration policy. At the same time, its impact so far has been highly differentiated. In 2000 half of the foreign-born population was concentrated in just thirteen metropolitan areas (Logan 2003). The previous categories of city, suburb, Sunbelt, and Snowbelt no longer suffice to categorize spatial inequality.[14] Whether at the level of description, explanation, or policy intervention, a new matrix algebra must replace the old universal calculus.

Concentrated Poverty

Of all the recent changes in the spatial organization of inequality, none has been more startling than the sharp deconcentration of poverty in the 1990s after two decades of expansion. As Table 10.6A shows, when defined as neighborhoods (i.e., census tracts) with at least 40 percent of residents poor by federal standards, the number of high-poverty neighborhoods in metropolitan areas declined from 2,791 in 1990 to 2,222 in 2000, and the proportion of the poor residing in such neighborhoods dropped from 17 to 12 percent.[15] If we count the total numbers of people—poor and nonpoor—who reside in such neighborhoods, the figures point in the same direction, whether they describe the United States as a whole,

Table 10.5

Immigration.

A. U.S. foreign-born population

	Number (millions)	Percentage of Population
1900	10.3	13.6%
1910	13.5	14.7%
1930	14.2	11.6%
1970	9.6	4.7%
1980	14.1	6.2%
1990	19.8	7.9%
2000	31.1	11.1%
2005	35.2	12.1%

Sources: Singer (2005), Figure 2.1; 2005 data from Camaraota (2005), Figure 2.

B. Population growth in the 69 largest metropolitan areas, 1990–2000 (thousands)

	Total	Cities	Suburbs
All persons	16,520	4,964	11,556
Native born	8,263	1,510	6,753
Foreign born	8,258	3,454	4,804

Source: Logan (2003), Table 4.

central cities, metropolitan suburbs, or non-metropolitan areas (Table 10.6C). Finally, the reduction in concentrated poverty was experienced by members of all races, but most notably by the black and Hispanic populations (Table 10.6D). For example, 30 percent of the black poor resided in high-poverty neighborhoods in 1990; only 19 percent did in 2000. In the case of Hispanics, the corresponding figures were 21 and 14 percent. In sum, concentrated poverty declined in all locations for all groups.[16]

The decline in highly impoverished places and in the population living in concentrated poverty reflects two trends: the overall reduction in poverty during a period of economic boom and the movement of poor people into new city and suburban neighborhoods.[17] Given the strong emphasis in the literature on the causal importance of place (neighborhood effects) in perpetuating poverty, one would have expected high-poverty neighborhoods to be self-sustaining. Instead, the drop in poverty itself seemed to explain the reduced concentration of the poor—rather than the reverse—and that decline reflected aggregate economic

Table 10.6

Trends in concentrated poverty, 1990–2000.

	1990	2000
A. Poverty rate 40% or more[a]		
Number of neighborhoods	2,791	2,222
Percentage of the poor	17%	12%
B. Poverty rate 30% or more		
Number of neighborhoods	5,433	5,224
Percentage of the poor	31%	26%
C. Residents of high-poverty[b] neighborhoods (thousands)		
United States	10,394	7,946
Central cities	7,560	5,988
Suburbs	1,089	1,041
Non-metropolitan	1,745	917
D. Percentage of the poor in high-poverty neighborhoods		
Black	30%	19%
Hispanic	21%	14%
Asian	13%	10%
White	7%	6%

[a]All data reflect federal poverty definitions.
[b]Poverty rate 40% or more.
Sources: Section A and B of Table 10.6, Kingsley and Pettit (2003), Table 1; Section C and D of Table 10.6 Jargowsky (1997), Figures 5.5, 5.4.

growth and employment demand.[18] Among the leading researchers on poverty, it was Paul Jargowsky who earlier predicted precisely this result when concentrated poverty was increasing sharply from 1970 to 1990. He concluded that concentrated poverty was an effect and not a cause[19]:

> Although a "tangle of pathology" may emerge in such [high-poverty] neighborhoods, the pathologies are a symptom of the problem, not the cause. The root causes of the increases in ghettos and barrios [i.e., black and Hispanic neighborhoods with poverty levels of at least 40 percent] in many northern cities are the changing opportunity structure faced by the minority community and, to a lesser degree, the changing spatial organization of the metropolis. (Jargowsky 1997)

Of course, even at the peak of concentrated poverty for the black poor, 70 percent of the population in poverty did not live in high-poverty neighborhoods, and the percentage of Hispanics, Asians, and whites not living in such places was much higher still. Most poor people have always resided in places where most of their neighbors were drawn from the working and middle classes. For these "deconcentrated" or, in the case of non-Hispanic whites, "dispersed" poverty populations, it never made sense to dwell on neighborhood effects.

When we think about racial and economic segregation and other spatial expressions of inequality, context matters. Some low-income neighborhoods should be cleared and put to better use, and some poor households would be better off if they were provided housing and social amenities elsewhere. Others would not. In research examining the effects on New Orleans residents of moving involuntarily to more affluent regions as a consequence of Hurricane Katrina, Vigdor (2007) found that they fared worse than comparable people who stayed in the city. The costs of relocation often are high in the disruption of family life and social networks. Many neighborhoods of concentrated poverty are well situated; again, we need to know the particular context to make a judgment. Social services usually are most available in central rather than peripheral locations. Immigrants may benefit substantially from living with their co-ethnics, even in neighborhoods that are largely poor. So the antidote to the very real hardships endured in poor neighborhoods may be worse than the disease.[20]

Space, Political Jurisdiction, and Social Structure

Even though place-based policies cannot go far in reducing poverty, the case can certainly be made to improve public amenities, housing, schools, and policing in poor neighborhoods. There is little question that these resource differences reinforce the gap between rich and poor. High tax rates, poorly financed schools, inadequate public facilities, limited opportunity to develop housing equity, impaired access to employment, and depressing environments all limit opportunities and send a message of marginality (Dreier et al. 2004). Within a national socioeconomic structure where inequality has worsened substantially, that inequality will necessarily manifest itself geographically.[21]

The glaring differences in resources between political jurisdictions within metropolitan areas have prompted repeated calls for consolidation or tax base sharing so as to facilitate equity (Orfield 2002; Rusk 2003). To be sure, restructuring metropolitan areas could make access to opportunity fairer, even if it does not increase the sum of opportunities. But in an extensive review of the research on the effects of metropolitan government, Margaret Weir (2004) concludes,

> Nor has consolidation been shown to have a positive impact on equity. Several case studies have concluded that consolidation increased the power of regional

elites at the expense of poor central city residents, especially regarding economic development decisions. . . . The consensus from this literature is that consolidated metropolitan governments are most effective at regional infrastructure issues and least effective at redistributive measures.[22]

Changing the boundaries of political jurisdictions so that central city majorities lose political power to the suburban diaspora weakens the ability of low-income people, particularly people of color, to affect resource allocation and gain political office.[23] Tax base sharing, which allocates revenues according to a formula that automatically favors poorer areas, is likely to be more efficacious than political consolidation in improving equity. Only marginally does tax base sharing address issues of inferior schooling, poor services, and other spatial expressions of inequality.

Bluntly, recalibrating political jurisdictions will never remedy inequality because it cannot change the class structure of society. However, it does have the potential to better the quality of life of people who suffer from various forms of disadvantage.[24] Reducing the rigidity of boundaries between neighborhoods and jurisdictions means that poor people can take greater advantage of the benefits of urban life. Henri Lefebvre (1996) discusses the right to the city, by which he means not simply that each person has a right to partake in urban life but also that the character of urban life should be fulfilling. As will be detailed in the next section, metropolitan areas can be improved through public policy so that everyone can benefit more from the advantages of urban agglomeration. Policy also can be shaped so that it does not, as is so often the case, make the poorest even worse off.

Equitable Spatial Policy

Much of the discussion related to the recent enthusiasm for metropolitan consolidation and regional institutions bears on governance structures rather than the actual content of programs.[25] Because representative institutions do not conform to actual agglomerations, advocates of consolidation and regional planning believe that redrawing boundaries would result in political institutions incorporating a broader range of interests, and more equitable policy would result. The difficulty here is that although metropolitan areas and regions constitute economic and environmental entities, they do not have a political meaning to most people. Therefore, it is unlikely that metropolitan or regional institutions would better represent groups, especially low-income groups, than do present forms.

In order to make public policy more equitable as it affects regions and metropolitan areas, it is necessary to consider the components of policy rather than to assume that more rationally designed institutions will produce better policy.

Equitable policy here is defined as the distribution of benefits to people in such a way that those who are the neediest receive disproportionate benefits. In the words of the *Cleveland Policy Planning Report* (Cleveland City Planning Commission 1982), policies should be designed to benefit the most disadvantaged, especially in agglomerations such as northern Ohio, where there are extremes of disadvantage that affect large numbers of people.[26] However, poor people alone are an ineffective political constituency. Moreover, policies benefiting low-income and minority groups should not be the product of a zero-sum game whereby the middle majority loses out. Thus, we propose policies in light of the following principles:

- Programs should aim at both poor and middle-majority populations and should combine people- and place-directed strategies (Fainstein and Markusen 1993). Moreover, they should be designed in ways that allow flexibility in response to particular local and metropolitan contexts.
- Redistribution without growth is not politically feasible or preferable; therefore, growth with equity must be the aim of policy.

Programs that provide benefits to middle-income people are obviously not as strongly redistributive as highly targeted programs. They can be justified as contributing to equity on two grounds. First, as the data in the first part of this chapter show, the middle majority of the population has seen its incomes stagnate and its relative position worsen; second, as many observers have pointed out, highly targeted policies are politically unpopular and become vulnerable to dissolution (as has been the case with public housing and Aid to Families with Dependent Children). Our support for growth as a public policy aim runs against progressive arguments that the striving for competitiveness characteristic of urban policy throughout the United States is counterproductive in terms of both equity and the environment (see McCann 2007). Nonetheless, although the side effects of growth can indeed be deleterious, the consequences of no growth in cities such as Detroit and Cleveland are worse. Under capitalism the only places we find that benefit from severe restrictions on growth are upper-class residential enclaves. At the same time, growth should not be the only or even primary aim of policy.

As noted earlier, we see little likelihood that the establishment of new metropolitan or regional institutions will improve the situation of disadvantaged people. Instead, and for several reasons, we believe that state governments already possess the power to rectify intra-metropolitan disparities through a variety of programs that will be described in the next section.[27] First, no constitutional change would be needed in order for them to fulfill this role. Second, they have at their disposal a broad tax base and need no permission from any other level of government in order to use it. Third, they possess regulatory powers that can be used to improve wages and working conditions. And fourth, their activities would not weaken urban political constituencies.

Clearly, our argument that focusing on existing state governments is more realistic than building metropolitan institutions invites the criticism that existing state governments have shortchanged urban interests and, given shrinking city population size relative to suburbs, will continue to do so. Weir et al. (2005) trace urban loss of influence in state legislatures to three factors: the weakening of state party organizations; term limits and diverging interests breaking up previous coalitions that brought together large cities with small depressed cities and poor rural areas; and impediments to governors' playing the role of broker in holding together coalitions favoring cities. Nevertheless, the authors hold out hope for new coalitions developed by grassroots organizers who link the interests of central city residents with suburbanites who also suffer from low income and environmental injustice. Such a political organizing strategy, along with a progressive agenda, offers the most promising subnational approach to dealing with equity issues. It is through mobilization and lobbying that the interests of disadvantaged people become represented in government, not through tinkering with jurisdictional boundaries.

Programmatic Goals

Policies to ameliorate spatial inequalities require people- and place-based approaches. The major redistributive programs addressed to individuals, such as Medicare, Medicaid, Social Security, Food Stamps, Temporary Aid to Needy Families, and the Earned Income Tax Credit are all federally funded.[28] Except in relation to educational support and subsidiary roles in some federal programs, states largely do not finance people-based programs and in fact are not the appropriate levels of government for income support.[29] Thus, the principal emphasis when looking for programs that states can sponsor to promote equity should fall largely on place-based programs. These can broadly be categorized into supply-side and demand-side programs.

Supply-Side Programs

Economic development programs have been significant state activities. They include industrial revenue bonds that make low-interest loans available to private investors; enterprise zones, which relieve businesses of tax liabilities and may also offer regulatory relief and various subsidies; and capital expenditures, especially on transportation facilities. Except for enterprise zones, most of these efforts are not specifically targeted to low-income areas. Analysis of the overall effect of the various tax incentive programs has demonstrated that they do not particularly benefit poor areas (Fisher and Peters 1998). Moreover, even when a subsidized firm locates in a low-income area, for example as the consequence of an enterprise zone, there is no guarantee that residents of the area will gain from its presence (Peters and Fisher 2002).

When state governments select capital expenditure projects, equity considerations rarely figure into their criteria. Customarily, states have reserved their capital spending, aside from their own office facilities, for sites in unincorporated areas, tourist attractions, transportation, and higher education facilities, with disproportionate resources for the latter going to flagship university campuses. Thus, commuter rail rather than bus services, highways instead of urban transit, and sports venues rather than public parks or recreation centers tend to get the bulk of funding. For example, the State of New York is contributing hundreds of millions of dollars to new stadiums for the Yankees and Mets baseball teams.[30] At the same time, while it develops and maintains parks in rural areas, it does not invest in poorly served areas of New York City, despite the needs of people who live there. A recent article commenting on two new city-built parks in the South Bronx notes,

> To some people in this neighborhood—where residents have waged long fights against what was a growth industry in waste transfer stations and scrap yards—the larger issue is how projects are planned in their out-of-the-way community. Despite the reassurance of officials, residents choose to remain a bit skeptical, noting for example that the parks are still closing before dusk and that sometimes no park workers are visible.
>
> "We got the parks, that is great and dandy, but how are we going to maintain them?" said Majora Carter, the founder of the environmental group Sustainable South Bronx, who was among the first to envision a riverside park on what had been a dump. "There is a fundamental problem we have had for a long time: unless it is a big, sophisticated project with value to tourists or businesspeople, it's forgotten. Our parks only serve the people here. But people up here need to know they have access to open space."

Greater equity requires that state-level investment in physical facilities be reoriented to promote economic development of a kind that would particularly target unskilled workers, provide affordable housing, and enhance access to recreational facilities in low-income communities. Other areas deserving greater state investment are higher education institutions that serve low-income students, especially community colleges, and local public schools, which currently receive state foundational support for annual expenses but usually not for construction. Most states have brownfield programs, and remediation sites often are located in poor areas; planning for reuse must prioritize functions that provide jobs, recreation, or housing for people who are unemployed or low income.

One very successful model for housing programs, which served a middle- as well as a low-income clientele, was New York State's Mitchell–Lama program. Established in 1955, the program financed 269 privately developed complexes with more than 105,000 units of housing, both rental and cooperatively owned, designed for working-class and lower middle-class occupants.[31] By the time the last building went up in 1979, the city and state had granted private developers more than $4.1 billion in low-interest, long-term loans and had also given them partial real estate tax exemptions. Because such housing produces a guaranteed cash flow, it can be financed by revenue bonds; therefore, it provides an excellent example of the way in which the financial power of state government can be used for a program remedying housing deficits at minimal cost to the taxpayer.

A number of states already have programs that subsidize first-time homeowners through loan guarantees. These programs could be expanded so that initial down payments are reduced or eliminated, either through a lease–purchase arrangement or, as was the case under the GI bill, brought down to zero. Such a program would be immensely popular, could be self-supporting, and would serve a range of households. Those currently subject to predatory lending and members of the middle class who are increasingly priced out of the ownership market could benefit.

State governments are able to enter into compacts with other states to develop regional programs that provide support for programs with equity-enhancing potential. The model here is the Appalachian Regional Commission (ARC). Although the ARC is a federally funded entity, a counterpart performing a similar function could be established by a compact between states. For instance, a compact in northern New England or along the Gulf Coast could benefit these areas of substantial deprivation. An evaluation of the ARC, 26 years after its inception, found that counties included in its mandate grew faster than a control group that did not receive similar assistance (Isserman and Rephann, 1995). Another evaluation of the ARC, though cautious in attributing improvements in the region to the ARC concluded that its "provision of local infrastructure and human resource investments ha[s] often made it possible for local areas to take advantage of the changes [caused by external economic forces]" (Bradshaw 1992:142). European Union structural funds have been important sources of capital spending for depressed regions there. Counterparts in the United States would require a federal commitment.

Regulatory and Demand-Side Programs

State regulatory programs have been instruments for enforcing equity since the days of Progressive reform in the nineteenth century. States pioneered wages and hours, occupational safety, workers' compensation, and public health regulation. Although eventually the federal government took control of many of these programs, states have retained the ability to superimpose their own more stringent controls on top of federal ones. For example, take the case of the minimum wage. Recently the State of Maryland enacted the nation's first statewide living wage statute, under which employers with state contracts will generally have to pay workers an amount well above the state and federal minimum wage (Greenhouse 2007).

Revision of state land use statutes to encourage infill and mixed-use development, inclusionary zoning, multifamily housing and equitable siting of noxious facilities represents an additional method available to state governments for redressing inequities between municipalities and improving access of low-income and minority households to housing. Because local land use law must conform to state statute, changes at the state level would filter down to municipalities. The experience of the State of New Jersey with the framing of its fair housing law and its state land use plan points in this direction. Under the former, municipalities lacking their fair share of affordable housing must either zone for it or contribute to a fund whereby it can be built elsewhere. Under the land use plan, higher densities are encouraged in certain parts of the state identified as growth corridors. The caveat regarding these often-cited precedents is that their implementation has had little effect on growth patterns in the state. What this indicates is that although state institutions offer a vehicle for forcing regional and metropolitan equity, institutional availability is insufficient to ensure results.

In terms of direct assistance to individuals, states do not have the financial capacity of the federal government to make a substantial difference. Still, some programs addressed to individuals and families are within the capacity of state government. Assistance to households in obtaining housing loans, daycare programs, and improved job training programs both directly benefit people and indirectly benefit their locations. Most importantly, alleviating fiscal inequities between jurisdictions, especially in regard to education spending, would be an important step toward improving the lives of the disadvantaged.

Conclusions

Our thesis is that only a strongly redistributional national state has the power to significantly ameliorate inequality within the United States. Spatial inequity certainly exists, and state-level policies could do much to improve the lives of those who, as a consequence of jurisdictional boundaries, receive inferior services from government. However, we cannot assume that equalization of services, or even disproportionate advantaging of poorer areas, provides a sufficient impetus to overcome the differentiation of earnings produced by the employment system or the disadvantages suffered by those raised in poverty and subjected to discrimination.

Furthermore, we argue that changing institutional structures so that municipalities encompass a greater diversity of inhabitants offers no guarantees concerning the content of policies. Undoubtedly, the present system of municipal government promotes a beg-thy-neighbor approach to policymaking. This causes central cities to have a weaker tax base than well-off suburbs and limits the possibility of coordinated metropolitan land use planning. However, we do not see evidence that enlarging central city boundaries or creating regional institutions would produce a political will to redress inequities within the new boundaries. State governments already possess the power to move toward this goal. That they do not exercise this power reflects the political weakness of low-income communities, not the lack of instruments that would allow it.

Notes

1. The United States is a metropolitan nation, with 83 percent of Americans residing in metropolitan areas. The number of metropolitan areas with populations larger than 1 million has grown from twenty-four in 1960 to forty-nine in 2005, and nearly two thirds of the population live within the bounds of the largest 100 (Katz et al. 2006). Following Census Bureau definitions, we will define regions as multicity sections of the country. Metropolitan areas are population concentrations that usually encompass a central city of at least 50,000 people and its surrounding jurisdictions (which we call suburbs). A few of the more than 300 metropolitan areas consist of a densely populated county or contiguous counties with no primary, central city.

2. By the early 1980s, all these forces were being played out on an even larger geographic scale as huge movements of people and jobs produced the regional shifts characterized by the decline of the Rustbelt and rise of the Sunbelt. The Sunbelt cities of the West and to a lesser extent the South displayed a different pattern from the older cities of the East and Midwest. Here, as a consequence of much larger areas being incorporated into central cities, economic, racial, and ethnic differences largely played themselves out within the boundaries of unified municipalities. However, the extent of inequality was not less.

3. However, black median household income is still only 64 percent of the white figure, compared with 61 percent in 1970. (Calculation based on U.S. Census Bureau 2005, Table A1.)

4. See Table A1 in U.S. Census Bureau 2005. In the quarter century ending in 2005, the median household income grew by only 13 percent, whereas that of the wealthiest quintile increased 27 percent and that of the richest 5 percent by 42 percent. The income share of the bottom quintile declined from 4.1 to 3.4 percent, and that of the middle quintile declined from 16.8 to 14.6, whereas the share of the wealthiest quintile grew from 44.2 to 50.4 percent. The Gini coefficient measures the deviation of the actual income distribution curve from an equal distribution; it varies from 0.000, where all households have the same income, to 1.000, where income is totally concentrated in the richest households. In 1979 the Gini coefficient stood at

.404; by 2005 it had grown steadily to .469, which made income inequality in the United States by far the greatest of any of the world's richest nations.

5. Following the current convention, we call individual census tracts "neighborhoods." They average 4,000 in population. Depending on population density, tracts may be larger or smaller geographically. Census tracts are drawn to coincide with boundaries that may also define neighborhoods. Nevertheless, it is somewhat misleading to characterize them as neighborhoods because we cannot assume that tracts with similar social composition are contiguous, much less coincide with what residents or local officials would call a neighborhood.

6. This is a commonly used relative definition of poverty that is sensitive to differences in metro standards of living and automatically controls for inflation. It defines a larger population as poor than does the federal definition. The data are for the 100 largest metropolitan areas.

7. Because much of the variance in family income is found within neighborhoods, median neighborhood incomes always cluster more strongly around the metro mean than do family incomes.

8. We again examined the 100 largest metropolitan areas, but with a slightly different set of income categories and a shorter timeframe.

9. This is the income at the fifth percentile and the ninety-fifth percentile of the distribution of per capita income for all suburban municipalities in the given Metropolitan Statistical Area (MSA) The ratio of those incomes is then averaged across the fifty SMAs at each decade.

10. However, central cities increasingly consist of minority groups because such a large percentage of whites reside in the suburbs.

11. Or of the city population, if that is the universe in which smaller units are located.

12. The Hispanic population may be either black or white, so we should expect Hispanic segregation to be lower than black.

13. When first Puerto Ricans and then foreign-born Hispanic immigrants entered the dichotomized racial world of the 1950s and 1960s, they called themselves minority groups. Later, a single category comparable to African American or black was made operative for the great variety of people who were of Hispanic linguistic background or Asian geographic background. In the 2000 Census, the government for the first time permitted the use of multiple ethnic and racial categories. All data collected by government agencies since 2000 permit multiple racial identities for individuals.

14. Singer (2005) creates a typology of metropolitan areas that depends on their history of immigration since the early 1900s. In recent years the pattern of immigration has differed substantially between these types with regard to both extent and ethnic composition.

15. A similar trend may be seen when the criterion for concentration is lowered to 30 percent poor in a census tract (Table 10.5B).

16. These findings are based on the federal definition of poverty. If a larger income category is used to define the poor—typically a relative measure of poverty, such as income below 50 percent of the median—then concentrated poverty remains largely unchanged in the 1990s (Swanstrom et al. 2006). But, of course, the meaning of *concentration* changes substantially when we change the definition of poverty so as to encompass a much larger percentage of the population.

17. It will be interesting to see what happens to the concentrated poverty figures after the next decennial census. If present trends continue, they may go up again. Little of the economic growth of the current decade has trickled down, and there has been a sharp rise in poverty among all groups. As of 2005, the national poverty rate had gone up to 12.6 percent (from 11.3 percent in 2000) and stood precisely where it had been in 1970; in a much larger U.S. population, however, almost 37 million people were poor in 2005, compared with about 25 million in 1970.

18. Strong support for the importance of macroeconomic factors is provided by the decline of non-Hispanic white poverty, because poor whites have never been concentrated in low-income neighborhoods. (This fact raises further serious questions about the importance in the first

place of neighborhood effects in causing or perpetuating poverty.) Thus, the percentage of non-Hispanic whites in poverty declined from 8.8 percent in 1990 to 7.4 percent in 2000, in absolute numbers a decrease in the number of poor, non-Hispanic whites of 1.2 million people.

19. Jargowsky (1997) found that 80 percent of the variance in concentrated poverty across metro areas could be explained by two variables: the relative robustness of the metro economy ("the metro-level opportunity structure") and the extent of racial segregation. He further concluded that the supposed "spatial mismatch" between high-poverty neighborhoods and job opportunities did not exist, except weakly in Northeast metro areas, and that travel times to employment were on average lower for high-poverty neighborhood residents in 1990 than for others in the same metro area (103–106).

20. Goetz (2003) provides an excellent discussion of the social science and public policy literature on concentration of poverty. He also reviews the findings on efforts in recent years to deconcentrate public housing and the low-income population. Most of his book examines a program for deconcentrating the poor in Minneapolis. Using several criteria, he assesses the effects on low-income households of both voluntary and forced deconcentration. (One of his cases focuses on a Southeast Asian immigrant neighborhood where residents are mainly opposed to moving.) Overall, he concludes that there are, at best, mixed benefits for poor households in moving into better-off neighborhoods, in part because their very move changes the character of the places where they are able to afford housing. He also shows that by itself a strategy of deconcentration will not have much effect on poverty and, though leading to the improvement of some neighborhoods, will also contribute to the deterioration of others, as the poor are simply moved from one place to another.

21. In a study of income inequality in global city regions, S. Fainstein (2001) showed that equity-oriented subnational governments were associated with nations supporting strong welfare states.

22. When using the term *region* here, Weir is referring to metropolitan areas.

23. Imbroscio (2006) calls the conventional approach of promoting regional growth "liberal expansionism." He notes that it is not simply a question of increasing resources to fund an equity agenda; "the politics also must be supportive of redistributing these available funds."

24. For example, the disabled benefit from policies that improve accessible transit or make public facilities accessible. However, these improvements will not remove their disability. Similarly, shortening the commutes of minimum wage workers will improve their lives but is unlikely to change their incomes.

25. The subject is undergoing one of its periodic revivals, even though, as Weir (2004:8) asserts, research on institutional forms has underscored the limits of consolidation and interlocal agreements as solutions to the issues of efficiency and equity in metropolitan areas.

26. This is in accordance with Rawls's difference principle, which in *Justice as Fairness: A Restatement* (2001:43) he summarizes as arrangements "that are to be to the greatest benefit of the least-advantaged members of society." This 2001 declaration is a more succinct statement than in his original *Theory of Justice* (Rawls 1971).

27. Altshuler (1998) comments, "State policy deliberations are more likely than local to avoid site specificity. This may . . . enable state officials to adopt regulatory standards and programs of financial aid without stirring up the fierce passions typically observed in site-specific disputes."

28. To the extent that the federal programs require a state contribution and give states latitude in determining benefits, the results have been to increase inequities between regions.

29. In a much-disputed book Paul Peterson (1981) argues that only national governments have the capacity for major redistributive programs. To some extent he obfuscates the difference between people- and place-based programs. We argue that he is incorrect when denying the possibility of progressive local policy. Moreover, he does not consider that local development programs can have serious negative effects on poor people through displacement. Nevertheless, he is right when describing the serious limits of city and state capacity to achieve large-scale redistribution.

30. In April 2006 the city's Independent Budget Office (IBO) estimated the total subsidy to the Yankees at $247 million, with $70 million coming from the State of New York (www .ibo.nyc.ny.us/iboreports/yankeeStadiumUpdate.pdf; accessed May 8, 2007). For the Mets the IBO estimated direct subsidies and exemptions from state and local taxes and access to tax-exempt bonds for building the stadium to cost the city $155 million (present value) and the state an additional $89 million over a 40-year period (www.ibo.nyc.ny.us/ibore ports/ Metsanalysis.pdf; accessed May 8, 2007). The public cost of expanding the Javits Convention Center was estimated in 2005 to be $1.4 billion (www.fiscalpolicy.org/FPI% 202005% 20NYC%20 Budget%20Briefing.doc; accessed May 8, 2007). The state has pledged to contribute $350 million to the first phase (www.nyc.gov/portal/site/nycgov/menu item.c0935b9a 57bb4ef3daf2f1c701c789a0/index.jsp?pageID=mayor_press_release&catID=1194&doc_name =http%3A%2F%2Fwww.nyc.gov%2Fhtml%2Fom%2Fhtml%2F2004b%2Fpr341 -04.html&cc=unused1978&rc=1194&ndi=1; accessed May 8, 2007).

31. http://www.dhcr.state.ny.us/Publications/ accessed May 9, 2007. No new housing is being constructed under Mitchell–Lama, and a number of existing developments have withdrawn from the program. Restrictions on moving the buildings into the private market lapse after a certain number of years.

References

Altshuler, A. A. 1998. The ideo-logics of urban land-use politics. In M. Derthick, ed. *Dilemmas of Scale in America's Federal Democracy*. Cambridge University Press, Cambridge.

Berube, A., and E. Kneebone. 2006. *Two Steps Backward: City and Suburban Poverty Trends*. Brookings Institution, Washington, D.C.

Birch, E. L. 2006. Who lives downtown? Pp. 29–59 in A. Berube, B. Katz, and R. E. Lang, eds. *Redefining Cities and Suburbs: Evidence from Census 2000* (Vol. 3). Brookings Institution Press, Washington, D.C.

Booza, J., J. Cutsinger, and G. Galster. 2006. *Where Did They Go? The Decline of Middle-Income Neighborhoods in Metropolitan America*. Metropolitan Policy Program, Brookings Institution, Washington, D.C.

Borjas, G. J. 1999. *Heaven's Door: Immigration Policy and the American Economy*. Princeton University Press, Princeton, NJ.

Bradshaw, M. J. 1992. *The Appalachian Regional Commission: Twenty-five Years of Government Policy*. University Press of Kentucky, Lexington.

Camarota, S. A. 2005. *Immigrants at Mid-Decade: A Snapshot of America's Foreign-Born Population in 2005*. Center for Immigration Studies, Washington, D.C.

Cayton, H., and S. C. Drake. 1945. *Black Metropolis: A Study of Negro Life in a Northern City*. Harcourt, Brace, New York.

Clark, K. 1965. *Dark Ghetto*. Harper & Row, New York.

Cleveland City Planning Commission. 1982 *Cleveland Policy Planning Report*. Cleveland, OH.

Dreier, P., J. H. Mollenkopf, and T. Swanstrom. 2004. *Place Matters*. University Press of Kansas, Lawrence.

Fainstein, N. 1993. Race, class, and segregation: Discourses about African Americans. *International Journal of Urban and Regional Research* 17(3):384–403.

Fainstein, S. 2001. Inequality in global city-regions. Pp. 285–298 in A. J. Scott, ed. *Global City-Regions*. Oxford University Press, Oxford.

Fainstein, S., and A. R. Markusen. 1993. Urban policy: Bridging the social and economic development gap. *University of North Carolina Law Review* 71:1463–1486.

Fisher, P. S., and A. H. Peters. 1998. *Industrial Incentives: Competition among American States and Cities*. W.E. Upjohn Institute for Employment Research, Kalamazoo, MI.

Fishman, R. 2005. The fifth migration. *Journal of the American Planning Association* 71(4):357–366.

Gelfand, M. I. 1975. *A Nation of Cities: The Federal Government and Urban America, 1933–1965*. Oxford University Press, New York.

Goetz, E. G. 2003. *Clearing the Way: Deconcentrating the Poor in Urban America*. Urban Institute Press, Washington, D.C.

Greenhouse, S. 2007, May 9. Maryland is first state to require living wage. Retrieved 2007 from www.nytimes.com/2007/05/09/us/09wage.html.

Imbroscio, D. L. 2006. Shaming the inside game: A critique of the liberal expansionist approach to addressing urban problems. *Urban Affairs Review* 42(2):224–248.

Isserman, A., and T. Rephann. 1995. The economic effects of the Appalachian Regional Commission: An empirical assessment of 26 years of regional development planning. *Journal of the American Planning Association* 61(3):345–364.

Jargowsky, P. A. 1997. *Poverty and Place: Ghettos, Barrios, and the American City*. Russell Sage Foundation, New York.

Jencks, C. 1992. *Rethinking Social Policy: Race, Poverty, and the Underclass*. Harvard University Press, Cambridge, MA.

Jencks, C., and P. E. Peterson, eds. 1991. *The Urban Underclass*. The Brookings Institution, Washington, D.C.

Katz, B., ed. 1993. *The "Underclass" Debate: Views from History*. Princeton University Press, Princeton, NJ.

———. 2005. *The State of American Cities and First Suburbs*. Unpublished presentation to the National Development Council.

Katz, B., R. Lang, and A. Berube. 2006. *Redefining Urban and Suburban America: Evidence from Census 2000*. Brookings Institution Press, Washington, D.C.

Kingsley, G. T., and K. L. S. Pettit. 2003. *Concentrated Poverty: A Change in Course*. Urban Institute, Washington, D.C.

Lefebvre, H. 1996. *Writings on Cities*. Oxford University Press, Oxford.

Logan, J. R. 2002. *Regional Divisions Dampen 90s Prosperity: New Census Data Show Economic Gains Vary by Region*. University of Albany, Lewis Mumford Center for Comparative Urban and Regional Research, Albany.

———. 2003. Ethnic diversity grows, neighborhood integration lags. Pp. 235–256 in *Redefining Urban and Suburban America* (Vol. 1). Brookings Institution, Washington, D.C.

Massey, D. S., and N. A. Denton. 1993. *American Apartheid: Segregation and the Making of the Underclass*. Harvard University Press, Cambridge, MA.

McCann, E. J. 2007. Inequality and politics in the creative city-region: Questions of livability and state strategy. *International Journal of Urban and Regional Research* 31(1):188–196.

Muller, T. 1993. *Immigrants and the American City*. New York University Press, New York.

O'Connor, A. 2001. *Poverty Knowledge: Social Science, Social Policy, and the Poor in Twentieth-Century U.S. History*. Princeton University Press, Princeton, NJ.

Orfield, M. 2002. *American Metropolitics: The New Suburban Reality*. Brookings Institution Press, Washington, D.C.

Peters, A. H., and P. S. Fisher. 2002. *State Enterprise Zone Programs: Have They Worked?* W. E. Upjohn Institute for Employment Research, Kalamazoo, MI.

Peterson, P. E. 1981. *City Limits*. University of Chicago Press, Chicago.

Piketty, T., and E. Saez. 2003. Income inequality in the United States, 1913–1998. *Quarterly Journal of Economics* 118(1):1–39.

Piven, F., and R. A. Cloward. 1967. Black control of cities. *New Republic*, September 30.

Puentes, R., and D. Warren. 2006. *One-Fifth of America: A Comprehensive Guide to America's First Suburbs*. Brookings Institution (Metropolitan Policy Program), Washington, D.C.

Rawls, J. 1971. *A Theory of Justice*. Harvard University Press, Cambridge, MA.

———. 2001. *Justice as Fairness: A Restatement*. Belknap Press, Cambridge, MA.

Rusk, D. 2003. *Cities without Suburbs: A Census 2000 Update*. Woodrow Wilson Center Press, Washington, D.C.

Saez, E. 2007. *Update of Piketty and Saez (2003) through 2005.* Retrieved June 15, 2007 from elsa.berkeley.edu/~saez/TabFig2005prel.xls.

Simmons, P. A., and R. E. Lang. 2003. The urban turnaround. Pp. 51–62 in *Redefining Urban and Suburban America* (Vol. 2). Brookings Institution, Washington, D.C.

Singer, A. 2005. The rise of new immigrant gateways. Pp. 41–86 in A. Berube, B. Katz, and R. E. Lang, eds. *Redefining Urban and Suburban America* (Vol. 2). Brookings Institution, Washington, D.C.

Sohmer, R. R., and R. E. Lang. 2003. Downtown rebound. Pp. 63–74 in A. Berube, B. Katz, and R. E. Lang, eds. *Redefining Urban and Suburban America* (Vol. 2). Brookings Institution, Washington, D.C.

Swanstrom, T., C. Casey, R. Flack, and P. Dreier. 2006. Pulling apart: Economic segregation in US metropolitan areas 1980–2000. Pp. 143–166 in A. Berube, B. Katz, and R. E. Lang, eds. *Redefining Urban and Suburban America* (Vol. 3). Brookings Institution, Washington, D.C.

U.S. Census Bureau. 2002. *Racial and Ethnic Segregation in the United States: 1980–2000.* U.S. Bureau of the Census, Washington, D.C.

———. 2005. U.S. Bureau of the Census, Washington, D.C.

———. 2006. *Income, Poverty and Health Insurance in the United States, 2005.* U.S. Bureau of the Census, Washington, D.C.

Vigdor, J. L. 2007. *The Katrina Effect: Was There a Bright Side to the Evacuation of Greater New Orleans?* Unpublished working paper, NBER. Durham, NC.

Ward, D. 1989. *Poverty, Ethnicity, and the American City, 1840–1925: Changing Conceptions of the Slum and the Ghetto.* Cambridge University Press, New York.

Weir, M. 2004. *A Century of Debate about Regionalism and Metropolitan Government.* Unpublished working paper, McArthur Foundation.

Weir, M., H. Wolman, and T. Swanstrom. 2005. The calculus of coalitions: Cities, suburbs, and the metropolitan agenda. *Urban Affairs Review* 40(6):730–760.

Wilson, W. J. 1987. *The Truly Disadvantaged: The Inner City, the Underclass, and Public Policy.* University of Chicago Press, Chicago.

Wirth, L. 1928. *The Ghetto.* Chicago University Press, Chicago.

Part III

SPATIAL PLANNING FOR A FUTURE AMERICA

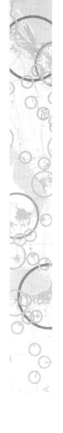

11

Novel Spatial Formats
Megaregions and Global Intercity Geographies

Saskia Sassen

Major shifts in the scales, spaces, and contents of economic activity are engendering novel spatial formats. Among the more prominent of these are global cities, megaregions, and global intercity geographies. These shifts call for shifts in our interpretations and policy frameworks to adjust to these novel spatial formats and maximize their benefits and distributive potential.

Rather than reviewing all components of this transformation, I examine the spatial features and economic contents of megaregions and global urban networks. The policy issues are sufficiently complex and diverse across administrative units to warrant a separate discussion. Furthermore, the ongoing formation of global cities is by now a well-documented trend and one that has elicited a rapidly growing scholarship worldwide; therefore, it seems less urgent to address in such a short chapter. I touch on global cities only insofar as they are part of the other two spatial formats I examine.

Megaregions and global intercity geographies are two very different formats. But I will argue that it is possible, analytically, to identify similar dynamics at work in both. Two such dynamics stand out. One is scaling and its consequences—in this case megaregional scaling and global scaling. The other dynamic is the interaction between geographic dispersal and new kinds of agglomeration economies, which in this case are operating within a megaregion and within the new global intercity geographies, respectively. Specifying a common analytic ground for these two very diverse spatial forms should enable us to develop a sharper approach to empirical research and possibly policy. These very diverse spatial forms also should help us assess the extent to which policy decisions can encourage greater economic integration between a country's more globalized cities and its other areas currently performing subordinate functions within the national territorial hierarchy. In other words, taking a megaregional scale might help in connecting the winners and the laggards; the megaregion here becomes a scale that includes both globalizing and provincial cities and areas. This raises a question as to whether this connecting of winners and laggards can also be extended to cross-border intercity networks by strengthening the connections between winners and laggards across borders.

One consequence is that not only winners get privileged, as is typical with targeting of resources to enable the formation of world-class cities and silicon valleys, but also laggards. More precisely, laggards can be enabled to become dynamically interconnected with winners within a megaregion in ways that replicate current practices at the global scale, notably outsourcing to low-cost areas, and in novel ways made possible because the low-cost area is within a megaregion. The hope would be that rather than pursuing the usual economic policies focused on the most advanced sectors, this would make a strong case for concentrating on the poorer regions, not as charity but as a recognition that they are part of the advanced sectors (again, as is the case when major firms outsource to low-cost areas across the world). Multiple components of major new economic dynamics combine a need for both lower-cost areas and dense high-cost areas. To mention just one of several examples, this type of framing would bring value to poorer areas in the most developed countries because these might be developed to become advantageous for the location of activities that are now being outsourced to low-wage countries. The aim would be to avoid a race to the bottom, as happens when these activities are offshored, and to provide alternative or complementary development paths to today's prevalent path, which is to privilege exclusively high-end economic activities such as biotech parks and luxury office parks.

Parallel to this effort to incorporate laggards or less successful areas into policy frames that today target mostly successful areas is the effort to understand how cities in the middle range of urban hierarchies fit in today's global intercity geographies. In the case of the United States, for instance, many of these midrange cities are also part of megaregions. The analytic bridge between megaregions and intercity geographies is the fact that the operational chains of a growing number of firms today are part of both these spatial formats. This opens up a whole new research agenda about economic globalization and place, in addition to the global city scholarship. Here I examine data from a recent study of the fifty global hubs, which includes nine U.S. cities. In addition, and using a different study, I developed a kind of "small world" sample of very diverse cities, from globally powerful to minor, and mapped their interconnections. This helps us get at cross-border networks connecting cities at diverse levels of each national urban hierarchy involved. The purpose here is to broaden the range of globalizing cities in the analysis beyond the usual top forty global cities in the world and to reduce their overwhelming analytical and empirical weight. Similarly, examining the top nine U.S. cities is a way of expanding the analysis beyond the familiar top three or four global cities in the United States. It shows that as corporate economic globalization has expanded, so have the numbers and types of territorial insertions of global city functions; in the case of the United States, today these go well beyond New York City. This expanded focus also allows us to capture the growth and diversification of global intercity flows.

These are some of the issues addressed in the chapter. The first section is a brief introduction of megaregions and global intercity geographies. The second section brings together critical analytic issues for the study of these two spatial formats. The third and fourth sections then apply these to megaregions and intercity geographies, respectively.

Two Novel Spatial Formats

One major tendency evident throughout the world is the formation of increasingly large urbanized areas, which at some point are best described as megaregions. Here I take the Regional Plan Association (RPA) definition of ten emergent megaregions in the United States, each at a different level of development (RPA 2006). Often these are merely seen as more of the same—more people, more endless urban landscapes. At its most elemental the megaregion results from population growth in a geographic setting where cities and metro areas blend into each other. And this does indeed call for cross-regional infrastructures, notably transport and electricity, and various forms of regional planning and coordination, as can be seen today. But are these conditions, which amount to an expanded version of urbanization economies, all there is to consider?

A basic starting point for my analysis is that a megaregion is sufficiently internally diverse that it can contain diverse spatial logics, particularly agglomeration and dispersal logics, which might translate into high-cost, high-density areas and low-cost, low-density areas. We know that large integrated firms need both types of areas for their operations. Thus the megaregional scale can enable the exploration of novel development strategies predicated on this diversity of spatial logics, ideally to the advantage of both the more advanced and the least advanced areas within that megaregion. It would take innovative governance umbrellas and new types of private–public arrangement.

The most common advantages of scales larger than that of the city, such as metropolitan and regional scales, come from sharing transport infrastructures for people and goods, enabling robust housing markets, and possibly supporting the development of office, science, and technology parks. More complex and elusive is whether the benefits of megaregional economic interaction can go beyond these familiar scale economies. There is no definitive research on this subject. Thus empirical specification can only be partial because the available evidence is fragmentary for the urban level, a shortcoming that becomes acute when dealing with the novel category of the megaregion.[1] However, we have enough analysis and evidence on one particular component of this subject—the advantages for global firms and markets of particular types of agglomeration economies at the urban level—that we can begin to use it as a lens for the megaregional scale that can take us beyond urbanization economies. Agglomeration economies are to be distinguished from such familiar urbanization economies. They involve complex interactions of diverse components, not simply, for instance, more people using a train line and the scale economies this might enable.

I argue that the specific advantages of the megaregional scale consist of and arise from the coexistence in one regional space of multiple types of agglomeration economies. These types of agglomeration economies are distributed across diverse economic spaces and geographic scales: central business districts, office parks, science parks, the transportation and housing efficiencies derived from large (but not too large) commuter belts, low-cost manufacturing districts (today often offshore), tourism destinations, specialized branches of agriculture (e.g., horticulture or organically grown food), and the complex kinds of agglomeration economies evident in global cities. Each of these spaces evinces distinct agglomeration economies and, empirically at least, is found in diverse types of geographic settings, from urban to rural, from local to global.

The thesis is that a megaregion is sufficiently large and diverse to accommodate a far broader range of types of agglomeration economies and geographic settings than it typically does today. This would take the advantages of megaregional location beyond the notion of urbanization economies. A megaregion can then be seen as a scale that can benefit from the fact that our complex economies need diverse types of agglomeration economies and geographic settings, from extremely high-agglomeration economies evinced by specialized advanced corporate services to fairly modest economies evinced by suburban office parks and regional labor-intensive low-wage manufacturing. It can incorporate this diversity into a single economic megazone. Indeed, in principle, it could create conditions for the return of particular activities now outsourced to other regions or to foreign locations.[2]

Thus the critical dimension for the purposes of this chapter is not just a question of the contents of a megaregion, such as its economic sectors, transport infrastructure, housing markets, and types of goods and services that get produced and distributed, exported and imported—a sort of X-ray of a megaregion. Also critical is the specification of economic interactions within the megaregion in order to detect what could be reincorporated into that region (e.g., factories or routine clerical work that is now outsourced to other national or foreign areas) and to detect emerging megaregional advantages.

One path into the question of megaregions and the global economy is through the particular global circuits that connect it across borders. The diversity of subeconomies in a megaregion signals a possibly equally diverse set of such cross-border circuits. Identifying these circuits is significantly easier in some of these subeconomies (e.g., Silicon Valley, Hollywood) than in others (e.g., the Midwestern machine- and tool-making export-oriented sector, Wall Street). The best data available today on these global circuits, beyond specialized firm studies and commodity chains (e.g., Wal-Mart), concern global financial and specialized services, which are mostly intercity networks. Particular networks connect particular groups of cities. This allows us to recover details about the diverse roles of cities in the global economy.

The formation of intercity geographies is contributing a sociotechnical infrastructure for a new global political economy, new cultural spaces, and new types of social networks. Some of these intercity geographies are thick and highly visible: the flows of professionals, tourists, artists, and migrants among specific groups of cities. Others are thin and barely visible: the highly specialized electronic financial trading networks that connect particular cities depending on the type of instrument involved. A bit thicker are the global commodity chains for diverse products that run from exporting hubs to importing hubs. Later in this chapter I briefly examine some of these specialized intercity geographies.

An often overlooked dimension underlying these intercity geographies, and one that I keep stumbling upon in my research, is that today's global economy brings to the fore the specialized capabilities of different cities and regions. The more common notion is that it homogenizes economies. This is only partly correct. It homogenizes standards, and it engenders global markets for standardized products. But it also captures the specialized differences of places. These intercity geographies contain multiple such specialized circuits, many connecting minor places with each other.

The specialized economic histories of major cities and regions matter in today's global economy because there is a globally networked division of functions. This fact is easily obscured by the common emphasis on competition and by the standardization (no matter how good the architecture) of built environments. This also means that today's megaregions need to extract these specialized capabilities; this might include some very different economies in different sites of a given megaregion. It is important to standardize transport infrastructures and various standards across a megaregion. But this should not obscure the fact that the value-adding potential of that region may well lie in the particular economic and cultural capabilities of the different types of sites, urban and nonurban, of that region. These types of particularities come to the fore in the evidence on the different types of advantages of U.S. cities in the global economy and in the small-world sample of intercity connections, both examined later in this chapter.

This also means that a city's or a region's role in these intercity geographies not only is determined by its rank but in fact can be critically shaped by its specialized capabilities. Elsewhere I have argued that the common notion of the homogenizing of the urban landscape in today's economy misses a critical point. It misses, or obscures, the diversity of economic trajectories through which cities and regions become globalized, even when the final visual outcomes look similar. Out of this surface analysis based on homogenized landscapes comes a second possibly spurious inference, that similar visual landscapes are a function of convergence. Both propositions—that similar visual landscapes are indicators of both similar economic dynamics and of convergence—may indeed capture various situations. But key conditions are not captured and in fact are rendered invisible by such notions. Similar landscapes may contain very different economies and therefore may not be competing but be complementary. At the scale of the megaregion this can become very significant.

The Diverse Spatial Logics of Megaregions: Does Their Interaction Add to Economic Growth?

Translocal chains of operations are increasingly common for many firms and for whole economic sectors. Establishing which segments of such chains are located in a given area becomes important in the specification of that area. One set of familiar categories through which to establish this is agglomeration versus dispersal of a firm's operations.

My thesis is that the megaregion is a scale that can accommodate a very broad range of the segments in a firm's or a sector's chain of operations (from those subject to agglomeration economies to those that can be dispersed to low-cost, low-density areas) and thus can derive multiplier growth effects from the fact that they are both part of the same operational chain. Thus this thesis captures one very specific and partial feature of megaregions, but it is one overlooked in the emergent discussion about these regions. Furthermore, by positing this particular dynamic I do not want to minimize the significance of urbanization economies and scale economies. Both matter and can make an enormous difference to the economic well-being of a region. I merely want to add yet another variable and argue that part of the specificity of the scale of the megaregion is that it can accommodate such diverse but mutually dependent spatial logics in ways that would be almost impossible in cities or suburbs. Today, these dependencies are largely organized at a global scale, with outsourcing the most familiar format. The substantive rationality for my pursuit of this thesis is that it contains the possibility of significant equity effects that are lost at the current global scale, where they are in fact transformed into a race to the bottom when it comes to workers' wages and work conditions.

Thus one first step is to examine why and when a firm's or a sector's agglomeration sites are articulated with its geographic dispersal sites. Examination of agglomeration economies in the current period is framed by two facts that are potentially in tension with each other. On one hand, new information technologies enable firms to disperse a growing range of their operations, whether at the metro, regional, or global level, without losing system integration.[3] This has the potential to reduce (but not eliminate) the benefits of urbanization economies for such firms; whether this also reduces agglomeration economies for these firms is a more complicated question. In my research I find that for some headquarters such a move brings with it a greater need to buy inputs, which used to be produced in house, and that it is these inputs whose production continues to evince agglomeration economies and therefore tend to be bought from firms located in cities. On the other hand, the evidence clearly shows a preference for high-density locations for firms in a large range of advanced economic sectors; such locational preferences point to the existence of agglomeration economies, although the character of the latter has also changed (Sassen 2006b, 2001).

I first address the most extreme instance: globalized firms with digitization of their production process and their outputs. In this case there are conceivably fewer and fewer agglomeration advantages, especially for the most advanced sectors, typically high-value producing, able to buy the latest technologies, and highly globalized, that is, with multiple operations across the world. Contesting this technologically driven explanation, one can show how and why these firms are subject to extreme agglomeration economies in some—though not all—of their components.[4] This fact matters for understanding megaregional advantage because megaregions contain extremely dense cities with diverse resources and types of talent that can deliver the agglomeration economies leading firms need. A second implication for the megaregion is that it can accommodate the second types of sites that characterize so many of the leading economic sectors, basically low-cost, underdeveloped areas.

The growth effects resulting from interactions of a firm's diverse types of sites give this finding added meaning for megaregions. Therefore, one of the hypotheses in my global city model is that a firm's central headquarter functions expand as a result of that firm's multi-sitedness (whether national or global).[5] The more affiliates, service outlets, and factories a firm has worldwide, the more its central management and servicing functions expand. This is a significant growth potential that can be endogenized into a megaregion. This growth effect goes beyond the mere addition of jobs resulting from that megaregion capturing more sites of a firm's chain of operations, in itself an attractive potential. It also adds a complex networked dynamic that begins to articulate very diverse parts of a megaregion.

Does Geographic Dispersal Feed Agglomeration Economies?

A good starting point is to focus on why the most advanced firms of the knowledge economy are subject to what often seem to be extreme agglomeration economies, even when they function in electronic markets and produce digitized outputs. Another way to ask the question is by focusing on the most globalized and digitized of all knowledge sectors: Why does global finance need financial centers? Or, more generally, why do highly specialized global corporate services that can be transmitted digitally thrive in dense downtowns? This means inserting place in an analysis of knowledge economies that are usually examined in terms of their mobility and space–time compression. Looking at the knowledge economy and, more broadly, global firms from the optic of regions, cities, or metro areas brings in different variables.[6]

In its sharpest formulation the question then becomes, "Why do cities matter for global firms, particularly global firms that are rich enough to buy whatever technical innovations free them from place, its frictions, and its costs? Furthermore, why do they matter in a way they did not as recently as the 1970s, when major headquarters were far more likely to leave cities?" Here are three logics that contribute to an answer.[7]

The first one is that no matter how intensive a user of digital technology a firm is, its operational logic is not the same as the engineer's logic for designing that technology. Confusing these two potentially very diverse logics has produced a whole series of misunderstandings. When new information and communication technologies began to be widely used in the 1980s, many experts forecast the end of cities as strategic spaces for firms in advanced sectors. Many routinized sectors did leave cities, and many firms dispersed their more routine operations to the regional, national, and global scale. But the most advanced sectors and firms kept expanding their top-level operations in particular types of cities.

Why were those experts so wrong? They overlooked a key factor: When firms and markets use these new technologies, they do so with financial or economic objectives in mind, not the objectives of the engineer who designed the technology. The logics of users may well thwart or reduce the full technical capacities of the technology.[8] When firms and markets disperse many of their operations globally with the help of the new technologies, the intention is not to relinquish control over these operations. The intention is to keep control over top-level matters and to be capable of appropriating the benefits of that dispersal.[9] Insofar as central control is part of the globalizing of activities, their top-level headquarter functions actually have expanded because it is more complex and risky to function in thirty or fifty or more countries, each with distinct laws, accounting rules, and business cultures.

As these technologies are increasingly helpful in maintaining centralized control over globally dispersed operations, their use has also fed the expansion of central operations. The result has been an increase in high-level office operations in major cities and a growth in the demand for high-level and highly paid professional services, either produced in house or bought from specialized service firms. Thus, the more these technologies enable global geographic dispersal of corporate activities, the more they produce density and centrality at the other end: the cities where their headquarter functions get done.

A second logic explaining the ongoing advantages of spatial agglomeration has to do precisely with the complexity and specialization level of central functions. These rise with globalization and with the added speed that the new information and communication technologies allow. As a result, global firms increasingly need to buy the most specialized financial, legal, accounting, consulting, and other services. These service firms get to do some of the most difficult and speculative work. It is increasingly these corporate service firms that evince agglomeration economies, because their work benefits from being in complex environments that function as knowledge centers because they contain multiple other specialized firms and high-level professionals with worldwide experience. Cities are such environments; the more than forty global cities in the world are the most significant of these environments, but a growing number of other cities are strong in particular elements of such environments. In brief, cities or central places provide the social connectivity that allows a firm to maximize the benefits of its technological connectivity.[10]

A third logic concerns the meaning of information in an information economy. There are two types of information. One is the datum, which may be complex yet is standard knowledge: the level at which a stock market closes, a privatization of a public utility, a bankruptcy. But there is a far more difficult type of information, akin to an interpretation, evaluation, and judgment. It entails negotiating a series of data and a series of interpretations of data in the hope of producing a higher-order datum. Access to the first kind of information is now global and immediate (even if often for a high fee) from just about any place in the highly developed world and increasingly in the rest of the world thanks to the digital revolution.

But the second type of information requires a complicated mixture of elements—the social infrastructure for global connectivity—which gives major financial centers a leading edge. When the more complex forms of information needed to execute major international deals cannot be gotten from existing databases, no matter what one can pay, then one needs to make that information; it becomes part of the production process in specialized corporate service firms, including financial services both as service providers and as firms in their own right. That making includes as a critical component: interpretation, inference, and speculation. At this point one needs the social information loop and the associated de facto interpretations and inferences that come with bouncing information off talented, informed people. It is the importance of this input that has given a whole new importance to credit rating agencies, for instance. Part of the rating has to do with interpreting and inferring. When this interpreting is considered authoritative, it becomes information available to all. For specialized firms in these complex domains, credit ratings are but one of these inputs; the making of authoritative information must be part of a production process, either in house or bought from specialized firms. This process of making inferences and interpretations into information takes an exceptional mix of talents and resources. Cities are complex environments that can deliver this mix.

The key implication of this analysis for megaregions is the possibility of containing at least some of the dispersed operations of a given firm and its central headquarters. The feedback effects of containing both can be significant, feeding growth in a megaregion's low-cost, possibly marginal areas and in its global cities, or cities that are national business centers.

One question at this point is whether the megaregions identified by RPA do contain cities with such global potentials, one of the poles for the type of megaregional multiplier effects discussed earlier.

Cities in the Global Economy: Connecting Their Megaregions

A new dataset shows nine U.S. cities rather than the usual four to be major commercial hubs in the global economy. In addition to New York, Chicago, Los Angeles, and Boston, the list includes San Francisco, Atlanta, Miami, Houston, and Washington, D.C. The data were collected from the perspective of firms and investors who want to do business globally. The study gets at equity issues through variables such as basic services and quality of life, which bring down some of the major centers characterized by large numbers of poor and degraded residential and commercial areas. But the study does not really get at issues of inequality per se, which we know from other sources are critical in global cities (Sassen 2006b).

The data come from the MasterCard Worldwide (2007) Centers of Commerce study of how major cities compare in performing critical functions that connect markets and commerce globally. The index was developed by a panel of eight experts from different parts of the world (including me) under the direction of Dr. Yuwa Hedrick-Wong from MasterCard Worldwide.[11] We started out with sixty-three cities that met the initial criteria. We used 100 data points organized into subindicators, which eventually were aggregated into six overall indicators (legal and political framework, economic stability, ease of doing business, financial flow, business center, and knowledge creation and information flow). The result was that fifty of these sixty-three qualified as major commercial hubs in the global economy, including nine U.S. cities (Table 11.1).

Of interest to the question of megaregions is that about half of the megaregions identified by RPA (2006) in the United States contain at least one, but typically more, of these global commercial hubs. The overall MasterCard Global Centers of Commerce (GCOC) Index finds that these nine cities are in the top twenty-three in the world, with New York, Chicago, and Los Angeles in the top ten, and the lower-ranked four (Atlanta, Miami, Houston, and Washington, D.C., in that order) grouped in the four lowest spots. For Tables 11.2–11.4, I selected only a few indicators and subindicators to bring to the fore the strengths of cities such as Atlanta (usually not listed in the top four) and the weaknesses of the top cities, notably New York. The purpose is to illustrate the strengths and weakness of U.S. cities in this global infrastructure for corporate capital and the variability of these strengths and weaknesses once we isolate specific criteria. Although the purpose here is not to describe the results of this study, it is worth highlighting a few results. Atlanta ranks above all other U.S. cities when it comes to the indicator "political and legal framework" and three of the subindicators it comprises (licenses, registering property, and trading across borders) listed in Table 11.1. This shows the strength of the U.S. system when it comes to large corporations, in contrast to increasing difficulties of the U.S. system in regulating particular financial markets, which helps explain New York's consistently low ranking on this indicator; I should add that I have left out several of the familiar variables where New York ranks at the top.

Next I briefly examine the emergence of a variety of cross-border circuits connecting cities in the midrange of the global hierarchy. This signals the possibility of expanded participation by a larger number of U.S. cities than the usual three or four (New York, Chicago, Los Angeles, and Boston). Insofar as these

Table 11.1

Top 30 cities for selected indicators.[a]

Rank	GCOC (Global Centers of Commerce) Index	Indicator 1: Political and Legal Framework	Indicator 3: Ease of Doing Business	Indicator 5: Business Center
1	London	Stockholm	Vancouver	Hong Kong
2	**New York**	Copenhagen	Toronto	London
3	Tokyo	Singapore	Montreal	Singapore
4	**Chicago**	**Atlanta**	Singapore	**New York**
5	Hong Kong	**Boston**	London	Tokyo
6	Singapore	**Washington, D.C.**	Dublin	**Los Angeles**
7	Frankfurt	**Chicago**	Copenhagen	Paris
8	Paris	**Houston**	San Francisco	**Chicago**
9	Seoul	**Los Angeles**	New York	Amsterdam
10	**Los Angeles**	**Miami**	Los Angeles	Shanghai
11	Amsterdam	**New York**	**Washington, D.C.**	Seoul
12	Toronto	**San Francisco**	Hong Kong	Frankfurt
13	**Boston**	Montreal	**Boston**	**Miami**
14	Sydney	Toronto	**Chicago**	Bangkok
15	Copenhagen	Vancouver	Stockholm	Toronto
16	Madrid	Berlin	Tokyo	Dubai
17	Stockholm	Frankfurt	**Miami**	**Atlanta**
18	**San Francisco**	Munich	Brussels	Sydney
19	Zurich	London	Sydney	Melbourne
20	**Atlanta**	Tokyo	**Atlanta**	**San Francisco**
21	**Miami**	Zurich	**Houston**	**Houston**
22	**Houston**	Geneva	Melbourne	Montreal
23	**Washington, D.C.**	Vienna	Zurich	Madrid
24	Berlin	Melbourne	Frankfurt	Vancouver
25	Milan	Sydney	Geneva	**Washington, D.C.**
26	Munich	Amsterdam	Amsterdam	Milan
27	Montreal	Barcelona	Munich	Brussels
28	Vancouver	Madrid	Berlin	**Boston**
29	Brussels	Dublin	Paris	Dublin
30	Vienna	Dubai	Vienna	Munich

[a]Aggregate of all indicators. U.S. cities are in bold.
Source: MasterCard Worldwide Centers of Commerce (2007).

cities are in megaregions other than the well-established Northeast corridor, it also signals expanded participation in the global economy by megaregions.

Global Intercity Geographies: From Hierarchical to Transverse

One way of thinking about the global economy is in terms of the many highly specialized circuits that make it up. Different circuits contain different groups of countries and cities. Viewed this way, the global economy becomes concrete and specific, with a well-defined geography. Globally traded commodities—gold, butter, coffee, oil, sunflower seeds—are redistributed to a vast number of destinations, no matter how few the points of origin might be. The expansion of global trade has brought hundreds and hundreds of locations into these networks.[12]

These circuits are multidirectional and criss-cross the world, feeding intercity geographies with both expected and unexpected strategic nodes. For instance, New York is the leading global market to trade financial instruments on coffee, even though it does not grow a single bean. But a far less powerful financial center, Buenos Aires, is the leading global market to trade financial instruments on sunflower seeds. Cities located on global circuits, whether few or many, become part of distinct, often highly specialized intercity geographies. Thus, if one were to track the global circuits of gold as a financial instrument, it is London, New York, Chicago, and Zurich that dominate. But if I track the direct trading in the metal, Johannesburg, Mumbai, Dubai, and Sydney all appear on the map.

In the last 20 years there has been a sharp increase in the capacity to control some of these economic circuits. Thus, although the commodities themselves may come from more than eighty countries and are sold in all countries of the world, about twenty financial exchanges control the global commodity futures trading. The map tightens when the seventy-three commodities thus traded are aggregated into three major groups. Five major global futures exchanges (NYME, LME, CBOT, TCOM, and IPE), located in New York, London, Chicago, and Tokyo, and concentrate 76 percent of trading in these seventy-three commodity futures traded globally. Aggregated into three major groups, one single market clearly dominates in each. For agricultural commodity futures, the CBOT (Chicago) controls most global trading, for energy it is the NYME (New York), and for metals, the LME (London).

This tighter map of commodity futures trading illustrates the role of cities in today's globalizing and increasingly electronic economy. This is one of those points where global cities enter the picture. They are not the places where commodities are produced, but they are the places where commodity futures are in-

Table 11.2

Top 30 cities for selected indicators and subindicators (part 1 of 3).

	GCOC (Global Centers of Commerce Index)	Dealing with Licenses	Registering Property	Trading across Borders	Political and Legal Frameworks[a]	Quality of Life	Basic Services
1	London	Copenhagen	Riyadh	Hong Kong	Stockholm	Los Angeles	Singapore
2	New York	Bangkok	Stockholm	Copenhagen	Copenhagen	San Francisco	Copenhagen
3	Tokyo	Tokyo	Atlanta	Singapore	Singapore	Sydney	Frankfurt
4	Chicago	Stockholm	Boston	Berlin	Atlanta	Melbourne	Munich
5	Hong Kong	Singapore	Washington, D.C.	Frankfurt	Boston	Milan	Vancouver
6	Singapore	Dublin	Chicago	Munich	Washington, D.C.	New York	Tokyo
7	Frankfurt	Paris	Houston	Montreal	Chicago	Rome	Zurich
8	Paris	Berlin	Los Angeles	Toronto	Houston	Berlin	Stockholm
9	Seoul	Frankfurt	Miami	Vancouver	Los Angeles	Boston	Vienna
10	Los Angeles	Munich	New York	Stockholm	Miami	Washington, D.C.	London
11	Amsterdam	Atlanta	San Francisco	Vienna	New York	London	Montreal
12	Toronto	Boston	Zurich	Dubai	San Francisco	Paris	Atlanta
13	Boston	Washington, D.C.	Geneva	Atlanta	Montreal	Vancouver	Paris
14	Sydney	Chicago	Dubai	Boston	Toronto	Chicago	Sydney
15	Copenhagen	Houston	Singapore	Washington, D.C.	Vancouver	Johannesburg	Toronto
16	Madrid	Los Angeles	London	Chicago	Berlin	Tokyo	Amsterdam

17	Stockholm	**Miami**	Montreal	**Houston**	Frankfurt	Vienna	**Boston**
18	**San Francisco**	**New York**	Toronto	**Los Angeles**	Munich	**Atlanta**	Brussels
19	Zurich	**San Francisco**	Vancouver	**Miami**	London	Brussels	**Washington, D.C.**
20	**Atlanta**	Seoul	Beijing	**New York**	Tokyo	Frankfurt	Geneva
21	**Miami**	Montreal	Chengdu	**San Francisco**	Zurich	**Miami**	Melbourne
22	**Houston**	Toronto	Shanghai	Amsterdam	Geneva	Toronto	Berlin
23	**Washington, D.C.**	Vancouver	Shenzhen	London	Vienna	Amsterdam	**Chicago**
24	Berlin	Mexico City	Bangkok	Tel Aviv	Melbourne	Barcelona	**New York**
25	Milan	Melbourne	Amsterdam	Barcelona	Sydney	**Houston**	**Houston**
26	Munich	Sydney	Santiago	Madrid	Amsterdam	Munich	**Los Angeles**
27	Montreal	Santiago	Copenhagen	Melbourne	Barcelona	São Paulo	**Miami**
28	Vancouver	Zurich	Moscow	Sydney	Madrid	Zurich	**San Francisco**
29	Brussels	Geneva	St. Petersburg	Paris	Dublin	Copenhagen	Dubai
30	Vienna	Copenhagen	Vienna	Tokyo	Dubai	Dublin	Hong Kong

U.S. cities are in bold.

[a]This indicator comprises more than the preceding set of subindicators.

Source: MasterCard Worldwide Centers of Commerce (2007).

Table 11.3

Top 30 cities for selected indicators and subindicators (part 2 of 3).

	Banking Services	Investor Protection	Corporate Tax Burden	Contract Enforcement	Ease of Doing Business	Financial Service Network	Starting a Business
1	Amsterdam	Singapore	Hong Kong	Copenhagen	Vancouver	London	Montreal
2	Barcelona	Hong Kong	Dubai	Stockholm	Toronto	**New York**	Toronto
3	Berlin	Kuala Lumpur	Riyadh	Hong Kong	Montreal	Hong Kong	Vancouver
4	Brussels	**Atlanta**	Dublin	Melbourne	Singapore	Tokyo	Melbourne
5	Zurich	**Boston**	Zurich	Sydney	London	Singapore	Sydney
6	Copenhagen	**Washington, D.C.**	Geneva	**Atlanta**	Dublin	Paris	Copenhagen
7	Dubai	**Chicago**	London	**Boston**	Copenhagen	Beijing	Stockholm
8	Dublin	**Houston**	Singapore	**Washington, D.C.**	**San Francisco**	Milan	**Atlanta**
9	Frankfurt	**Los Angeles**	Santiago	**Chicago**	**New York**	Shanghai	**Boston**
10	Geneva	**Miami**	Montreal	**Houston**	**Los Angeles**	Frankfurt	**Chicago**
11	Hong Kong	**New York**	Toronto	**Los Angeles**	**Washington, D.C.**	Madrid	**Houston**
12	London	**San Francisco**	Vancouver	**Miami**	Hong Kong	**Chicago**	**Los Angeles**
13	Madrid	Tel Aviv	Copenhagen	**New York**	**Boston**	Zurich	**Miami**
14	Munich	Montreal	Stockholm	**San Francisco**	**Chicago**	Sydney	**New York**
15	**New York**	Toronto	Melbourne	Tokyo	Stockholm	**Los Angeles**	**San Francisco**
16	Paris	Vancouver	Sydney	Zurich	Tokyo	Mexico City	**Washington, D.C.**

17	Singapore	Dublin	**Atlanta**	Geneva	**Miami**	Mumbai	Dublin
18	Stockholm	Johannesburg	**Boston**	London	Brussels	São Paulo	Hong Kong
19	Vienna	London	**Washington, D.C.**	Dublin	Sydney	Toronto	Singapore
20	Budapest	Tokyo	**Chicago**	Montreal	**Atlanta**	Bangkok	Paris
21	**Washington, D.C.**	Brussels	**Houston**	Toronto	**Houston**	Dublin	London
22	Kuala Lumpur	Copenhagen	**Los Angeles**	Vancouver	Melbourne	Seoul	Brussels
23	**Los Angeles**	Santiago	**Miami**	Budapest	Zurich	Amsterdam	Geneva
24	Milan	Bogotá	**New York**	Paris	Frankfurt	Buenos Aires	Zurich
25	Montreal	Warsaw	**San Francisco**	Singapore	Geneva	**Atlanta**	Amsterdam
26	Riyadh	Mumbai	Beirut	Vienna	Amsterdam	**Boston**	Tel Aviv
27	Sydney	New Delhi	Istanbul	Seoul	Munich	Jakarta	Moscow
28	Tokyo	Mexico City	Seoul	Moscow	Berlin	Johannesburg	St. Petersburg
29	Toronto	Bangkok	Johannesburg	St. Petersburg	Paris	Kuala Lumpur	Tokyo
30	Vancouver	Stockholm	Tokyo	Brussels	Vienna	**San Francisco**	Bangkok

Other U.S. cities

Boston (31)
Chicago (32)
Miami (34)
San Francisco (38)
Atlanta (40)
Houston (42)

Other U.S. cities

Houston (33)
Miami (39)
Washington, D.C. (50)

U.S. cities are in bold.

[a]This indicator comprises more than the preceding set of subindicators.

Source: MasterCard Worldwide Centers of Commerce (2007).

Table 11.4

Top 30 cities for selected indicators and subindicators (part 3 of 3).

	Employing Workers	Closing a Business	Air Passenger Traffic	Air Cargo Traffic	Conventions, Exhibitions, Meetings	Commercial Real Estate Development	Business Center[a]
1	Atlanta	Singapore	London	Hong Kong	London	Hong Kong	Hong Kong
2	Boston	Tokyo	Chicago	Tokyo	Berlin	New York	London
3	Chicago	Montreal	Atlanta	Seoul	Paris	Singapore	Singapore
4	Houston	Toronto	Los Angeles	Shanghai	Hong Kong	São Paulo	New York
5	Los Angeles	Vancouver	Paris	Frankfurt	Singapore	Buenos Aires	Tokyo
6	Miami	Brussels	Houston	Paris	Barcelona	Toronto	Los Angeles
7	New York	Amsterdam	New York	Singapore	Vienna	Vancouver	Paris
8	San Francisco	Dublin	Tokyo	Los Angeles	Munich	Milan	Chicago
9	Washington, D.C.	London	Frankfurt	London	New York	Seoul	Amsterdam
10	Singapore	Seoul	Washington, D.C.	Miami	Istanbul	Rio de Janeiro	Shanghai
11	Hong Kong	Melbourne	Madrid	New York	Prague	Dubai	Seoul
12	Melbourne	Sydney	Amsterdam	Chicago	Bangkok	Tokyo	Frankfurt
13	Sydney	Hong Kong	Shanghai	Amsterdam	Seoul	Madrid	Miami
14	Montreal	Atlanta	Beijing	Dubai	Madrid	Caracas	Bangkok
15	Toronto	Boston	Milan	Bangkok	Tokyo	Tel Aviv	Toronto
16	Vancouver	Chicago	Toronto	Beijing	Shanghai	Kuala Lumpur	Dubai

17	Copenhagen	**Houston**	São Paulo	**Atlanta**	Moscow	Istanbul	**Atlanta**
18	Riyadh	**Los Angeles**	Moscow	Brussels	Buenos Aires	**Miami**	Sydney
19	London	**Miami**	Rome	Kuala Lumpur	Dubai	Moscow	Melbourne
20	Kuala Lumpur	**New York**	Hong Kong	San Francisco	Beijing	Shenzhen	San Francisco
21	Bangkok	**San Francisco**	Munich	Milan	Brussels	**San Francisco**	**Houston**
22	Geneva	**Washington, D.C.**	Bangkok	Sydney	Budapest	**Chicago**	Montreal
23	Zurich	Stockholm	**Miami**	Shenzhen	Amsterdam	Montreal	Madrid
24	Santiago	Barcelona	Seoul	São Paulo	Milan	Amsterdam	Vancouver
25	Beirut	Madrid	**San Francisco**	Mumbai	São Paulo	Johannesburg	**Washington, D.C.**
26	Dubai	Copenhagen	**Boston**	**Houston**	Dublin	Santiago	Milan
27	Tokyo	Vienna	Barcelona	Mexico City	St. Petersburg	Sydney	Brussels
28	Tel Aviv	Bogotá	Mexico City	Toronto	Stockholm	Shanghai	**Boston**
29	Warsaw	Berlin	Jakarta	New Delhi	Melbourne	London	Dublin
30	Dublin	Frankfurt	Sydney	Jakarta	**Chicago**	New Delhi	Munich

Other U.S. cities   **Washington, D.C. (34)**

Other U.S. cities   **Boston (31)**

Atlanta (40)

Washington, D.C. (41)

Los Angeles (50)

Houston (55)

U.S. cities are in bold.

a This indicator comprises more than the preceding set of subindicators.

Source: MasterCard Worldwide Centers of Commerce (2007).

vented so as to facilitate the global trading of these commodities and partly manage some of the associated risks. This tighter map also makes concrete one of the main counterintuitive trends evident in today's global economy: that the more globalized and nonmaterial the activity (trading in financial instruments), the more concentrated the global map of those activities.

There are other such global maps, beyond commodities, commodity futures, and finance in general. Here I will focus on the global networks of global service firms, which show us yet another version of this mix of globally distributed operations and high-agglomeration economies. One way of tracking the global operations of firms is through their overseas affiliates. The top 100 global service firms have affiliates in 315 cities worldwide. For all multinational firms, the figure jumps to 1 million overseas affiliates.

Global Service Firms: Feeding Intercity Geographies

Mapping the global operations of specialized service firms gives us a mirror image of the sharp concentration of the financial futures exchanges mentioned earlier. Their central operations are about managing the sales of their services to as many places as possible, where futures trading markets seek to concentrate as big a share of the trade in commodities. The servicing operations of these firms are in demand in a growing number of cities as globalization expands. When countries open up to foreign firms and investors and allow their markets to become integrated into global markets, it is often foreign service firms that take over the most specialized servicing; it happened in cities as diverse as Buenos Aires and Beijing.

But the data point to a new pattern emerging along with this expanded globalization: the rise of cities such as Mumbai and Dubai as centers for servicing regional operations. More generally, the data show more transverse connectivities—that is, between cities in the midrange emerging as service centers for other midrange cities, rather than all international servicing originating in the leading global cities, as was the case in the 1980s and much of the 1990s. Returning to the question of megaregions in the United States, this growth of transverse midrange connectivities points to an opening up of possibilities for midrange cities in the United States.

What follows is clearly one particular mapping of connectivity in a group of very diverse cities. I derived a sample of 24 cities from a 315-city dataset developed by Peter Taylor and his colleagues (2004; see generally the GaWC Web site), who have generously put the data in the public domain. These 24 cities include some, not all, of the top global cities and middle-range cities in the global hierarchy. Except for Turin and Lagos, the 24 cities are in the top third of the 315 cities where these firms have headquarters or branches. The following analysis is confined to the intercity connectivities between these 24 cities, rather than the 315 cities in the original dataset.

The numbers capture the extent to which these 24 cities are connected through the office affiliates networks of these 100 global service firms, mostly headquartered in major global cities. This information is one microcosm of a pattern that repeats itself over and over with a variety of other types of transactions, such as the almost meaningless measure of a city with McDonald's outlets or the extreme concentration of the commodity futures discussed earlier. Against this background, the connectivity measures of such office networks are a middle ground, very much a part of the infrastructure for the new intercity geographies.

Table 11.5 shows the overall connectivity of these cities for six major corporate services. The table shows only the aggregate values, based on six different corporate service industries. Five of our cities are among the top 10 of the worldwide total for the 315 cities where these firms have operations. London and New York stand out in our sample, as they do in the world generally, with vastly higher levels of connectivity than any other city. A second diverse group for our 24 cities includes Tokyo, Milan, Los Angeles, and São Paulo. A third group includes Mexico City, Jakarta, Buenos Aires, Mumbai, Shanghai, and Seoul. A fourth group is Moscow, Johannesburg, Istanbul, Manila, and Barcelona. A fifth group includes Caracas, Bogotá, Berlin, Dubai, and Cairo. Turin and Lagos are at a much lower level of connectivity. Turin, with the lowest connectivity of the cities in the sample, nonetheless houses offices of fourteen of these global firms, pointing to the extent to which these firms network the world, albeit on their specialized and partial terms.

Some of these outcomes reflect key patterns in the remaking of space economies. (Tables for each of the specific service industries are on file with the author.) Thus Berlin and Turin rank low because the major international financial and business centers in their respective countries, Frankfurt and Milan, are extremely powerful in the global network and concentrate a growing share of the global components in their national economies. This is a pattern that recurs in all countries. In banking and finance, Jakarta's connectivity is high because it is a major and long-established banking center for the Muslim world in Indonesia's geopolitical region and hence of great interest to Western firms but also in need of these firms to bridge into the West. Shanghai's connectivity is high because it is one of the major financial and, especially, corporate centers for the region, and it has become the leading national stock market in China, with Hong Kong having regained its position as China's leading international financial center.

Table 11.5

Select cities: Ranking and relative global network connectivity between 24 cities (all sectors).[a]

Rank	All Service Sectors	Gross Connectivity	Proportional Connectivity	Relative Global Network Connectivity[b]
1	London[b]	11,789	0.0874	1
2	New York	11,524	0.0855	0.978
3	Tokyo	8,533	0.0633	0.724
4	Milan	7,178	0.0532	0.609
5	Los Angeles	7,068	0.0524	0.6
6	São Paulo	6,561	0.0487	0.557
7	Mexico City	5,824	0.0432	0.494
8	Jakarta	5,782	0.0429	0.49
9	Buenos Aires	5,779	0.0429	0.49
10	Mumbai	5,579	0.0414	0.473
11	Shanghai	5,293	0.0393	0.449
12	Seoul	5,210	0.0386	0.442
13	Moscow	5,079	0.0377	0.431
14	Johannesburg	5,026	0.0373	0.426
15	Istanbul	5,004	0.0371	0.424
16	Manila	4,847	0.0359	0.411
17	Barcelona	4,770	0.0354	0.405
18	Caracas	4,317	0.032	0.366
19	Bogotá	4,182	0.031	0.355
20	Berlin	4,117	0.0305	0.349
21	Dubai	4,033	0.0299	0.342
22	Cairo	4,011	0.0297	0.34
23	Lagos	1,997	0.0148	0.169
24	Turin	1,343	0.01	0.114

[a]We chose six major specialized corporate service sectors: banking, finance, management consulting, advertising, legal accounting, and insurance. Uses the Taylor method but applies it to a sample of 24 cities to measure the connectivity between these 24 cities.
[b]London = 100.

South Korea is the tenth largest economy in the world and has undergone significant deregulation since the 1997 Asian financial crisis. This has made Seoul an attractive site for Western financial firms as foreign investors have been buying up a range of holdings in both South Korea and Thailand since the 1997 financial crisis, even as many local firms, including factories, have gone under.

Dubai is an interesting case that points to the making of a whole new region, one not centered in the operational map of our top 100 global service firms. Only in the last few years has Dubai become an important financial and business center at the heart of a new emergent region that stretches from the Middle East to the Indian Ocean; its financial global connectivity is not derived principally from Western financial firms but increasingly its own and its region's firms. Its specific financial connectivity is not picked up when the focus is on the interactions between the cities, but its accounting connectivity is extremely high for the very simple reason that Western-style accounting rules the world.

When these global connectivity measures are disaggregated by specialized sectors, there is much reshuffling because of the high level of specialization that marks the global economy. In accountancy, Mexico City and, perhaps most dramatically, Dubai and Cairo move to the top. They are becoming deeply connected with global economic circuits, they mediate between the larger global economy and their regions, and thus they offer the top global accounting firms plenty of business. In contrast, Shanghai moves sharply down; the global accounting firms have set up their operations in Beijing because going through the Chinese government remains critical.

The other sectors evince similar reshufflings. The often sharp change in the degree of connectivity for different sectors in a given city generally results from misalignments between global standards for legal and accounting services and the specifics of the national systems. Global insurance firms have clearly decided that locating in Johannesburg and Shanghai makes sense; this move to the top ten among our cities signals that the domestic insurance sector either is not sufficiently developed or is too "un-Western" to satisfy firms and investors, and therefore foreign insurance firms can gain a strong foothold. The low connectivity of Seoul and Mumbai tell us that the domestic insurance sector is taking care of business. The high connectivity for legal services in the case of Moscow, São Paulo, and Shanghai, which all move into the top ten, signals the need for Western-style legal services in a context of growing numbers of foreign investors and firms. São Paulo, for instance, hosts about seventy financial service firms from Japan alone.

In management and consultancy, Buenos Aires, São Paulo, Seoul, and Jakarta move into the top ten cities in our sample, in good part because of the dynamic opening of their national economies in the 1990s and the resulting opportunities for foreign and national firms and investors. Barcelona, Mumbai, and Cairo have drawn far fewer of our global 100 service firms because either the domestic sector could provide the services, as is the case in Mumbai and Cairo, or the opportunities lay elsewhere, as is suggested by Spain's investments throughout Latin America, now even including banking in the United Kingdom.

For the top 100 global advertising firms, Mumbai and Buenos Aires, both with rich cultural sectors and industries, were a strong draw. Again, the weaker presence of global advertising firms in Cairo and Dubai results from these cities' stronger orientation to their emergent region.

London has the strongest presence of these global firms in accounting, banking, finance, and insurance, and New York is strongest in advertising and management consulting. It should be noted that this dominance is due mostly to the sharp concentration of headquarters and branches.

The global map produced by the operations of the top 100 service firms is dramatically different from that produced by the financial trading of commodity futures, which is in turn different from that of the trading in actual commodities. The extreme concentration evident in finance would stand out even more if a map were drawn of goods trading and the innumerable criss-crossing circuits connecting points of origin and destination. It does suggest that the specialized services are a sector that seeks out cities; as far as these firms are concerned, the more the better.

Implications for Megaregions

There is much to be said about megaregions.[13] Here the concern is to identify possible types of intraregional economic interactions that could be enabled by the megaregional scale. The focus is on two key issues. The first is whether such interactions might mean moving beyond economic planning styles that focus on only the most advanced economic sectors, such as "knowledge economies," and begin to find value in the less developed areas of a region and lower-income jobs. The second is whether this co-presence of high- and low-value areas might give megaregions particular advantages in today's global economy. If both of these are indeed the case, it is useful to ask whether and how novel types of megaregional coordination and governance could help in extracting and realizing these advantages. The central effort is to take the benefits of megaregions beyond familiar scale economies—that is, beyond the advantages of bigger and more of the same, whether mega-parking lots or longer train routes.

One component of this analysis is whether a megaregion can seek to accommodate a larger range of the operations constituting a firm's value chain—

from high-agglomeration sites to dispersal sites. Practically speaking, this points to the possibility of bringing into or back to a megaregion some of the services and goods producing jobs and operations now offshored to take advantage of lower wages and fewer regulations. Can these services and goods be reinserted into the low-growth, low-cost areas of a megaregion? What type of planning would it take, and can it be done so as to optimize the benefits for all involved, not only firms but also workers and localities? This would expand the project of optimizing growth beyond office parks and science parks, the preferred options today, and move across far more diverse economic sectors. It would use the lever of the megaregional scale to provide diverse spaces catering to different types of activities, ranging from those subject to high-agglomeration and those subject to low-agglomeration economies. And, finally, the megaregional scale would help in optimizing the growth effect arising from the interactions of some of these diverse agglomeration economies. This growth effect would be optimized by reregionalizing some of the low-cost operations of firms today spread across the country or the world.

This way of thinking about the megaregional scale raises the importance of planning and coordination to secure optimal outcomes for all parties involved, including the challenge of securing the benefits firms are after when they disperse their operations to low-wage areas. This would work for some types of economic sectors and types of firms, not for all. Some activities that have been outsourced to other countries have not worked out and have been repatriated; they range from airline sales agents to particular types of design work in industries as diverse as garments and high-tech. But many of these outsourced activities are doing fine as far as the firms are concerned. Research and specific policies are needed to establish the what, how, and where of the advantages for the pertinent firms of accessing low-wage workers in the United States; this includes understanding how location of these low-cost components in the megaregion where a given firm is headquartered could compensate for higher costs. This may require megaregional investment in developing low-cost areas for such jobs—a kind of rural enterprise zone.

There is possibly a positive macro-level effect from repatriating some of these jobs if a race to the bottom can be avoided and a certain level of consumption capacity secured in low-income areas of a region through reasonable wages or particular indirect subsidies. This brings a specific positive effect for a megaregion's less developed areas because lower-wage households tend to spend a much larger share of their income in their place of residence; they lack the investment capital of upper-income strata, who can allocate most of their income to overseas investments. Finally, this is also one element in the larger challenge of securing more equitable outcomes.[14] It is important to ask about the distributive effects of the current configuration and of potentially optimized outcomes, as described in this chapter; there is sufficient evidence of how inequitable distribution of the benefits of economic growth is not desirable in the long run.

These ways of specifying the meaning of a megaregion (or a region) take us from a "packaging" approach to a more dynamic concept of the megaregion: Beyond urbanization advantages, a megaregion may well turn out to be a sufficiently large scale to optimize the benefits of containing diverse and interacting agglomeration economies.

Today's information technologies and communication capabilities can deliver system integration no matter how far-flung the operations of a firm or sector might be. If all firms and sectors can buy and use these technologies to reduce or neutralize agglomeration economies and advantages, the result would be a decline in the benefits of locations that deliver agglomeration economies, most notably global cities. Such a decline would be further strengthened by the possibility of rising shares of e-commuters working online from home.

In its most extreme version this scenario suggests that the advantages of locating in a megaregion would be limited to urbanization economies. Firms need to locate somewhere, and so do their workers, so why not a megaregion? Furthermore, regardless of whether there are specific megaregional location advantages, there would be a demand for local suppliers of final and intermediate goods and services that must be produced in situ—those that cannot be imported from far away, or at least not yet. The fact of population growth itself is enough to feed this type of demand.

Under these conditions, the specificity of megaregional locational advantages comes down to the fact that there is a market, or rather a whole range of markets for needed goods and services, both final and intermediate. Transportation, housing, office buildings, factory buildings, and so on all meet a real demand by households, governments, and their multiple instances, from schools to courts, institutions of all sorts, and firms. As populations and distances grow, novel types of demand emerge: for high-speed rail, superhighways, and more diversity in the housing supply. No matter how complex the components of this final and intermediate demand, this is, in some ways, a very elementary version of the advantages of the megaregional scale.

Is there more to megaregional advantage? Location is a variable. The firm that can replace agglomeration advantages with the new information technologies represents one extreme case on the location variable; it evinces minor if any agglomeration economies. The fact of population growth, and the associated need for housing and all that comes with it, is in many ways the same type of point on that variable; the difference is that it is subject to urbanization advantages. At the other end of these two cases are high-agglomeration economies; this is well established for very specialized branches of global finance and the most innovative branches of high-tech industries, with global cities and silicon valleys the respective emblematic spatial forms.

The advantages of location in a megaregion in these three diverse types of instances must be empirically specified. In the first two cases the particular advantage is some very broad, geographically expanded notion of urbanization advantages: the bundle of infrastructures, labor markets, buildings, housing, basic institutional resources, and amenities. In a megaregion these advantages spread over a vast geographic terrain, engendering the specific components of final and intermediate demand (e.g., rapid transit systems).

The question then becomes how to enhance these urbanization advantages and how to avoid excessive growth and its negative effects on congestion, prices, costs, and so on. Whether markets or planning is the desirable instrument to optimize "urbanization" economies (broadly understood to include not only urban locations) depends on a range of variables. One potentially innovative line of analysis here is the extent to which the megaregion allows novel ways of handling negative externalities.

On the other hand, in the case of sectors subject to agglomeration economies, it may well be the case that the megaregion does not contain distinctive advantages over other scales, notably cities and metro areas. What these sectors seem to need is a bundle of resources that correlate with high-density and, at the extreme, very dense central places, such as global cities and silicon valleys. The question then becomes whether one or several specific types of agglomeration economies can develop and be enhanced at the scale of the megaregion. Megaregions contain high-density locations; a firm subject to agglomeration economies may well find the mix of highly specialized diverse resources it needs in one of those locations. But does it need a whole megaregion attached to that location?

One critical hypothesis developed for the global city model is that insofar as the geographic dispersal of the operations of global firms (whether factories, offices, or service outlets) feeds the complexity of central headquarter locations, the more globalized a firm, the greater the advantages its headquarters derives from central locations.[15] One inference is that the advantage of a megaregional scale is that it could, in principle, contain both the central headquarters and at least some of those dispersed operations of global firms. In other words, is a megaregion a scale at which such firms can also outsource jobs and suburbanize headquarter functions—both in search of cheaper costs—and benefit from the region's major cities, including in some cases global cities or cities with significant global city functions?

Can megaregions deliver particular advantages if they can also contain some of the geographically dispersed operations of a firm? The evidence shows that increasingly the spatial organization of firms and economic sectors contains both points of spatial concentration and points of dispersal. Furthermore, the evidence also shows that in many cases these points of spatial concentration contain segments in a firm's chain of operations that evince strong agglomeration economies. One underlying (and disciplining) trend here, becoming visible already in the 1970s, is that spatial concentration is costlier for many firms so that the push is to disperse whatever operations can be dispersed; this contrasts with earlier periods when even large headquarters kept all functions in one place. This dispersal of a firm's operations can be at a regional, national, or global level, and agglomerations might vary sharply in content and in the specifics of the corresponding spatial form.[16] For instance, among U.S. cases, consider Chicago's financial center, Los Angeles's Hollywood, and northern California's Silicon Valley: Each delivers agglomeration economies to firms and sectors that also contain often vast geographic dispersal of some of their other operations.

A focus on the fact that much economic activity contains both spatial concentration and translocal chains of operations helps us situate the specifics of a city, a metro area, or a megaregion in a far broader systemic condition, one that might include both points subject to sharp agglomeration economies and points that are not—where geographic dispersal is an advantage. What the megaregion offers in this context is a bigger range of types of locations than a city or a metro area—from locations subject to high-agglomeration economies all the way to locations where the advantage comes from dispersal.

Taking it a step further, most globalized and innovative firms were characterized by the fact that agglomeration economies are themselves partly a function of dispersal. That is to say, the more globalized and thus geographically dispersed a firm's operations, the more likely the presence of agglomeration economies in particular moments (the production of top-level headquarter functions) of that firm's chain of operations.[17] For the purposes of this chapter, it underlines the fact of a single dynamic with diverse specializations (i.e., both agglomeration and dispersal) across diverse geographic scalings; a megaregion would then conceivably be a scaling that could incorporate these different settings.

One way of specifying some of this empirically is to posit a direct relationship between growth in a megaregion's locations for dispersed economic activities and locations for activities subject to high-agglomeration economies. The more the former grow, the more the latter will also grow. The trick is then to maximize the co-presence in a given megaregion of these two types of locations. It is important to notice that this also sets limits to the advantages of urbanization economies. The latter turn out to be a curve: They grow with scale, up to a point. That point typically is specified in terms of negative externalities. But what my analysis here suggests is that this point can also be specified in terms of the economic losses derived from not allowing the "development" of dispersal locations; because this means locations where firms can send their low-wage jobs requiring little education, it clearly goes against the prevailing aims of most places, which is to get high-wage, capital-intensive jobs. Finally, if what is today the point on the curve where familiar negative externalities set in (e.g., excess congestion) can be made to coincide with the development of "dispersal locations" for firms, an advantage could be made out of what is now a disadvantage.

In practical terms, there are clearly enormous challenges for a megaregion to achieve this type of co-presence, maximizing the extent to which a megaregion can contain both the agglomeration and dispersal segments of a firm's chain of operations. For one, it is a counterintuitive proposition. It is not easy to see why a megaregion's highly dynamic economic spaces (the central areas of its global cities and silicon valleys), anchored by the headquarters of global and national firms, might actually be partly fed and strengthened by development of the "dispersal locations" of those same firms. Thinking of developing such "dispersal locations" as one way of making the most of negative externalities might make it more acceptable to the skeptics; you might as well go for activities that benefit from geographically dispersed arrangements once you hit excess congestion disadvantages. But one option at this point is such items as golf courses and exurban luxury housing. This argument could be countered because megaregions tend to contain much land that is not optimal for such uses but could be optimal for developing "dispersal locations"; furthermore, and critical to some of my substantive concerns for disadvantaged areas, these could benefit from such development if a race to the bottom is avoided.

The megaregion can then be seen as an interesting scalar geography: It can contain some of the dispersals of a firm's operations that feed these new kinds of agglomeration economies. It would suggest that strategic regional planning could aim at maximizing the combination of different locational logics. It is this combination that in my view marks the specificity of the project contained in the notion of the megaregion.

Notes

1. For a definitive examination of the shortcomings of the data on subnational scalings, see the report by the National Academy of Sciences (2003). See also OECD (2006, 2007).
2. Besides regionalizing various segments of a firm's chain of operations, one might also propose to regionalize more segments of various commodity chains. See Gereffi et al. (2005).
3. For one of the best datasets on dispersal at the global scale of the operations corporate service firms, see Globalization and World Cities Study Group and Network GWAC (2008).
4. A parallel issue here, not fully addressed in this chapter, is the articulation of technical connectivity with social connectivity. See Garcia (2002) and Ernst (2005).

5. This is a type of agglomeration economy I found in my research on global cities, but it can also be applied to national or regional scales. The hypothesis was that the greater the capabilities for geographic dispersal a firm has, the higher the agglomeration economies it is subject to in some of its components, notably top-level headquarter functions. See Sassen (2001) for a brief explanation of the nine hypotheses that specify the global city model. The most specialized functions of the most globalized firms are subject to the highest agglomeration economies. The complexity of the functions that must be produced, the uncertainty of the markets such firms are involved in, and the growing importance of speed in all these transactions constitute a new logic for agglomeration. It is not the logic posited in older models, where weight and distance (cost of transportation) are seen to shape agglomeration economies. The mix of firms, talents, and expertise in a broad range of specialized fields makes a certain type of dense environment function as a strategic knowledge economy wherein the whole is more than the sum of its parts.

6. This spatial lens is also to be distinguished from the more common angle of firms and markets (see Ernst 2005).

7. For a full development of this subject, see Sassen (2006a, Chapters 5 and 7; 2001).

8. For a detailed explanation of this thwarting of technical logics by the economic, financial, or cultural and political logics of users, see Sassen (2006a, Chapter 7).

9. Today's multinationals have more than 1 million affiliates worldwide. Affiliates are but one mode of global operation. For empirical details about the range of formats of global operations, see Sassen (2006b, Chapter 2; Taylor 2004; World Federation of Exchanges 2007 and annual updates).

10. For a detailed examination of the importance of the subnational scale for a global market, see Harvey (2007).

11. The members of the group were Professor Fan Gang, director, National Economic Research Institute, Beijing; Manu Bhaskaran, partner and head, economic research, Centennial Group, Singapore; Dr. Michael Goldberg, professor emeritus, Sauder School of Business, University of British Columbia; Professor William Lever, emeritus professor of urban studies, University of Glasgow; Professor Maurice D. Levi, chair of Bank of Montreal, professor of international finance, University of British Columbia; Dr. Anthony Pellegrini, partner and director of the Urban and Infrastructure Policy and Finance Practice, Centennial Group, Washington, D.C.; Professor Peter J. Taylor, co-director, Globalization and World Cities Research Group and Network, Loughborough University, UK; and me.

12. This networked system also feeds unnecessary mobilities because the intermediary economy of specialized services thrives on any kind of mobility. Thus in the case of the United Kingdom, a study by the New Economics Foundation and the Open University of London found that in 2004, the United Kingdom exported 1,500 tons of fresh potatoes to Germany and imported 1,500 tons of the same product from the same country; it sent 10,200 tons of milk and cream to France and imported 9,900 tons of the same dairy goods from France; and so on over a vast spectrum of items.

13. This portion of the chapter is based on a paper prepared for the RPA, presented at Princeton University's Institute for Regional Policy, and subsequently published in the institute's papers series.

14. For an analysis of options see Henderson (2005).

15. But there is a caveat. A second key hypothesis used to specify the global city model is that the more headquarters buy some of their corporate functions from the specialized service sector rather than producing them in house, the greater their locational options become. These options include moving out of global cities and, more generically, out of dense urban environments. This is an option precisely because of the existence of a networked specialized producer service sector that can increasingly handle some of the most complex global operations of firms and markets. It is precisely this specialized capability to handle the global operations of

firms and markets that distinguishes the global city production function in my analysis, not the number of corporate headquarters of the biggest firms in the world, as is often suggested.

16. One of the best and most detailed analyses comparing two different formats for high-tech districts is Saxenian (1996).

17. Indeed, certain contemporary forms of dispersal are a function of particular capacities developed in settings marked by high-agglomeration economies (exemplified by global cities). And they are not only happening in the narrowly understood sphere of the economy; for instance, it is possible to identify the growth of an international curatorial class, and major museums allow their most valued collections to go on tour in a foreign country.

References

Ernst, D. 2005. The new mobility of knowledge: Digital information systems and global flagship networks. Pp. 89–114 in R. Latham and S. Sassen, eds. *Digital Formations: IT and New Architectures in the Global Realm*. Princeton University Press, Princeton, NJ.

Garcia, D. L. 2002. The architecture of global networking technologies. Pp. 39–69 in S. Sassen, ed. *Global Networks/Linked Cities*. Routledge, London.

Gereffi, G., J. Humphrey, and T. Sturgeon. 2005. The governance of global value chains. *Review of International Political Economy* 12(1):78–104.

GWAC. 2008, September 24. *Globalization and World Cities Research Network*. Loughborough University. Retrieved September 25, 2008 from www.lboro.ac.uk/gawc/.

Harvey, R. 2007. The sub-national constitution of global markets. In S. Sassen, ed. *Deciphering the Global: Its Spaces, Scales, and Subjects*. Routledge, New York.

Henderson, J. 2005. Governing growth and inequality: The continuing relevance of strategic economic planning. Pp. 227–236 in R. Applebaum and W. Robinson, eds. *Towards a Critical Globalization Studies*. Routledge, New York.

MasterCard Worldwide. 2007. *Worldwide Centers of Commerce Index 2007*.

National Academy of Sciences Fifteenth Annual U.S. Frontiers of Science Symposium. Irvine, California, 2003

OECD/ESRC/DfES Seminar. London , July 2006

OECD/DAC, Paris21 Steering Committee Meeting. Paris, May 2007

Regional Plan Association (RPA). 2006. *America 2050: A Prospectus*. Regional Plan Association, New York.

Sassen, S. 2001. *The Global City: New York, London, Tokyo* (2nd ed.). Princeton University Press, Princeton, NJ.

———. 2006a. *Cities in a World Economy* (3rd ed.). Sage/Pine Forge, Thousand Oaks, CA.

———. 2006b. *Territory, Authority, Rights: From Medieval to Global Assemblages*. Princeton University Press, Princeton, NJ.

Saxenian, A. 1996. *Regional Advantage: Culture and Competition in Silicon Valley and Route 128*. Harvard University Press, Cambridge, MA.

Taylor, P. J. 2004. *World City Network: A Global Urban Analysis*. Routledge, New York.

World Federation of Exchanges. 2007. *Annual Statistics for 2006*. World Federation of Exchanges, Paris.

12

Governing American Metropolitan Areas
Spatial Policy and Regional Governance

Myron Orfield and Thomas F. Luce Jr.

The U.S. Constitution grants powers to both the federal government and state governments. It makes no provision for local governments; all of their powers come from the states. At the same time, America has a tradition of local control. In large metropolitan areas, the sheer number of local governments, each making decisions in its own self-interest, makes developing regional solutions or regional institutions increasingly difficult. Regional governments fall awkwardly between the state and local levels: They have no power unless mandated by the state, but they threaten local control and therefore find it difficult to gain political support. Megaregions encompassing more than one metropolitan area and parts of multiple states present even greater governance challenges. Coordination attempts at this scale must deal not only with the American tradition of local control but also with even more deeply embedded interstate rivalries.

This chapter explores the obstacles to and possible opportunities for regional governance by examining two case studies: the regional governments of Portland, Oregon (Portland Metro) and Minneapolis and St. Paul, Minnesota (the Twin Cities Metropolitan Council). Similarities and differences between the two

The authors wish to acknowledge the excellent assistance of research assistant Jeff Rosenberg. Other Institute on Race and Poverty staff also contributed to portions of this chapter, including research associates Baris Gumus-Dawes and Eric Myott and geographic information system specialist Bill Lanoux.

experiences provide valuable lessons for those considering larger-scale efforts in megaregions.

The Case for Regional Institutions

Advocates of planning and service provision on a regional scale often argue that such regional governance would be more efficient. Many of the services that are best planned at a regional level are also best provided at the same level. Requiring local funding of regional improvements would result in a mismatch between the costs and the benefits; regional governments with taxing authority can spread the costs equitably around the region. Creating a regional plan for orderly infrastructure provision, tied to a land use plan, can also reduce per capita costs (Orfield 2002).

By contrast, highly fragmented local government systems create incentives for local areas to compete for activities that provide high tax revenues and low service costs, such as office parks, industrial development, and expensive single-family homes. From a regional perspective, the resources expended in such competition contribute little or nothing to the economy. Interlocal competition can also create vicious cycles of decline in places that lose desirable uses (Orfield 2002).

Planning for regional systems can avoid duplication and produce efficiency and equity. For example, individual municipalities have no incentive to include affordable housing because it provides few tax revenues and high service costs at the local level. The costs of providing affordable housing are endured locally, whereas the benefits are largely regional. Integrating affordable housing throughout a region, then, requires regional planning. Similarly, allowing purely local decisions on the siting of wastewater treatment facilities could lead to negative effects on adjacent localities. Finally, certain components of transportation systems must meet the travel needs of residents from all over a metropolitan area. The benefits are regional; therefore, the planning is best done regionally.

There is also growing awareness that regions, not localities, are the competitive unit in national and international competition. Firms deciding where to locate, expand, or relocate evaluate entire metropolitan labor and housing markets, not local areas. Regions that can improve the operation of these markets stand to gain in interregional competition for economic activity.

Finally, regional governance and planning can be used to address equity issues not currently addressed in a system of local fragmentation. The capacities of local governments to finance public services vary dramatically from place to place. The lowest-income areas where public service needs are greatest usually are the places with the least ability to raise revenues to finance services.

Region-wide provision of services can ease fiscal inequities by spreading the cost of services across the full income spectrum, and regulation of metropolitan housing and labor markets can trump local incentives toward exclusionary behavior in higher-income, higher-opportunity communities.

Metropolitan Planning Organizations and Regional Governance

Metropolitan planning organizations (MPOs) are the most widespread form of regional governance in the United States today. Created to assist with federal transportation planning, they are responsible for developing long-range transportation plans and hold the authority to approve or deny state and local applications for transportation aid (Federal-Aid Highway Act of 1973; Weiner 1992).

The passage of the Intermodal Surface Transportation Efficiency Act (ISTEA) in 1991 enhanced MPOs' role in regional coordination and planning. ISTEA allowed MPOs discretion to use Federal Highway Trust Fund money and general funds appropriated to various highway programs for other projects, including recreational trails, pedestrian and bicycle facilities, congestion mitigation, air quality programs, and mass transit.

Some MPOs have also taken on additional responsibilities, including air quality conformity planning, local and regional economic development, land use plan review and coordination, rideshare services, and regional demographic and economic forecasting. A few MPOs, including those in Seattle, San Diego, Los Angeles, and Denver, also conduct limited, voluntary land use and growth management planning and have the authority (given by state mandate) to review the land use and transportation plans of local jurisdictions to ensure that they are coordinated and comply with state goals and laws.

In some cases, the functions that MPOs serve are embedded in multipurpose governments that provide a variety of services at the regional level. Regional multipurpose governments are meant to provide the same types of economies at the regional scale that municipal governments do at the local scale. The Twin Cities' Metropolitan Council and Portland's Metro are the only existing multipurpose regional governments in the United States.[1] These governments do not attempt to duplicate or replace local government services. Instead, they have extensive authority for planning and policy review, especially related to planning for metropolitan growth. They also deliver certain services that are more efficiently provided by a regional government, including transportation planning. The following sections examine the Metropolitan Council and Metro to see how well they have been able to address equity issues and create new efficiencies on a regional scale.

Case Study: Twin Cities Metropolitan Council

The Twin Cities Metropolitan Council is a good case study of regional governance in the United States for a variety of reasons. Table 12.1 shows very clearly that the council serves more roles than any other council in the twenty-five largest metropolitan areas.[2] The Metropolitan Council also operates in one of the most fragmented local government systems in the country, presenting the council with more difficult coordination problems than most regional bodies.

History

A spirit of regional cooperation developed slowly but steadily in the Twin Cities. Over several decades, a number of regional organizations were formed, including the Twin Cities Sanitary District (1933), the Metropolitan Airports Commission (1943), the Metropolitan Area Sports Commission (1956), the Twin Cities Metropolitan Planning Commission (1957), and the Metropolitan Mosquito Control District (1958). The requirement, by the federal government, of MPO oversight of transportation planning spurred further interest in a regional body and paved the way for the creation of the Metropolitan Council (hereafter Met Council) in 1967.

Since its creation the Met Council has grown in both size and scope. Originally formed as a coordinating body with no authority to provide service or set policy (Naftalin 1986), it has since been able to expand its oversight. In 1974 it received the authority to approve the Metropolitan Transit Commission's and the Metropolitan Waste Commission's budgets and long-range plans and to appoint the members of these commissions. In 1976 the state legislature gave the Met Council the authority to adopt a "comprehensive development guide" for the metropolitan area and the ability to modify the comprehensive plans of local governments (Minn. Stat. §§ 473.851–473.872; Naftalin 1986). A 1994 act gave the Met Council the functions of the Metropolitan Transit Commission, Regional Transit Board, and Metropolitan Waste Control Commission.

Current Responsibilities and Fiscal Capacity

In addition to regional comprehensive planning, the Met Council is responsible for providing regional services and for overseeing the Metropolitan Urban Service Area, which provides regional services and facilities under its jurisdiction (Metropolitan Council 2004). The Met Council engages in transportation planning as the MPO for the Twin Cities region. It also operates most Twin Cities transit through its Metro Transit Division. The Met Council advises but does not control the Metropolitan Airports Commission and participates in aviation planning and budgeting. It plans and operates the regional wastewater system (the

Table 12.1

Regional councils and their functions.

Region	Regional Council	Transportation	Land Use	Growth Management	Transit	Waste Water	Solid Waste
Atlanta	Atlanta Regional Commission	•	•	•			
Boston	Metropolitan Area Planning Council	•	•				
Chicago	Northeastern Illinois Planning Commission						
Cincinnati	Ohio–Kentucky–Indiana Regional Council of Governments	•	•				
Cleveland	Northeast Ohio Areawide Coordinating Agency	•					
Dallas–Fort Worth	North Central Texas Council of Governments	•					
Denver	Denver Regional Council of Governments	•	•				
Detroit	Southeast Michigan Council of Governments	•					
Houston	Houston–Galveston Area Council	•					
Kansas City	Mid-America Regional Council	•	•				
Los Angeles	Southern California Association of Governments	•	•				•
Miami	South Florida Regional Planning Council						

City	Regional Council				
Milwaukee	Southeastern Wisconsin Regional Planning Commission	•			
New York	Long Island Regional Planning Board	•			
New York	Hudson Valley Regional Council				
Philadelphia	Delaware Valley Regional Planning Commission	•			
Phoenix	Maricopa Association of Governments	•			
Pittsburgh	Southwestern Pennsylvania Commission	•			
Portland	Metro	•	•		•
St. Louis	East–West Gateway Coordinating Council	•			
San Diego	San Diego Association of Governments	•			•
San Francisco	Association of Bay Area Governments	•	•		
Seattle	Puget Sound Regional Council	•			
Tampa	Tampa Bay Regional Planning Council				
Twin Cities	Metropolitan Council of the Twin Cities Area	•	•	•	
Washington, D.C.	Metropolitan Washington Council of Governments	•			

Source: National Association of Regional Councils.

largest part of its budget) and engages in water supply planning. It engages in regional park planning and acquires and dedicates parkland for regional uses. Finally, it serves as the region's housing authority (Metropolitan Council 2008).

The Met Council's annual budget is roughly $650 million, significantly less than that of its component counties, school districts, or cities and townships. However, because of its role in providing regional infrastructure, the council is very active in bond markets. In 2005, its bonded debt exceeded $1 billion, more than that of its seven component counties combined. Revenue from regional borrowing is spent on wastewater (76 percent), transit (20 percent), and parks (4 percent) (Metropolitan Council 2006).

The council's primary source of revenue is charges to consumers (for transit services) and municipalities (for wastewater collection and treatment), representing 39 percent of current revenue in 2005. However, it also receives significant amounts of money from the state and federal governments (24 percent) and taxes (28 percent). It assesses property taxes and receives a share of the state-administered motor vehicle excise tax.

Addressing Regional Issues

Despite the fact that the Met Council's power has increased over time, its stance on urban growth has gradually weakened. Early in its history, it focused on the connection between land use and the cost of providing services and gave heavy priority to directing growth to existing infrastructure over new development (Metropolitan Council 1975, 1988). Since the mid-1990s, the Met Council has been more reluctant to curb urban growth and increase density in the Twin Cities area. Its planning documents, such as Blueprint 2030, have contained smart growth recommendations and advocated strengthening the area's land use connections but have also indicated that increased density is not a high priority (Metropolitan Council 2002). Rural zoning also became less restrictive and more tolerant of large-lot exurban development.

Case Study: Portland Metro

Although Portland Metro does not have as many statutory powers as the Met Council, its powers are supported by a strong statewide planning law, and it has shown a greater willingness to exercise the powers that it has. Until recent years it has had a better record of enforcing its urban growth power than the Met Council has had with its Urban Services Area. Metro is different from the Met Council in another important way: It is an elected body, not an appointed one. This difference may partially explain its greater willingness to exercise its statutory powers.

History

The formation of Metro was the end result of a decades-long experiment by Portland-area governments to establish regional planning and service delivery (Abbott and Abbott 1991). From 1957 through 1966, Portland and the three counties in the region formed the Metropolitan Planning Commission (MPC), which acted more as a research organization than a true regional planning agency (Abbott and Abbott 1991). The new regional government was approved by voters in May 1978 and began work January 1, 1979 (Abbott and Abbott 1991).

Current Responsibilities and Fiscal Capacity

Metro has been slowly acquiring new responsibilities. Initially, it was involved only with solid waste planning. Eventually, in 1976 it began operating the Washington Park Zoo (Abbott and Abbott 1991). In 1979, it became Portland's MPO, responsible for transportation planning. In 1989, it began work on the regional urban growth goals and objectives, its first major foray into prescriptive regional planning. Regional planning has since become its primary function (Metro 2003, preamble). In 1995, and again in 2006, voters approved bond measures giving Metro a mandate and funding to develop a system of regional parks. In a sense, Metro "is a 'government-in-waiting' for a time when the voters agree that a regional approach to a specific delivery is warranted" (Gustafson 1994; Abbott and Abbott 1991). Although the Tri-County Metropolitan Transportation District is a separate organization, Metro also does transportation planning, including transit planning, as part of its MPO responsibilities. In addition to planning, Metro is responsible for regional solid and liquid waste disposal, the metropolitan zoo, the convention center, sporting and cultural facilities, regional parks, open spaces, and recreational facilities. In addition, their responsibilities extend to natural disaster planning and response coordination, development and marketing of data, and other functions required by state law, assigned by the voters, or declared a "metropolitan concern" by the council (Metro 2003 §§ 6, 7(1)). It does not have control over regional sewage and water services or airports,[3] and thus it has less control over services than the Met Council, which provides most regional services.

Metro's budget has been described as "piddling by comparison to many other governmental units" (Nelson 1996). Almost half of Metro's revenue (46 percent) comes from enterprise fees from services provided by Metro. The enterprise fees, approximately half of which comes from Metro's solid waste facilities, remain an important component of its business model. Other important sources of revenue include property taxes (19 percent), grants (9 percent), excise taxes (7 percent), and intergovernmental revenues (5 percent) (Metro 2007a). For fiscal year 2007–2008, Metro's budget includes just over $328 million in expenditures. Its total bonded debt in 2007 was approximately $185 million. However, this figure does not include $227.4 million that was approved by voters in 2006 for natural areas, parks, and streams, which had not been issued at the time the budget was proposed (Metro 2007a).

Addressing Regional Issues

Portland's growth management policy has called for greater densities over time. Portland is unusual in its adoption of an urban growth boundary (UGB), which Metro helps develop and enforce. Since the initial planning process, UGB expansions have been guided by analyses of land needs. Metro and other governments must show that land within the UGB can accommodate estimated housing needs for 20 years (Or. Rev. Stat. § 197.296(2)). After developing such an estimate in 2002 (Metro 2002), Metro added more than 18,000 acres to the UGB (Metro 2005). Since the large 2002 addition to the UGB, Metro has not designated any new urban reserve land. However, it has already added as much land to the UGB as called for in Metro's Region 2040 plan; it remains to be seen whether that will prove sufficient until 2040.

Metro also envisions increasing densities within the UGB. Twenty-nine percent of the growth expected to occur between 2000 and 2022 is expected to be "refill"—redevelopment or infill (Metro 2002). Metro's Urban Growth Management Functional Plan sets recommended average densities (Table 12.2).

Table 12.2
Metro's recommended average densities.

Planning Area	Recommended Density
Central city	250 people per acre
Regional centers	60 people per acre
Station communities	45 people per acre
Town centers	40 people per acre
Main streets	39 people per acre
Corridors	25 people per acre
Employment areas	20 people per acre
Inner neighborhoods	14 people per acre
Outer neighborhoods	13 people per acre
Industrial areas	9 employees per acre
Regionally significant industrial areas	9 employees per acre

Source: MetroCode § 3.07.170(A).

Metro's transportation plans have also become more focused on producing a compact urban form. The 1982 Regional Transportation Plan (RTP), and its 1989 update, focused on using freeway and transit investments and travel demand management to provide a cost-effective solution to continuing growth. The 2000 RTP is less focused on keeping down costs and is more idealistic. It is designed to implement the Regional Framework Plan, which explicitly linked urban form to transportation. It calls for infrastructure investments to be focused on the primary components of that plan: the central city, regional centers, industrial areas, and intermodal facilities. The plan also calls for increasing transportation choices and eliminating dependence on one mode of transportation.

Twin Cities and Portland: Using Regional Governance to Address Issues of Efficiency and Equity

Prior sections show that the Twin Cities and Portland place more emphasis than other large metropolitan areas on regional institutions to manage their regional economies and housing markets. This section compares the two metropolitan areas with each other and, where possible, with other large metros to see how regional outcomes vary in several policy areas most directly affected by regional governments. These include urbanization rates (sprawl), housing affordability, racial segregation, job clustering and job change, traffic congestion, and fiscal equity.

Sprawl

To measure sprawl, we look at changes over time in the amount of urbanized land that metropolitan areas consume to accommodate population growth. The chosen measure defines urbanized land as land with more than one housing unit per 4 acres, a measure roughly equal to the definition used by the Bureau of the Census for outlying regions in metropolitan areas in 2000. The sprawl measure is the ratio of urban land in 2000 to urban land in 1970, divided by the ratio of metropolitan population in 2000 to metropolitan population in 1970.

Figures 12.1 and 12.2 show urbanization trends in the Twin Cities and Portland between 1970 and 2000. The Twin Cities experienced more sprawl than Portland; the gap between urban land growth and population growth was significantly greater in the Twin Cities. This was most noticeable from 1990 to 2000, a decade in which the Met Council's focus on growth management was diminished. In Portland, the rate of population growth actually exceeded the rate of urban land growth in the 1980s and 1990s. This was most pronounced from 1990 to 2000, when Metro became more heavily involved in regional planning.

In order to compare Portland and the Twin Cities to each other and to other large metros, Figure 12.3 shows how local government fragmentation and sprawl

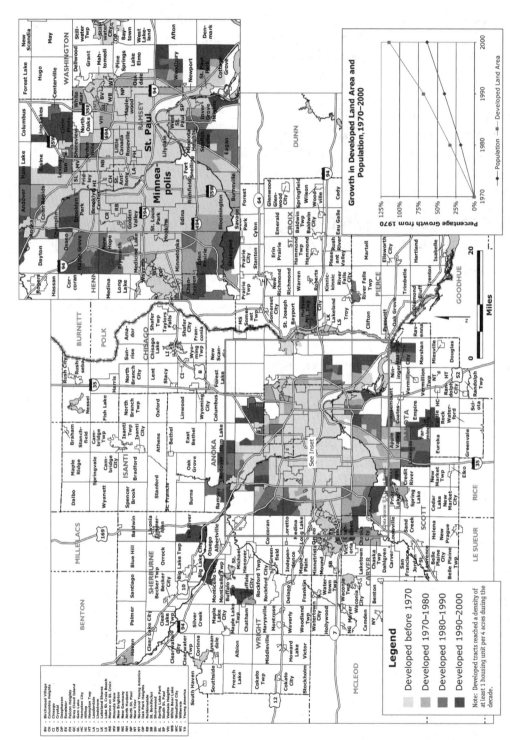

Figure 12.1 Twin Cities Region: Housing Development by Census Tract, 1970–2000.

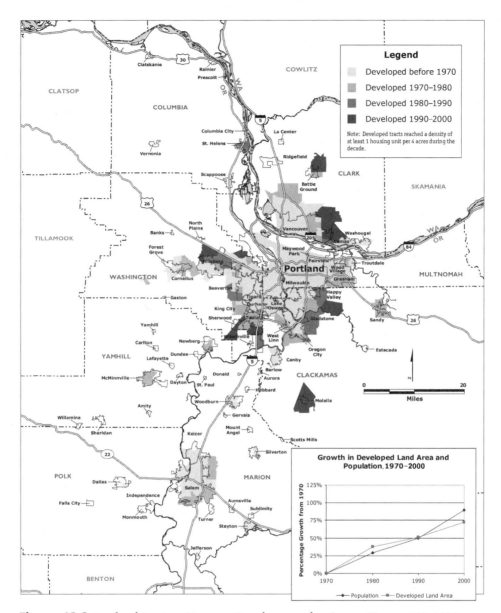

Figure 12.2 Portland Region: Housing Development by Census Tract, 1970–2000.

relate in the fifty largest metropolitan areas. Local government fragmentation is measured as the number of municipal governments per 10,000 residents. Higher levels of political fragmentation are clearly correlated with greater sprawl rates. The curved line ("Predicted Sprawl") in Figure 12.3 shows the curvilinear relationship between the sprawl and fragmentation in the fifty largest metropolitan areas.[4] Interestingly, both Portland and the Twin Cities experience less sprawl than would be expected given the fragmentation of local governments in

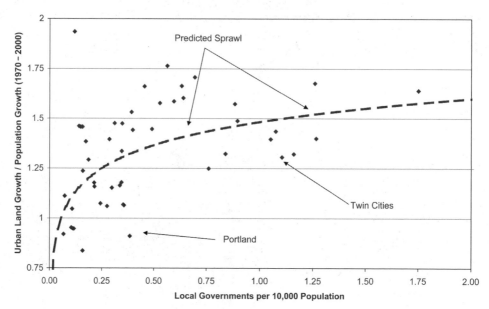

Figure 12.3 Fragmentation and Sprawl in the 50 Largest Metropolitan Areas.

their regions. Both regions experienced a smaller ratio of urban land growth to population growth than other regions with similar levels of fragmentation. In the Twin Cities, the sprawl ratio was approximately 1.3 from 1970 to 2000. This is roughly 15 percent lower than would be expected given the region's high degree of political fragmentation. In Portland, the growth in urban land was actually slower than the growth in population; the sprawl ratio was approximately 0.9. This is roughly 30 percent lower than would be expected given the area's moderate degree of political fragmentation.

The difference between the two regions is largely the result of Portland's smaller, more strictly enforced UGB. Between 1979 and 2007, the area within the boundary increased less than 20 percent and is now approximately 400 square miles (Leonard 1983; Metro 2007b). In that time, the population inside the UGB increased by more than 46 percent (Metro 2008). In contrast, the Twin Cities Metropolitan Urban Services Area (or MUSA)—the part of the region designated by the Met Council to receive regional services such as wastewater collection—is larger, grew by more during this period, and saw less population growth than Portland. The area inside the Twin Cities MUSA line grew by 26 percent between 1975 and 2007 to more than 1,000 square miles. During that time population inside the MUSA grew by about 42 percent.

However, recent developments in Portland put Metro's ability to maintain this discipline at risk. Measure 37 was passed by Oregon voters in 2004. The measure requires that when a land use regulation reduces the value of a property, the owners of that property be compensated for the amount of the loss or have the regulation waived. It applies retroactively to any law put into place after a property owner acquired his or her property (Liberty 2006). Although a later referendum (Measure 49) weakened Measure 37, the combined effect is still to undermine Metro's power to regulate development of previously undeveloped land, especially land outside the UGB. Measure 37 claims are scattered across undeveloped, suburban areas, often noncontiguous with already developed areas.[5] Already, more than 20,000 acres of land in the Portland area have had regulations modified under the measure—an area just under half of the total increase in the UGB between 1979 and 2007.

Affordable Housing

Growth management policies such as growth boundaries and urban service areas are often blamed for high housing costs. However, despite the fact that Portland and the Twin Cities use these policy instruments, their housing costs are not high in comparison to those of other large metros. Housing in the Twin Cities was actually more affordable than in the twenty-five largest metropolitan areas on average in both 1990 and 2000. In Portland, affordability went from being comparable to the Twin Cities in 1990 to a level slightly less affordable than in the twenty-five largest metros in 2000. In 2000, the Twin Cities had a significantly smaller proportion of owner-occupied housing affordable to households with 30 percent of the regional median household income, compared with Portland and the twenty-five largest. For rental housing, the Twin Cities, Portland, and the twenty-five largest regions had similar levels of affordability (Figure 12.4).[6]

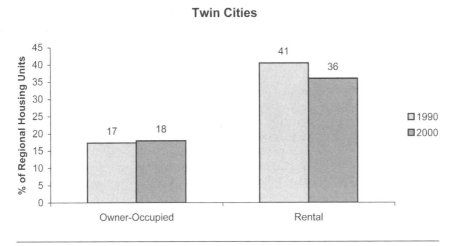

Figure 12.4 Percentage of Housing Units Affordable to Households with 30 Percenet of the Regional Median Household Income.

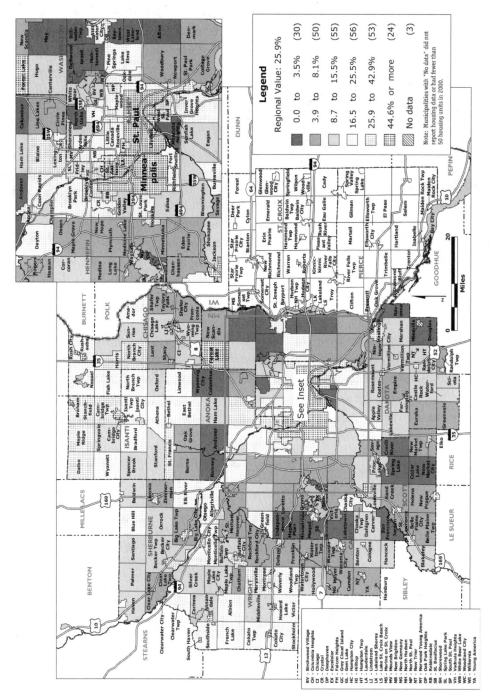

Figure 12.5 Twin Cities Region: Percentage of Housing Units Affordable to Households with 30 Percent of the Regional Median Household Income by Municipality, 2000.

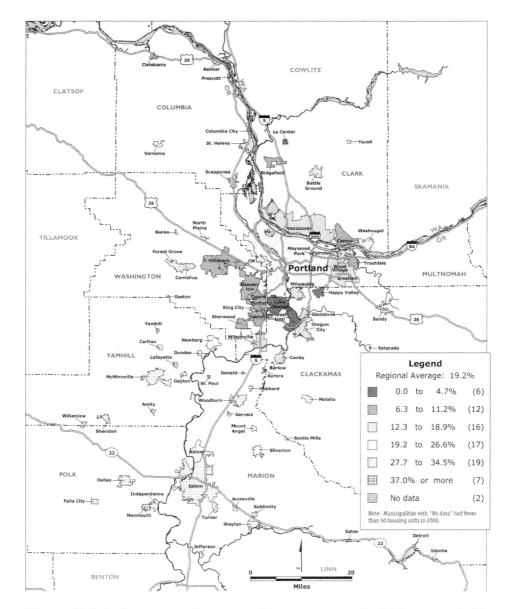

Figure 12.6 Portland Region: Percentage of Housing Units Affordable to Households with 30 Percent of the Regional Median Household Income by Municipality, 2000.

Most of the affordable housing stock in the Twin Cities is concentrated in the core of the central cities, although small pockets also exist in suburban areas (Figure 12.5).[7] Portland does not have equivalent pockets (Figure 12.6). However, data on affordable housing are not available for unincorporated portions of the Portland metropolitan area, which are likely to contain a substantial portion of the supply.

These statistics show that housing affordability in Portland is close to that of the twenty-five largest metropolitan areas. Unlike in the Twin Cities and the twenty-five largest metropolitan areas, though, housing affordability in Portland dropped sharply between 1990 and 2000. The reason for Portland's decreasing affordability has been a subject of much debate.[8] Most scholars agree that government regulation such as zoning and growth management leads to rising land prices (see Black and Hoben 1985; Malpezzi 1996; Green 1999), particularly when it reduces the supply of buildable land (Nelson et al. 2004). However, some argue that regulation is not as important a force as market demand (Knaap and Nelson 1992; Phillips and Goodstein 2000; Jun 2004). Similarly, although it is apparent that Portland's housing prices have been rising rapidly, it is unclear whether the UGB has caused this increase. Indeed, housing appreciation in Portland has been comparable to that of other Western cities (Downs 2002).

Racial Segregation

The degree of political fragmentation is correlated with racial segregation, just as it is with sprawl. Figure 12.7 shows this relationship in the fifty largest metropolitan areas. Higher degrees of fragmentation are associated with greater seg-

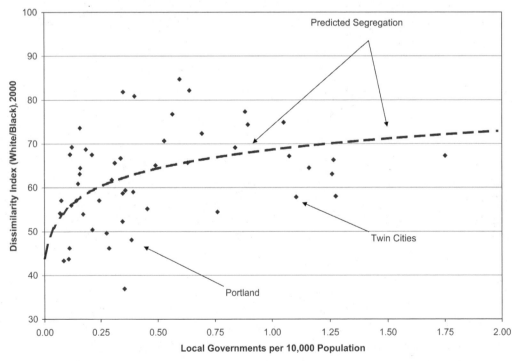

Figure 12.7 Fragmentation and Segregation in the 50 Largest Metropolitan Areas, 2000.

regation, as measured by the dissimilarity index for white and black residents.[9] However, the data again suggest that regional coordination of land use planning can lessen the overall degree of segregation. The Twin Cities and Portland each shows less segregation than would be expected given their levels of political fragmentation. Portland's dissimilarity index of 48 is 23 percent lower than its expected index, and the Twin Cities' index of 58 is 16 percent lower than expected.

However, the results for specific racial groups are less positive. Hispanics in particular show increasing rates of segregation. This can be seen by classifying neighborhoods and calculating the percentage of individual racial groups living in segregated settings.[10] By this measure, black segregation declined a bit in the largest twenty-five metropolitan areas in both the 1980s and the 1990s. In 1980, 72 percent of black residents lived in segregated settings in these metros on average, and this declined to 68 percent in 1990 and 66 percent in 2000 (Figure 12.8). However, the percentage of Hispanics and other races (largely Asian) living in segregated settings increased in each decade, from 56 to 61 to 67 percent for Hispanics and from 16 to 22 to 29 percent for other races.

In contrast with the overall segregation index measured in a single year, the trend data for individual races do not look better in the Twin Cities and Portland than in other large metros. Indeed, the share of black residents living in segregated settings actually went up in the Twin Cities region in the 1990s, from 19 percent to 23 percent. Similarly, the share of Hispanics and other races living in segregated settings climbed more rapidly in the region than in the largest twenty-five metropolitan areas. In contrast to the Twin Cities, blacks and other racial groups in Portland became less segregated during the entire period. However, Portland showed similar increases in Hispanic segregation.

Growth in Employment

There was a great deal of variation in metropolitan growth rates in the 1990s and 2000s. The period saw a continuation of the Frostbelt–Sunbelt disparities evident in prior decades. This was particularly true among large metros. From 1990 to 2006, the eleven metros with the fastest job growth rates among the twenty-five largest were in the South and West, and twelve of the fourteen slowest-growing regions were in the Northeast and Midwest. Portland ranked sixth and the Twin Cities ranked twelfth, outgrowing all other Northern and Midwestern metros.

Consistent with the sprawl and segregation results, there is a clear correlation between political fragmentation and job growth rates across metropolitan areas (Figure 12.9). The Twin Cities and Portland again stand out with growth rates significantly above what would be expected given their political fragmentation. The Twin Cities' growth rate was nearly twice the expected rate (29

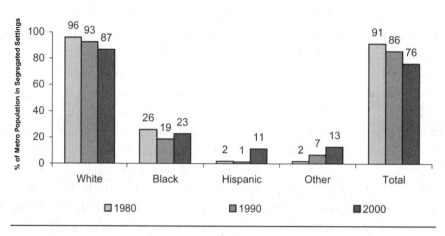

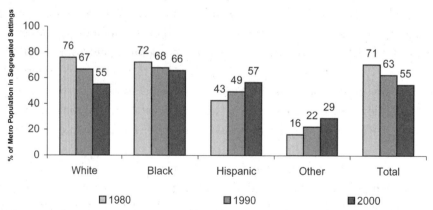

Figure 12.8 Population in Segregated Settings, 1980–2000.

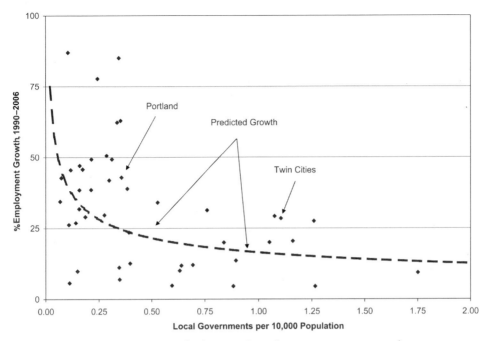

Figure 12.9 Fragmentation and Job Growth in the 50 Largest Metropolitan Areas.

percent versus 16 percent), and Portland's was about two-thirds higher than expected (39 percent versus 24 percent).

One would expect that regional organizations would try to reduce decentralization rates and to encourage job clustering in order to avoid new infrastructure needs and to encourage transit usage whenever possible. The record in the Twin Cities and Portland is mixed on these measures.

Table 12.3 and Figures 12.10 and 12.11 show the distribution of jobs and job growth rates by location in the two regions. Both regions show a roughly 50/50 split between the number of jobs in clusters and the number in scattered sites.[11] Each metro also shows roughly a quarter of clustered jobs in central city job centers. Jobs are decentralizing in both metros as well: Growth rates for job clusters increase with distance from the core. However, Portland shows a better balance between growth in job clusters and growth in scattered site jobs. The two rates are roughly equal in Portland, whereas nonclustered jobs grew much more rapidly than clustered jobs in the Twin Cities (31 percent versus 14 percent).

Figures 12.10 and 12.11 show the geography of job growth in Portland's and the Twin Cities' employment centers. In Portland, faster job center growth tends to be uniformly spread across the developed part of the region, and job centers are often much closer to the core of the central cities of Portland and Salem than in the Twin Cities. With the exception of the southeast quadrant of Portland, moderate to high job growth rates are found throughout the region. In the Twin

Table 12.3

Jobs and job growth by type of employment center.

Employment Center	Percentage of Regional Jobs		Percentage Change, 1990–2000	
	Portland	Twin Cities	Portland	Twin Cities
Central business district	9	11	15	6
Other central city	20	13	33	4
Inner suburb	10	12	28	19
Middle suburb	9	13	60	22
Outer suburb	4	3	117	37
Total, employment centers	52	52	36	14
Nonclustered employment	48	48	34	31
Total, metropolitan area	100	100	35	22

Source: Calculated from 1990 and 2000 Census Transportation Planning Package.

Cities job growth is stronger southwest of Minneapolis and weaker south and northwest of Minneapolis. Similar to Portland, the Twin Cities area tends to have employment centers closely bundled near the central cities.

Transportation and Congestion

In contrast with other policy areas, all metros in the country are required by the federal government to have regional organization planning and managing funds for transportation. Not surprisingly, Portland and the Twin Cities do not stand out in comparisons with other large metropolitan areas.

Table 12.4 shows that both metros have below-average levels of congestion in absolute terms, but congestion has been increasing more rapidly than average in the Twin Cities. Interestingly, both the Twin Cities and Portland increased freeway lane miles by much less than average, despite the fact that population was growing more quickly than average in both places. A possible reason for this is that they use their regional planning capacities to rely more on land use approaches to congestion control than other metros.

Fiscal Equity

The disparities between wealthier and poorer local communities can be eased in a variety of means, including direct ways such as tax base sharing and indirect activities such as regional planning to distribute economic activity and affordable

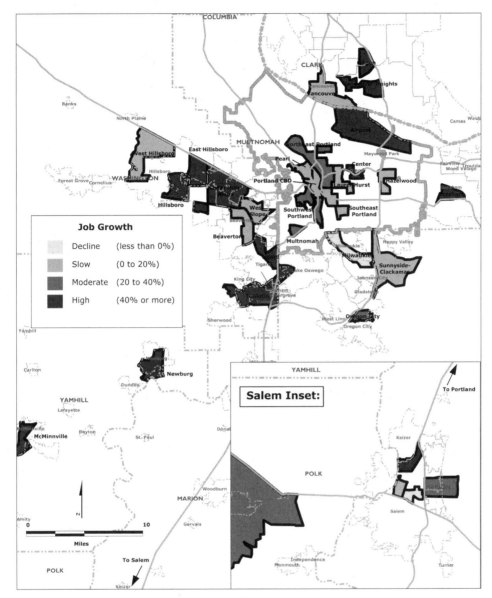

Figure 12.10 Portland Region: Job Growth in Employment Centers.

housing more equitably. The Twin Cities uses both methods, whereas Portland relies on more proactive planning activities.

In the Twin Cities, the Fiscal Disparities Act of 1971 instituted a tax base sharing program that reduces the disparities between the "winners" and "losers." Each taxing jurisdiction must contribute 40 percent of the growth of its commercial and industrial tax capacity since 1971 to a regional pool, which is then shared by all local governments, with a larger proportion going to municipalities

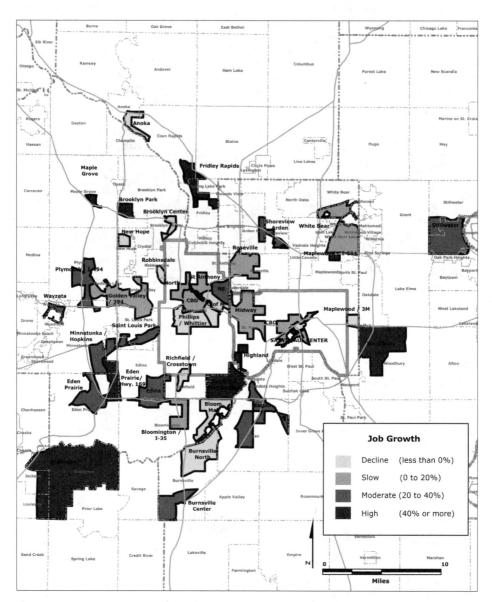

Figure 12.11 Twin Cities Region: Job Growth in Employment Centers.

with lower-than-average market value per capita. This has had the effect of re-ducing inequality by approximately 20 percent. The program was created during the same wave of regionalism that led to the Met Council, although it is admin-istered by the seven counties included in the program rather than the Met Council.

Portland does not have anything similar to tax base sharing, but it uses its planning and transportation powers to achieve similar ends. Indeed, Portland

Table 12.4

Selected transportation statistics, 1993–2003.

Metropolitan Area	Population Growth (%)	Hours of Delay per Traveler		Change in Delay per Traveler (%)	Change in Lane Miles (%)	Change in Lane Miles per Capita (%)
		1993	2003			
Atlanta	38	38	67	76	8	3
Boston	7	38	51	34	18	1
Chicago	10	42	59	38	3	0
Cincinnati	8	18	30	67	24	2
Cleveland	0	10	10	0	14	0
Dallas–Fort Worth	30	47	60	28	10	3
Denver	26	38	51	34	14	4
Detroit	3	77	57	−26	8	0
Houston	25	38	63	66	13	3
Kansas City	12	13	17	31	10	1
Los Angeles	10	113	93	−18	16	2
Miami	22	39	51	31	10	2
Milwaukee	3	19	23	21	22	1
New York	8	34	49	44	14	1
Philadelphia	4	25	38	52	13	1
Phoenix	44	42	49	17	95	42
Pittsburgh	−3	14	14	0	7	0
Portland	22	33	37	12	4	1
St. Louis	5	31	35	13	10	1
San Diego	12	29	52	79	11	1
San Francisco	8	62	72	16	9	1
Seattle	15	56	46	−18	12	2
Tampa	17	42	46	10	39	7
Twin Cities	15	30	43	43	2	0
Washington, D.C.	18	51	69	35	7	1
Average	14	39	47	27	16	3

Source: Texas Transportation Institute.

Table 12.5

Gini coefficients for tax capacity per household.

Metropolitan Area	1993	2001	Change, 1993–2001
Atlanta	.13	.14	.01
Boston	.22	.25	.03
Chicago	.30	.30	.00
Cincinnati	.44	.45	.00
Cleveland	.34	.31	−.03
Dallas–Fort Worth	.22	.26	.03
Denver	.20	.36	.16
Detroit	.32	.30	−.02
Houston	.14	.15	.01
Kansas City	.19	.21	.02
Los Angeles	.20	.23	.03
Miami	.19	.21	.02
Milwaukee	.25	.29	.04
New York	.27	.34	.06
Philadelphia	.30	.28	−.03
Phoenix	.13	.20	.07
Pittsburgh	.26	.26	.00
Portland	.12	.11	−.01
St. Louis	.36	.39	.03
San Diego	.10	.11	.01
San Francisco	.18	.19	.02
Seattle	.32	.22	−.10
Tampa	.17	.15	−.02
Twin Cities	.19	.17	−.02
Washington, D.C.	.29	.37	.08
Average	.23	.25	.02

Source: Computed from various state and local sources.

shows even lower fiscal disparities than the Twin Cities, as measured by the Gini coefficient. Table 12.5 shows that both metros are in the top five of the twenty-five largest metros in this dimension.[12]

Portland and the Twin Cities also have less inequality than would be expected given their levels of local government fragmentation. The curved line ("Predicted Inequality") in Figure 12.12 shows the curvilinear relationship between local

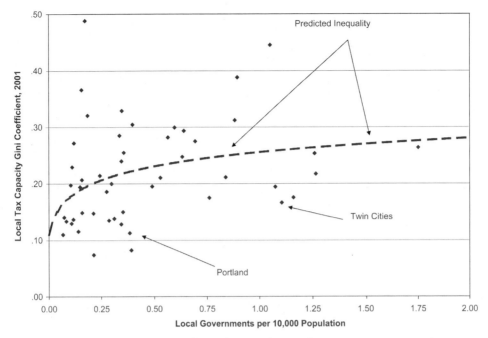

Figure 12.12 Fragmentation and Fiscal Inequality in the 50 Largest Metropolitan Areas.

fragmentation and a commonly used measure of fiscal inequality, the Gini coefficient.[13] Although the Twin Cities has the fifth-highest level of fragmentation out of the fifty largest metropolitan areas, its Gini coefficient is below average, and 35 percent below the level predicted by the rate of fragmentation (.17 compared to .26). Portland fares even better, with a Gini coefficient 50 percent below the level predicted (.11 compared to .22). This implies that Portland's tax base is distributed more evenly across the region.

Conclusions

It appears that the Met Council and Metro have been able to offset many of the drawbacks associated with highly fragmented local government systems. Both metros consistently fared better than other large metros on the outcome measures included here—sprawl, segregation, job growth, and fiscal equity—especially given their degrees of local fragmentation. The clear implication is that regionalism provides a means to enjoy many of the benefits of highly fragmented systems (smaller units of government that are closer to voters, for instance) without many of the drawbacks.

The comparison also suggests that a regional governing structure does not need total control of regional systems to be effective. Despite the Met Council's greater authority, Portland is urbanizing land at lower rates than are the Twin Cities, is less segregated, and has done a better job of directing new job growth toward existing job centers. And despite experiencing greater growth rates, Portland experienced smaller increases in annual hours of delay per traveler, perhaps because its transit system covers a wider area with greater usage rates. Finally, Portland's tax base is distributed more evenly across the region than that of the Twin Cities.

There are two likely explanations for these differences in the context of this analysis. First, Portland Metro's planning activities are complemented by a strong state planning program that regulates activity outside Metro's service area. This enhances Metro's ability to enforce its urban growth boundary. The Met Council, on the other hand, operates on its own in a seven-county service area that no longer includes all of the metropolitan area, which now includes four Minnesota counties and two Wisconsin counties outside the council's purview. This means that developers, potential residents, and businesses have options that limit the council's ability to pursue aggressive growth management activities.

Second, Portland Metro is an elected body whose representatives must answer to voters, whereas the Met Council is appointed by the governor. Counterintuitively, this means that Metro is the more stable body, because its partisan mix reflects the mix among voters, which changes only gradually over time. The Met Council, on the other hand, can go from 100 percent Democratic to 100 percent Republican as the result of a single statewide election. This means that Metro's growth management activities have been more consistently administered over time. The case can also be made that an elected body is likely to be more aggressive than an appointed one because elected officials may be more likely to use the powers available to them to show the results needed for reelection.

What does this imply for megaregions? As metropolitan economies merge into loosely connected megaregions, the incentives for interlocal and interregional competition are likely to intensify, not diminish, because a whole new layer of inter-metropolitan competitive pressures will be added to the system. Given the institutional, cultural, and historical difficulties associated with organizing entire megaregions, the best solution is for metropolitan-level bodies to work together to manage issues of common interest to these larger, more loosely connected economies.

Notes

1. MPOs that have been given additional state-mandated powers, such as Seattle, San Diego, Los Angeles, and Denver, are arguably evolving into multipurpose governments, although the Twin Cities and Portland regional governments remain more powerful.
2. The Metropolitan Council also serves as the Twin Cities' regional housing authority, a role filled by only two other councils.

3. Wastewater services are provided by numerous agencies, including the Portland Bureau of Environmental Services and the Washington County Unified Sewerage Agency. Water services are provided individually by almost every city in the Portland region (see Regional Water Providers Consortium 2008). Aviation is the responsibility of the Oregon Department of Aviation.

4. The line shows a log-linear relationship. The simple correlation between the sprawl measure and the log of the fragmentation measure is .53, a value significant at the 99 percent confidence level.

5. See www.oregon.gov/LCD/docs/measure37/number_of_claims_102505.pdf.

6. An affordable rental unit is defined as one for which contract rent is less than 30 percent of the 30th percentile of regional median household income. An affordable owner-occupied unit is defined as a house valued low enough that mortgage costs plus the average local regional property tax are less than 30 percent of the 30th percentile regional median household income.

7. The maps define affordable housing as housing units (owner occupied and rental) that cost less than 30 percent of total income at 50 percent of the regional median income.

8. For a review of this literature, see Nelson et al. (2002), on which the brief summary given here is based.

9. The simple correlation between the natural log of the fragmentation measure and the dissimilarity index is .42, significant at 99 percent confidence.

10. For the purposes of this chapter, people in segregated settings are defined as members of the predominant group in segregated neighborhoods. This includes white people in neighborhoods less than 10 percent black and less than 10 percent Hispanic; black people in neighborhoods more than 50 percent black and less than 10 percent Hispanic; Hispanic people in neighborhoods less than 10 percent black and more than 50 percent Hispanic; black and Hispanic people in neighborhoods less than 40 percent white, more than 10 percent black, and more than 10 percent Hispanic; "other" people in neighborhoods less than 40 percent white and more than 50 percent "other"; and "other" and black or Hispanic people in neighborhoods with more than 10 percent "other" and more than 10 percent black or with more than 10 percent "other" and more than 10 percent Hispanic.

11. The data are from the Census of Transportation Planning Package, 1990 and 2000. Employment centers were defined as contiguous traffic analysis zones with greater than average numbers of jobs per square mile and total employment exceeding 1,800 jobs. Large job agglomerations such as those in the central business districts were divided into multiple employment centers based on job densities in different parts of the larger clusters. Salem, Oregon also included a central business district that was allocated to "other central city" employment centers, because the number of jobs and job density of Salem were more typical of other central city job centers and less typical of central business districts in the selected regions.

12. The Gini coefficient, shown in Table 12.5, measures the difference between the actual distribution of tax base and a perfectly equal distribution. It varies between 0 and 1, taking on a value of 0 if the distribution is perfectly equal (all jurisdictions have the same tax base per household) and 1 if the distribution is perfectly unequal (one jurisdiction with only one household has the entire tax base).

13. The line shows a log-linear relationship. The simple correlation between the inequality measure and the log of the fragmentation is .35, a value significant at the 98 percent confidence level.

References

Abbott, C., and M. P. Abbott. 1991. *A History of Metro*. Retrieved 2007 from www.metro-region.org/index.cfm/go/by.web/id/2937.

Black, J. T., and J. E. Hoben. 1985. Land price inflation and affordable housing. *Urban Geography* 6(1):27–47.

Downs, A. 2002. Have housing prices risen faster in Portland than elsewhere? *Housing Policy Debate* 13(1):7–50.

Green, R. K. 1999. Land use regulation and the price of housing in a suburban Wisconsin county. *Journal of Housing Economics* 8(2):144–159.

Gustafson, R. 1994. Metro: Finding its niche, finally. *The Oregonian,* April 10.

Jun, M. J. 2004. The effects of Portland's urban growth boundary on urban development patterns and commuting. *Urban Studies* 41(7):1333.

Knaap, G. J., and A. C. Nelson. 1992. *The Regulated Landscape: Lessons on State Land Use Planning from Oregon.* Lincoln Institute of Land Policy, Cambridge, MA.

Leonard, H. J. 1983. *Managing Oregon's Growth: The Politics of Development Planning.* Conservation Foundation, Washington, D.C.

Liberty, R. 2006. Give and take over Measure 37: Could Metro reconcile compensation for reductions in value with a regional plan for compact urban growth and preserving farmland. *Environmental Law* 36:187–220.

Malpezzi, S. 1996. Housing prices, externalities, and regulation in U.S. metropolitan areas. *Journal of Housing Research* 7:209–242.

Metro. 2002. *2002–2022 Urban Growth Report: A Residential Land Need Analysis.* Retrieved May 30, 2007 from www.irpumn.org/uls/resources/projects/Chapter_2_12.17.07.pdf.

———. 2003. *Metro Charter.* Retrieved May 30, 2007 from www.metro-region.org/library_docs/about/charter.nov2000.may2002.clean.03.pdf.

———. 2005. *2002 Urban Growth Boundary Decision.* Retrieved May 30, 2007 from www.oregonmetro.gov/index.cfm/go/by.web/id=1.

———. 2007a. *Proposed Budget* (Vol. 1). Retrieved May 30, 2007 from www.oregonmetro.gov/index.cfm/go/by.web/id=1.

———. 2007b. *Urban Growth Boundary.* Retrieved May 24, 2007 from www.metro-region.org/article.cfm?articleID=277.

———. 2008. *Data Resource Center.* Retrieved November 6, 2008 from www.oregonmetro.gov/index.cfm/go/by.web/id=1.

Metropolitan Council. 1975. *Metropolitan Development Guide.* Metropolitan Council of the Twin Cities Area, St. Paul, MN.

———. 1988. *Metropolitan Development and Investment Framework.* Metropolitan Council of the Twin Cities Area, St. Paul, MN.

———. 2002. *Blueprint 2030.* Metropolitan Council of the Twin Cities Area, St. Paul, MN.

———. 2004. *Framework 2030.* Metropolitan Council of the Twin Cities Area, St. Paul, MN.

———. 2006. *Financial Summary and Fiscal Analysis.* St. Paul, MN.

———. 2008, October 13. *About the Metropolitan Council.* Retrieved October 20, 2008 from www.metrocouncil.org/about/about.htm.

Naftalin, A. 1986. *Making One Community out of Many: Perspectives on the Metropolitan Council of the Twin Cities Area.* Metropolitan Council of the Twin Cities Area, St. Paul, MN.

Nelson, A. C. 1996. Portland: The metropolitan umbrella. In H. V. Savitch and R. K. Vogel, eds. *Regional Politics: America in a Post-City Age.* Sage, Thousand Oaks, CA.

Nelson, A. C., R. Pendall, C. J. Dawkins, and G. J. Knaap. 2002. *Growth Management and Housing Affordability: The Academic Evidence.* The Brookings Institution, Washington, D.C.

———. 2004. The link between growth management and housing affordability: The academic evidence. Pp. 117–175 in A. Downs, ed. *Growth Management and Affordable Housing: Do They Conflict?* Brookings Institution Press, Washington, D.C.

Orfield, M. 2002. *American Metropolitics: The New Suburban Reality.* Brookings Institution Press, Washington, D.C.

Phillips, J., and E. Goodstein. 2000. Growth management and housing prices: The case of Portland, OR. *Contemporary Economic Policy* 18(3):334–344.

Regional Water Providers Consortium. 2008. *About Us*. Retrieved November 6, 2008 from www.conserveh2o.org/about.

Weiner, E. 1992. *Urban Transportation Planning in the United States: An Historical Overview*. Praeger/Greenwood, Westport, CT.

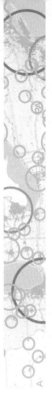

13

The Megaregion and the Future of American Planning

Catherine L. Ross and Jessica L. H. Doyle

The quality of a new idea can be judged by the possibilities it creates, especially when such possibilities stimulate new and unbounded interpretations and allow more innovative and beneficial outcomes. The mind is free to wander without a map; the map gets created in the form of possibilities and a future that might otherwise not have been envisioned. The implications of a new idea can be examined through different lenses; some allow vastly different expectations, goals, and objectives. Previous knowledge can be considered without reducing the potential of the new idea. Yet the pursuit and formulation of new concepts can be both extraordinarily frustrating and exhilarating, and so it is with the concept of megaregions. In many ways our progress toward building a clearer understanding of the possibilities of this construct is being held captive by the rising expectations and impatience of those who want to know how this new theoretical construct will help solve the urgent problems that confront them.

Megaregion as a construct has both the benefits and the disadvantages of being new. Scholars from various disciplines, as represented in this volume, have taken the idea, held it up to the light, weighed it, played with it, adjusted it, considered its implications, and pointed out its potential flaws and possibilities. Furthermore, the very newness of the idea means that much of its potential is still unexplored.

As many of the writers in this volume have noted, the magnitude of the challenges facing us (the rapid depletion of environmental resources, the increasing magnitude of climate change, growing economic uncertainty, and increasing congestion on deteriorating transportation infrastructures) will require a response soon. If the growing theoretical and practical investment in megaregions can produce positive results, then it is in our best interest to begin implementing megaregional planning as quickly as possible. However, we cannot implement change until we have carefully vetted megaregions as a concept and framework for action. If the vetting is not done first, our efforts may fail to produce positive outcomes and may divert scarce resources from efforts that might produce better results. As is always the case with new paradigms, the stakes are high.

This book has brought together multiple perspectives and viewpoints on the concept of megaregions. In this regard, the volume has attempted to mine the potential of the megaregion by tapping into the experiences and perceptions of the noted contributors. Their views vary, ranging from those who consider it to have fairly limited scope to those who think it has wide-ranging applicability in the global economy. We regard this book as a first step in defining the concept of the megaregion. It is the beginning, rather than the end, of the discussion. This concluding chapter summarizes the case for megaregions, describes the theoretical challenges remaining, and examines the potential implications for regional policy development in the United States.

The Case for Megaregions

As we have seen, demographic shifts within the United States and changes in the global economy mandate greater creativity, productivity, and effectiveness in planning. Our current planning efforts are not taking place at the appropriate speed or scale to accommodate new economic, environmental, infrastructure, or demographic challenges. Some of these dynamics make a case for a megaregion-based approach:

- Regions play a larger and faster-changing role in the global economy than do individual cities and states, and therefore any efforts to plan in a global context must consider the region (megaregion) as a basic unit of analysis and operation in American planning.
- Specific systems and resources (transportation and water use are two of the most obvious) cannot be planned effectively within the constraints of traditional jurisdictional boundaries. Our current planning system encourages competition and standoffs rather than regional cooperation. The megaregion is a way to emphasize regional, national, and global priorities rather than, and in addition to, individual local needs.
- Natural disasters (earthquakes, forest fires, floods, mass extinctions, and even climate change) and other extreme weather events are not neatly

confined within political boundaries. They too have implications at the megaregion level.

- Megaregional planning will allow policymakers to take advantage of and add to urban agglomeration economies, positioning them to be more competitive in an increasingly globalized economy.
- Megaregions offer a more appropriate geographic scale for the construction and development of a twenty-first-century transportation system; they provide global connections to existing and emerging markets of opportunity for the United States.
- The construction of green infrastructure and rail systems is better accommodated at the megaregion level, offering great potential to facilitate natural resource management, emission reduction, and greater mobility.

A megaregional approach confers significant advantages: regional connectivity over local isolation, interdependence over autonomy, and system-wide thinking over confinement to particular jurisdictions. These authors suggest that the concept of the megaregion, if applied skillfully, could allow increased economic growth and better accommodate the rising urban population while reducing negative impacts on the natural environment. The megaregion also enhances the potential to influence areas beyond its economic and political core.

Further Questions for Megaregional Research

"It's not at all clear to me that world competition is between mega-regions," wrote Paul Krugman in April 2008 (Krugman 2008). He is not the only person expressing some skepticism about the concept of the megaregion. Regional planning has not flourished in the United States for a variety of reasons (Levine 2001; Frisken and Norris 2001); why should the megaregion idea be any different? Advocates of the megaregion idea will have to carefully distinguish the potential staying power—that is, the potential usefulness—of the megaregion while answering some of the criticisms and skepticism voiced by others.

The opinions about megaregions are not uniformly favorable. Susan and Norman Fainstein, evaluating the megaregion in terms of persistent income inequality, are not convinced that a regional planning initiative would address these problems. Tridib Banerjee fears the propagation of megasprawl, and Scott Campbell wonders whether the megaregion growth machine might trump longstanding concerns about the negative impacts of growth. Campbell correctly asserts that a megaregion is not by definition a sustainable region: Conscious choices must be made to create a greener megaregion. Finally, Andreas Faludi refers to a discussion centered on European Union (EU) regional policies; in particular he notes the unresolved internal debate as to whether the promotion of polycentricity will allow the EU to be more globally competitive or whether regional policy should focus on particular successful centers of business and innovation. Within the EU as well, there are dissenting voices about the necessity of continued growth, even as the EU extends its polycentric approach to new members with significantly smaller average incomes.

At this early stage in the development of the idea, supporters of the megaregion run the risk of promising too much and touting it as a cure-all. Simply adding a layer of regional planning will not lead to smarter and more efficient government administration or settle the long-standing differences regarding class and racial disparities, sustainable practices, and clean energy sources. Therefore, it is both necessary and useful to have a clearer understanding of what the megaregion can and cannot accomplish.

With this in mind we pose the following questions that we hope will guide future research in the megaregion:

- How should megaregions be governed? Who will make final decisions? Mike Meyer and William Ankner have made some suggestions in addressing this question in regard to transportation investment. They suggest the formation of multistate organizations and multistate infrastructure banks.
- How does the megaregion ensure future global competitiveness? It should be noted at this point that the megaregional framework does not touch all of the factors that influence global investment patterns, as laid out in Sassen's chapter, most notably financial and business regulations.
- How does the megaregion encompass different ideas and preferences about growth and quality of life? Committed to a regional approach to economic growth (and to infrastructure investment), the EU nevertheless has come under fire by activists in Western Europe who question the necessity of continued growth. How is such dissent to be handled at the megaregional level? How are such conflicts to be resolved?
- How will culture be propagated and supported in megaregions? To put the question somewhat more concretely, what would happen to the megaregion currently defined as the "Cascadia Ecolopolis" if Vancouver were to continue to devote significant resources to environmental issues, but the governments of Seattle and Portland were to declare other issues, economic or social, of greater importance?
- How will megaregions react to demographic change? As Robert Lang and Arthur Nelson explain in their chapter, the megaregion has become an important construct because of recent demographic shifts, expected to continue to 2050. Does that mean that future demographic shifts could weaken the

megaregion? Might there come a time when a particular megaregion ceases to exist?

These questions will not be answered easily, even by those who believe most strongly that incorporating megaregions into American governance and planning thought will result in greener, richer, more sustainable regions. The stakes are high, and the costs of proceeding incorrectly could be as great as or greater than the costs of neglecting to plan at all. Thus it is all the more important that the idea of the megaregion and all that it promises be embraced and evaluated in regard to the promises it keeps.

It might be helpful to revisit the theoretical foundations on which the megaregion concept is based before turning to the policy implications of megaregions.

Megaregion Development

The idea of the megaregion is based in part on the idea that regions, as opposed to cities or states, contribute to economic growth. By facilitating economic transactions within a region, we can increase economic activity, which may contribute to the region's comparative advantage within the global economy. The importance of regional and interregional trade in the shaping of cities has been studied since the nineteenth century. What is new today is that globalization forces a greater use of technology, lowers costs of capital mobility, integrates national economies into the global economy, increases direct foreign investment, and more generally increases the access to goods and services produced in foreign countries.

The idea of the "central place" and the hierarchy of urban centers, first put forward by Christaller in 1933, remains very influential. As Higgins and Savoie (1995) describe it, to some degree all urban centers are now central places, both generating and receiving spread effects. What has increased dramatically since World War II is the reach of these spread effects, as transportation costs have declined. Fujita, Krugman, and Venables (1999) show the importance of transportation links in contributing to urban agglomerations. It is not a coincidence that some of the poorest countries in the world, especially in Africa, also have some of the poorest transportation links to the global economy (Limão and Venables 1999). Transportation links, both to and within the region, become crucial to ensuring and enhancing economic activity at the global scale. The region's most central places—New York, Boston, and Washington, D.C. in the Northeast Megaregion; Atlanta, Charlotte, and Birmingham in the Piedmont Atlantic Megaregion; Houston, Dallas, and San Antonio in the Texas Triangle—reinforce their own importance in the global economy. They have or are creating transportation links to other parts of the region, by road and rail; and to other parts of the country and the world, by road, rail, air, and sea connections.

As Saskia Sassen skillfully pointed out, economic sectors contain both points of spatial concentration and points of spatial dispersal. The dispersion effect is easy to see, as companies take advantage of cheaper production costs associated with the use of processing facilities far from their home country. The reasons for spatial concentration can be more difficult to articulate. Sassen (2001) concentrates on agglomeration advantages in business and financial services. Other theorists suggest that comparative advantage lies in attracting agglomerations of a certain type of labor (Florida 2002). Hall (1999) discusses the extent to which certain activities associated with global cities—information services and cultural activities—require a high degree of face-to-face interaction and thus tend to agglomerate spatially. The evidence suggests that spatial agglomerations still matter in a global economy.

The relevance of much of the earlier discussion is more readily associated with central cities or with connected metropolitan areas that form the economic core of megaregions. We might ask, "What is the immediate relevance to surrounding areas or areas of influence in the megaregion?" Many argue that the earlier discussion supports the idea that economic considerations should largely be targeted or concentrated on central cities. However, Levine (2001) summarizes the case for emphasizing the region rather than the city:

- Regional economies can be superior in realizing production economies.
- Regions can draw on larger pools of resources, both human and fiscal.
- By limiting interjurisdictional competitions, regions can limit the waste of resources and duplication of efforts.

Sassen's chapter in this volume extends the idea of economic development in such a way that the development of the region and the global city go hand in hand, even as global competition seems to support the city at the expense of the region. She argues that the megaregion can offer a variety of locations, some spatially concentrated, that can suit different parts of a firm's supply chain. The megaregion thus offers a number of advantages for the locating firm, such as coordination of bureaucracy, agglomeration economies of the central cities, transportation links throughout the region, and production locations that can be located in the hinterlands of the megaregion.

The regional efforts within the EU, as Faludi describes them, are concerned not with improving the economic activities of the Blue Banana or pentagon but integrating poorly performing regions into the larger EU in order to improve the viability of the EU as a whole. Thus, a hypothetical firm in London is able to consider locations with skilled workers, lower transportation costs, and higher quality of life in Vilnius, Turin, or Lisbon.

Policy Implications

The contributions by writers focusing outside the United States further highlight the challenges that further globalization will bring to the American economy. As more and more cities and regions become competitive, American cities, especially those overdependent on gasoline-powered cars, will struggle to maintain their economic attractiveness. A primary purpose of this book is to examine the potential of megaregions as an approach to meet those challenges. To that end, we suggest some specific potential policy implications of a megaregional approach:

- Develop a national transportation and infrastructure investment strategy that can respond to the mobility and economic needs of the global economy. This might include introducing new financial resources to support infrastructure improvements to the regions, corridors, and places critical to economic productivity and performance.
- Enable transportation system redundancy to ensure the ability to respond to emergency preparedness and national security needs.
- Invest in and facilitate commodity and person movement by constructing high-speed rail systems and improved rail connections through partnerships with the private sector to construct strategic mobility plans. Such partnerships should focus on removing existing bottlenecks, particularly those that prevent landside access to ports.
- Implement a nationwide green infrastructure development plan in conjunction with major infrastructure investment to enhance national resource management, protect cultural resources, and direct growth away from lands not appropriate for development.
- Use innovative financial tools, including user fees and tolls, private sector initiatives, and expanded capacity for local areas to finance and implement public works.
- Create the opportunity for cooperation and joint financing within and between megaregions in regard to economic development and education. The education may be linked to specific educational needs and support the economic activity and preferences of the particular megaregion.
- Improve access to trade corridors, airports, intermodal hubs and connectors, gateways, border crossings, and freight bottlenecks. Establish a system of performance metrics and indicators to monitor transportation system performance between and within megaregions.
- Establish strategies and funds for the maintenance and preservation of the National Highway System, approximately 160,000 miles (256,000 kilometers) of roadway important to the nation's economy, defense, and

mobility. This includes other principal arterials, including highways in rural and urban areas that provide access between an arterial and a major port, airport, public transportation facility, or other intermodal transportation facility. It also includes the Strategic Highway Network, a network of highways that provide defense access, continuity, and emergency capabilities for defense purposes.

- Implement megaregion climate change initiatives that include emission reduction targets and a cap-and-trade initiative appropriate to the scale and particularities of the region.

These are not the only potential policy implications of a megaregional approach. Yet they do give an idea of how the megaregion would allow for planning at a larger scale than has historically been possible in the United States. Larger-scale planning would reduce inefficiencies and allow American planners to tackle problems that do not fit neatly inside political jurisdictions, such as climate change and natural resource management. It would give regional leaders a chance to view their regions holistically and perhaps provide an overarching vision with which to reduce infighting between localities. Finally, the megaregion encourages a larger sense of community, an understanding that residents of the region are dependent on each other for the improvement of their short- and long-term quality of life. It is our hope that, with this book, the megaregion can be put forward as a potential tool to help make Americans' lives better.

References

Florida, R. 2002. *The Rise of the Creative Class and How It's Transforming Work, Leisure, Community and Everyday Life*. Basic Books, New York.

Frisken, F., and D. F. Norris. 2001. Regionalism reconsidered. *Journal of Urban Affairs* 23(5).

Fujita, M., P. Krugman, and A. J. Venables. 1999. *The Spatial Economy: Cities, Regions, and International Trade*. MIT Press, Boston.

Hall, P. 1999. The future of cities. *Computers, Environment and Urban Systems*. 23(3):173–185.

Higgins, B., and D. J. Savoie. 1995. Growth poles and central places. Pp. 89–113 in *Regional Development Theories and Their Application*. Transaction, New Brunswick, NJ.

Krugman, P. 2008, April 12. *The Conscience of a Liberal: Mega-skepticism*. Retrieved April 14, 2008 from krugman.blogs.nytimes.com/2008/04/12/mega-skepticism/.

Levine, J. N. 2001. The role of economic theory in regional advocacy. *Journal of Planning Literature* 16(2):183–201.

Limão, N., and A. J. Venables. 1999. *Infrastructure, Geographical Disadvantage, and Transport Costs* (Policy Research Working Paper). World Bank, Washington, D.C.

Sassen, S. 2001. *The Global City: New York, London, Tokyo* (2nd ed.). Princeton University Press, Princeton, NJ.

Contributors

Adjo A. Amekudzi is an associate professor at the School of Civil and Environmental Engineering at the Georgia Institute of Technology. She earned a B.S. in civil engineering from Stanford University and an M.S. in civil engineering (transportation) from Florida International University, an M.S. in civil infrastructure systems, and a Ph.D. in civil and environmental engineering from Carnegie Mellon University. Professor Amekudzi studies systems problems on the integrated built and natural environment with the objective of improving built systems decision making to promote sustainable development. Her current research focuses on the development and application of sustainability evaluation methods to built systems. Professor Amekudzi is the associate director of the Georgia Transportation Institute and the Georgia Tech University Transportation Center.

William D. Ankner has a B.A. from Stonehill College in North Easton, Massachusetts, a master's degree and a doctorate from the University of Ottawa, and a certificate in executive management from Duke University. He was appointed secretary of the Louisiana Department of Transportation and Development in January 2008. Dr. Ankner, who had previously served as head of the Missouri Transportation Institute, directed the Rhode Island Department of Transportation from 1996 to 2003 and has held senior management positions with the Delaware and New Jersey departments of transportation. He chaired the Transportation Research Board's Third National Transportation Finance Conference and has presented at numerous workshops and conferences. He is a member of the National Surface Transportation Policy and Revenue Study Commission's Blue Ribbon Expert Advisory Panel and the Transportation Research Board's Transportation Finance Committee. Dr. Ankner is the former president of the Northeast Association of State Transportation Officials.

Tridib Banerjee holds the James Irvine Chair of Urban and Regional Planning at the School of Policy, Planning, and Development at the University of Southern California. His research, teaching, and writing focus on the design and planning of the built environment and related human and social consequences. In particular, he is interested in the political economy of urban development, the effects of globalization in the transformation of urban form, and urbanism from a comparative international perspective. His publications include *Beyond the Neighborhood Unit* (with William C. Baer), *City Sense and City Design: Writings and Projects of Kevin Lynch* (co-edited with Michael Southworth), and *Urban Design Downtown: Poetics and Politics of Form* (with Anastasia Loukaitou-Sideris).

Jason Barringer, American Institute of Certified Planners, is a research scientist at Georgia Tech's Center for Quality Growth and Regional Development (CQGRD). He received a master's degree in city and regional planning from Georgia Tech. His research and practice experience has focused on demographic and geographic information system analysis, population projections, infrastructure asset management, and regional sustainable development. He recently completed a community impact assessment of freight movement for the Atlanta metropolitan region and has spoken on megaregions in many forums around the country.

Dr. Scott Campbell is an associate professor and coordinator of doctoral studies in the Urban Planning Program at the University of Michigan. His research and teaching focus on sustainable development and regional planning. His publications include two books co-edited with Susan Fainstein: *Readings in Planning Theory* and *Readings in Urban Theory*. He has published numerous articles and monographs, including the award-winning article in the *Journal of the American Planning Association*, "Green Cities, Growing Cities, Just Cities? Urban Planning and the Contradictions of Sustainable Development."

Dr. Cheryl K. Contant is vice-chancellor for academic affairs and dean at the University of Minnesota, Morris. Dr. Contant served as professor and director of the City and Regional Planning Program at the Georgia Institute of Technology from 1999 to 2008. She has published on water quality issues in agricultural regions of the United States and on watershed planning and management. She has recently conducted research funded by the Robert Wood Johnson Foundation and the Centers for Disease Control and Prevention assessing the impact of parks and mixed-use development community design on physical activity and travel patterns. She received her Ph.D. in civil engineering and infrastructure planning from Stanford University.

Jessica L. H. Doyle is a doctoral researcher at the Center for Quality Growth and Regional Development. She is currently enrolled in the doctoral program in City and Regional Planning in Georgia Tech, focusing on economic development and transportation. From April 2001 to August 2005 she served as editor of Economist.com Global Executive, *The Economist* magazine's online portal for new ideas in business education and management theory. She also reported on the Southeastern United States for *The Economist*, having covered topics from economic redevelopment in Alabama's Black Belt to John Edwards's 2004 presidential campaign. Doyle received a B.A. in history from Swarthmore College.

Norman Fainstein teaches sociology and urban studies at Connecticut College. Fainstein holds a B.S. and Ph.D. in political science from the Massachusetts Institute of Technology. He has published several books and numerous articles on urban history and politics, planning, economic development, race relations, social movements, and public policy.

Susan S. Fainstein is professor of urban planning in the Graduate School of Design at Harvard University. She previously taught in the Columbia University planning program and was a long-time faculty member in the Department of Urban Planning and Policy Development at Rutgers University. She is widely regarded as a leading figure in the field of urban planning, and her teaching and research have focused on the political economy of urban redevelopment, tourism, comparative urban and social policy, planning theory, and issues of gender and planning. She is completing a book titled *The Just City*, to be published by Cornell University Press. Among her books are *Urban Political Movements, Restructuring the City*, and *The City Builders: Property, Politics, and Planning in London and New York*. She is a recipient of the Distinguished Planning Educator award of the Association of Collegiate Schools of Planning. Her Ph.D. is in political science from the Massachusetts Institute of Technology.

Dr. Andreas Faludi is a professor of spatial policy systems at the Research Institute for Housing, Urban, and Mobility Studies at Delft University of Technology. He is a prolific writer about European models of spatial planning and territorial cohesion policy. Among his numerous books are *Critical Rationalism and Planning Methodology, A Decision-Centered View of Environmental Planning, Rule and Order: Dutch Planning Doctrine in the Twentieth Century* (with A. van der Valk), *The Making of the European Spatial Development Perspective: No Masterplan* (with Bas Waterhout), and he is editor of *European Spatial Planning*. He received his doctorate in urban planning at Vienna University of Technology and an honorary doctorate at Blekinge Institute of Technology at Karlskrona, Sweden.

Dr. Richard Florida is academic director of the Martin Prosperity Institute and professor of business and creativity at the Rotman School of Management, University of Toronto. Previously, Florida has held professorships at George Mason University and Carnegie Mellon University and taught as a visiting professor at Harvard and the Massachusetts Institute of Technology. Florida earned his bachelor's degree from Rutgers College and his Ph.D. from Columbia University. He is a former senior scientist with the Gallup Organization. As a result, he provides unique, data-driven insight into the social, economic, and demographic factors that drive the twenty-first-century world economy. In the last 5 years, Florida has penned two national bestsellers: *The Rise of the Creative Class* and *The Flight of the Creative Class.*

Shirley Franklin was elected the fifty-eighth mayor of the City of Atlanta in 2001; at that time she became the first African American woman to serve as mayor of a major city in the Southeastern United States. Mayor Franklin's accomplishments include the oversight of a $3.2-billion sewer upgrade for the city, the launching of a citywide sustainability initiative, the addition of a fifth runway to Hartsfield–Jackson Atlanta International Airport, and the implementation of wide-ranging ethics reform. Mayor Franklin co-chaired the 2008 National Democratic Convention. She serves as a member of the Board of Trustees of the United Nations Institute for Training and Research, chairs the Atlanta Development Authority, and is secretary of the board of the Atlanta Regional Commission and chair of its Ethics Committee. Mayor Franklin earned her B.A. in sociology from Howard University in Washington, D.C. and was awarded her M.A. in sociology from the University of Pennsylvania. She has received honorary degrees from Howard University, the Atlanta College of Art, Cambridge College, Spellman College, Morehouse College, Clark Atlanta University, Tuskegee University, Oglethorpe University, and the University of Pennsylvania.

Robert E. Lang, Ph.D., is a professor of urban planning and director of the Urban Affairs and Planning Program at Virginia Tech in Alexandria. He is also a co-director of the Metropolitan Institute at Virginia. Dr. Lang is the editor of the scholarly journal *Housing Policy Debate*, a senior fellow of the Brookings Institution, and a fellow at the Urban Land Institute. Dr. Lang received a Ph.D. in sociology and urban planning from Rutgers University, where he also taught sociology and urban studies, and was a research associate at the Center for Urban Policy Research. Dr. Lang has held several fellowships; in 2008 he was a Fulbright Fellow at the École Normale Supérieure in Paris. Dr. Lang's research specialties include suburban studies, real estate development, world cities, demographic and spatial analysis, housing and the built environment, and metropolitan governance. He has authored more than 130 academic and professional publications on a wide range of topics. Dr. Lang also authored the book *Edgeless Cities: Exploring* *the Elusive Metropolis* and has co-authored three other books. His research has been featured in *USA Today*, *The New York Times*, *The Washington Post*, *The Wall Street Journal*, and *U.S. News & World Report* and reported on by NPR, CNN, MSNBC, Fox News, and ABC World News Tonight. Before joining Virginia Tech, Dr. Lang was director of urban and metropolitan research at the Fannie Mae Foundation.

Karen Leone de Nie, American Institute of Certified Planners, is a researcher in community development at the Federal Reserve Bank of Atlanta, where she studies neighborhood stabilization, green development and lending, and the effects of an aging population on communities. Previously, Leone de Nie was a research scientist at Georgia Tech's Center for Quality Growth and Regional Development, where she focused on the evaluation of development regulations for consistency with community goals and sustainable development principles, and the impact of the built environment on public health. Leone de Nie received a master's degree in city and regional planning from the Georgia Institute of Technology in 2005, where she participated in initial research on the Piedmont Atlantic Megaregion.

Dr. Thomas F. Luce Jr. is research director of the Institute on Race and Poverty. His work focuses on state and local finance, metropolitan development, and intergovernmental relations. He is co-author (with Myron Orfield) of a forthcoming book on regionalism in the Twin Cities, and his other work includes studies of growth pressures on environmentally sensitive areas in the Twin Cities, fiscal and demographic patterns in a wide range of American metropolitan areas, the Twin Cities Fiscal Disparities Tax-Base Sharing Program, the effects of tax rate disparities on metropolitan growth patterns, and other work on various aspects of metropolitan development patterns. He has a Ph.D. in public policy analysis from the University of Pennsylvania and has served on the faculties of the Humphrey Institute of Public Affairs, University of Minnesota and the Department of Public Administration, Pennsylvania State University.

Dr. Michael D. Meyer is director of the Georgia Transportation Institute, a professor of civil and environmental engineering, and former chair of the School of Civil and Environmental Engineering at the Georgia Institute of Technology. From 1983 to 1988, Dr. Meyer was director of transportation planning and development for Massachusetts, where he was responsible for statewide planning, project development, traffic engineering, and transportation research. Before this, he was a professor in the Department of Civil Engineering at the Massachusetts Institute of Technology. Dr. Meyer has written more than 180 technical articles and has authored or co-authored numerous texts on transportation planning and policy, including a college textbook titled *Urban Transportation Planning: A Decision Oriented Approach.*

Arthur C. Nelson, Ph.D., Fellow of the American Institute of Certified Planners, is Presidential Professor of City and Metropolitan Planning and director of metropolitan research at the University of Utah. Dr. Nelson has conducted pioneering research in land use planning, growth management, public facility finance, and urban development policy. He has made notable contributions to the areas of public facility finance, growth management, and metropolitan development patterns. His research and practice have led to the publication of nearly 20 books and more than 200 scholarly and professional publications. He received his Ph.D. from Portland State University.

Myron Orfield is the Julius E. Davis Professor of Law at the University of Minnesota Law School, executive director of the Institute on Race and Poverty, nonresident senior fellow at the Brookings Institution in Washington, D.C., affiliate faculty member at the Hubert H. Humphrey Institute of Public Affairs, and the 2005–2006 Fesler–Lampert Chair in Urban and Regional Affairs. Orfield has published two widely read and influential books on metropolitan governance: *American Metropolitics: The New Suburban Reality* and *Metropolitics: A Regional Agenda for Community and Stability*. Orfield served five terms in the Minnesota House of Representatives and one term in the state senate. He received his J.D. from the University of Chicago.

Dr. Catherine L. Ross is the Harry West Professor and director of the Center for Quality Growth and Regional Development at the Georgia Institute of Technology. Her publications include numerous chapters, articles, and reports on transportation planning, quality growth, infrastructure policy, urban economic development, and health impact assessment. Her recent research projects include studies for the Ford Foundation, the Robert Wood Johnson Foundation, the U.S. Department of Transportation, the Georgia Department of Transportation, and the MacArthur Foundation. She is co-author of *The Inner City: Urban Poverty and Economic Development in the Next Century*. She received her Ph.D. in city and regional planning from Cornell University. Dr. Ross is a member of the National Academy of Public Administration and a Fellow of the Urban Land Institute. She was recently named as a Georgia Institute of Technology Advance Professor. Dr. Ross served as the first director of the Georgia Regional Transportation Authority.

Dr. Saskia Sassen is the Lynd Professor of Sociology and a member of the Committee on Global Thought at Columbia University. Her recent books are *Territory, Authority, Rights: From Medieval to Global Assemblages* and *A Sociology of Globalization*. She wrote a lead essay in the *2006 Venice Biennale of Architecture Catalogue* and has completed for the United Nations Educational, Scientific, and Cultural Organization a 5-year project on sustainable human settlement based on a network of researchers and activists in more than thirty countries; it is published as one of the volumes of the *Enclyclopedia of Life Support Systems*. Dr. Sassen's books have been translated into sixteen languages. Her comments have appeared in *The Guardian*, *The New York Times*, OpenDemocracy.net, *Le Monde Diplomatique*, *The International Herald Tribune*, *Newsweek International*, and *The Financial Times* among others.

Dr. Myungje Woo is a research scientist at the Center for Quality Growth and Regional Development at the Georgia Institute of Technology. He holds a Ph.D. in city and regional planning from Ohio State University. He was previously employed at the Ohio Supercomputer Center, the Seoul Development Institute, and the University of Seoul's Metropolitan Research Institute. His research focuses on growth management policies, residential mobility, relationship between land use policies and transportation, and urban spatial structure. He has also studied revitalization of brownfields and residential zoning systems in Seoul, Korea. Dr. Woo is researching megaregions and transportation planning using geographic information systems and quantitative methods.

Dr. Jiawen Yang is an assistant professor in the city and regional planning program at the Georgia Institute of Technology. His teaching and research interests focus on spatial development, transportation planning, and international planning. He received his B.S. and M.S. degrees from Beijing University and his Ph.D. in urban planning from the Massachusetts Institute of Technology.

Index